FEDERALISTS AND ANTIFEDERALISTS

CONSTITUTIONAL HERITAGE SERIES

JOHN P. KAMINSKI AND RICHARD LEFFLER
General Editors

FEDERALISTS AND ANTIFEDERALISTS
The Debate Over the Ratification of the Constitution
Edited by John P. Kaminski & Richard Leffler
SECOND EDITION

A NECESSARY EVIL?
Slavery and the Debate Over the Constitution
Edited by John P. Kaminski

THE ESSENTIAL *Federalist*
A New Reading of the Federalist Papers
Edited by Quentin P. Taylor

CONSTITUTIONAL HERITAGE SERIES

Volume I

FEDERALISTS AND ANTIFEDERALISTS

The Debate Over the Ratification of the Constitution

Edited by

JOHN P. KAMINSKI AND RICHARD LEFFLER

SECOND EDITION

MADISON HOUSE

A Madison House Book
Rowman & Littlefield Publishers, Inc.
4720 Boston Way, Lanham, Maryland 20706
www.rowmanlittlefield.com

Printed in the United States of America

Library of Congress Cataloging-in-Publication Data

Federalists and antifederalists : the debate over the ratification of
    the Constitution / edited by John P. Kaminski and Richard Leffler. —
    2nd ed.
        p.   cm.—(Constitutional heritage series, issn 0895-9633; v.1)
    Includes bibliographical references and index.
    isbn 0-945612-57-5 (cloth : alk. paper).—isbn 0-945612-58-3 (pbk. :
    alk. paper)
    1. Constitutional history—United States—Sources.   I. Kaminski,
    John P.   II. Leffler, Richard.   III. Series.
    KF4515.F44 1998
    342.73'029—dc21   98-16872
                                                                            CIP

Volume I in the
Constitutional Heritage Series
issn 0895-9633

Published for
The Center for the Study of the American Constitution
by
MADSION HOUSE PUBLISHERS, INC.

SECOND EDITION

Contents

2. THE HOUSE OF REPRESENTATIVES 37

Antifederalist

Federalist

3. THE SENATE 67

Antifederalist

Federalist

4. THE PRESIDENT 84

Antifederalist

Antifederalist and Federalist

Federalist

5. THE JUDICIARY *120*

Antifederalist

Federalist

6. THE BILL OF RIGHTS *151*

Antifederalist

Federalists

7. THE CONSTITUTION: DEBATE OVER PROPERTY, CLASS, AND GOVERNMENT *178*

Outsiders View American Society

Antifederalists

Federalists

Introduction

FOR A QUARTER CENTURY between 1763 and 1788 Americans intensely debated the nature of government and the need to protect individual liberties and the rights of local government. This was not a purely theoretical debate. Americans had fought a war for seven years over these issues. This public discussion climaxed in the debate over the ratification of the United States Constitution in 1787–1788.

This book looks at six issues in that constitutional debate: the House of Representatives, the Senate, the President, the Judiciary, the Bill of Rights, and the Nature of Republican Government. Each of these topics is discussed in documents written by eighteenth-century writers, some of whom were the leading theorists and politicians of the day. Antifederalists and Federalists are both represented. The documents sometimes originated in newspapers or as pamphlets; sometimes they were private letters or speeches in state ratifying conventions. The issues discussed in this book are important because they are the basic components of the new federal government, form the character of the government, and in great measure determined the direction that new government would take.

The debate over the House of Representatives centered on three issues: the apportionment of representatives among the states according to population, the two-year term of office, and the ability of the House to adequately represent the interests of all the people.

The Senate was one of the most controversial elements in the new Constitution. Antifederalists charged that it would become a bastion of aristocracy and that it would continually be in session. Large states objected to the equal representation of the states in the Senate. Objections also were raised to the six-year term and the election by state legislatures. Gone was the state power to recall Senators and Representatives and the mandatory requirement for rotation in office. Many Americans were also alarmed at the lack of separation of powers between the Senate and the President. Who would have major responsibility in the appointment of officeholders and in treaty-making? Would shared responsibility result in irresponsibility? Also, would the Senate function properly as the court of impeachment when it had confirmed the appointments of officeholders?

The Presidency reminded many Americans of the British king. Predictions of monarchy were not uncommon, but Federalists demonstrated the significant differences between the new American Presidency and the British king. The appointment, treaty-making, pardoning, veto, and military powers of the President were as fully discussed in 1787–1788 as they are today.

The creation of a federal judiciary was of prime importance in the new government. Antifederalists, however, thought this new system of courts would annihilate state judiciaries and endanger the right to trial by jury. The overriding question in this debate was whether the new federal courts would bring justice to the land or serve as the instrument of oppression for a despotic government.

The most important issue discussed during the ratification debate was whether the Constitution should contain a bill of rights. A motion for a bill of rights was made late in the Constitutional Convention but was defeated. Federalists subsequently argued that a bill of rights was unnecessary and maybe even dangerous because the new federal government would be a government of delegated powers. Antifederalists, however, stressed the importance of such a written protection to liberties, especially in light of the Constitution's "necessary and proper," "general welfare," and "supremacy" clauses. This debate laid the groundwork for the proposal and adoption of the Bill of Rights in 1789 and 1791, respectively.

In addition to specific provisions of the Constitution, Americans also debated the general nature of the government to be created by the Constitution. Antifederalists alluded to the commonly held theory, most eloquently stated by Baron de Montesquieu, that republics could only exist over a small territory. When that territory became too large, republics degenerated into despotic regimes. Federalists, on the other hand, argued that the Constitution would create a new kind of government—a federal republic. Not only would this new type of government tie the states together in a strong union that would protect the liberties of the majority, but it would also protect minorities from the oppression of the majority. This new theory was developed most completely by James Madison in *The Federalist* No. 10.

Taken together, the documents in this volume present the hopes and fears of Americans as they debated the nature of the government to be established by the new Constitution. It is surprising how vital that debate 200 years ago has remained in our continuing effort to understand the changing nature of our federal system of government.

A Note on the Text

The texts of the documents used in this volume have been transcribed verbatim from the original sources. No punctuation has been added and misspellings have not been corrected except for obvious typographical errors. Because of space limitations, excerpts have often been printed. Footnotes provided by the editors have been marked with asterisks and daggers and have been placed at the bottom of the page. Footnotes provided by the original author of the document have been labeled alphabetically, i.e., (a), (b), etc., and have also been placed at the bottom of the page.

FEDERALISTS AND ANTIFEDERALISTS

1

———◆———

The Constitution
and the Nature of
Republican Government

ANTIFEDERALISTS ARGUED *that the Constitution would destroy the states and create one large, consolidated republic that would deteriorate into monarchy or despotism. They espoused a traditional position based on Montesquieu and other political theorists that a republic—by which they meant a government in which the people consent to be governed by representatives they elect either directly or indirectly on a regular basis—could exist only in a relatively small territory populated by people who shared similar values and interests.*

Antifederalists believed that in a small republic the representatives know the minds of their constituents and the people know their representatives. This enables the people to understand their government and the laws. Such a government commands the confidence and support of the people.

This intimacy between the people and their representatives is impossible in a large republic, where representatives would be little known and distant, and the government and laws would become complex. A large country would contain a diverse population, with different, sometimes conflicting, interests. The result would be a constant clashing and disorder. A large, peacetime standing army would be needed to enforce the central government's laws.

Instead of the single large republic, Antifederalists advocated a confederacy of smaller republics (the states), which would delegate to the central authority only such powers as were required to maintain the Union. The central government would act, not directly on the people, but through the states.

Federalists believed that a confederacy was not an adequate government for the United States. They denied that the Constitution would destroy the states or create one large, consolidated republic. The Constitution, they said, would create a government that was partly national and partly federal.

Federalists denied the charge that the Constitution violated traditional republican theory, and they cited Montesquieu whenever possible. More interestingly, they devised a theory that valued a large and diverse polity as the solution to the great problem of republican government: to secure the public good and private rights from the tyranny of the majority while still retaining popular government. The clashing of diverse interests in a large republic becomes not an evil to be avoided, but a cure for the ancient disease afflicting republican government.

Antifederalist

BRUTUS I
New York Journal, 18 October 1787*

To the CITIZENS *of the* STATE *of* NEW-YORK.

When the public is called to investigate and decide upon a question in which not only the present members of the community are deeply interested, but upon which the happiness and misery of generations yet unborn is in great measure suspended, the benevolent mind cannot help feeling itself peculiarly interested in the result.

In this situation, I trust the feeble efforts of an individual, to lead the minds of the people to a wise and prudent determination, cannot fail of being acceptable to the candid and dispassionate part of the community. Encouraged by this consideration, I have been induced to offer my thoughts upon the present important crisis of our public affairs.

Perhaps this country never saw so critical a period in their political concerns. We have felt the feebleness of the ties by which these United-States are held together, and the want of sufficient energy in our present confederation, to manage, in some instances, our general concerns. Various expedients have been proposed to remedy these evils, but none have

---

*This is the first of sixteen essays signed "Brutus" that appeared in the *New York Journal* between 18 October 1787 and 10 April 1788. James Madison may well have had this essay in mind when he wrote on 21 October, "a new Combatant . . . with considerable address & plausibility, strikes at the foundation [of the Constitution]." The author is not known. Several Antifederalists have been suggested, including New Yorkers Abraham Yates, Jr., Robert Yates, Melancton Smith, and Governor George Clinton. Richard Henry Lee of Virginia has also been mentioned. This essay was reprinted in the *Pennsylvania Packet*, 26 October; Boston *Independent Chronicle*, 22 November; and the Northampton, Mass., *Hampshire Gazette*, 19, 26 November.

succeeded. At length a Convention of the states has been assembled, they have formed a constitution which will now, probably, be submitted to the people to ratify or reject, who are the fountain of all power, to whom alone it of right belongs to make or unmake constitutions, or forms of government, at their pleasure. The most important question that was ever proposed to your decision, or to the decision of any people under heaven, is before you, and you are to decide upon it by men of your own election, chosen specially for this purpose. If the constitution, offered to your acceptance, be a wise one, calculated to preserve the invaluable blessings of liberty, to secure the inestimable rights of mankind, and promote human happiness, then, if you accept it, you will lay a lasting foundation of happiness for millions yet unborn; generations to come will rise up and call you blessed. You may rejoice in the prospects of this vast extended continent becoming filled with freemen, who will assert the dignity of human nature. You may solace yourselves with the idea, that society, in this favoured land, will fast advance to the highest point of perfection; the human mind will expand in knowledge and virtue, and the golden age be, in some measure, realised. But if, on the other hand, this form of government contains principles that will lead to the subversion of liberty— if it tends to establish a despotism, or, what is worse, a tyrannic aristocracy; then, if you adopt it, this only remaining assylum for liberty will be shut up, and posterity will execrate your memory.

Momentous then is the question you have to determine, and you are called upon by every motive which should influence a noble and virtuous mind, to examine it well, and to make up a wise judgment. It is insisted, indeed, that this constitution must be received, be it ever so imperfect. If it has its defects, it is said, they can be best amended when they are experienced. But remember, when the people once part with power, they can seldom or never resume it again but by force. Many instances can be produced in which the people have voluntarily increased the powers of their rulers; but few, if any, in which rulers have willingly abridged their authority. This is a sufficient reason to induce you to be careful, in the first instance, how you deposit the powers of government.

With these few introductory remarks, I shall proceed to a consideration of this constitution.

The first question that presents itself on the subject is, whether a confederated government be the best for the United States or not? Or in other words, whether the thirteen United States should be reduced to one great republic, governed by one legislature, and under the direction of one executive and judicial; or whether they should continue thirteen confederated republics, under the direction and controul of a supreme federal head for certain defined national purposes only?

This enquiry is important, because, although the government reported by the convention does not go to a perfect and entire consolidation,
yet it approaches so near to it, that it must, if executed, certainly and
infallibly terminate in it.

This government is to possess absolute and uncontroulable power,
legislative, executive and judicial, with respect to every object to which
it extends for by, the last clause of section 8th, article 1st, it is declared
"that the Congress shall have power to make all laws which shall be
necessary and proper for carrying into execution the foregoing powers,
and all other powers vested by this constitution, in the government of the
United States; or in any department or office thereof." And by the 6th
article, it is declared "that this constitution, and the laws of the United
States, which shall be made in pursuance thereof, and the treaties made,
or which shall be made, under the authority of the United States, shall be
the supreme law of the land; and the judges in every state shall be bound
thereby, any thing in the constitution, or law of any state to the contrary
notwithstanding." It appears from these articles that there is no need of
any intervention of the state governments, between the Congress and the
people, to execute any one power vested in the general government, and
that the constitution and laws of every state are nullified and declared
void, so far as they are or shall be inconsistent with this constitution, or
the laws made in pursuance of it, or with treaties made under the authority
of the United States.—The government then, so far as it extends, is a
complete one, and not a confederation. It is as much one complete government as that of New-York or Massachusetts, has as absolute and perfect
powers to make and execute all laws, to appoint officers, institute courts,
declare offences, and annex penalties, with respect to every object to which
it extends, as any other in the world. So far therefore as its powers reach,
all ideas of confederation are given up and lost. It is true this government
is limited to certain objects, or to speak more properly, some small degree
of power is still left to the states, but a little attention to the powers vested
in the general government, will convince every candid man, that if it is
capable of being executed, all that is reserved for the individual states
must very soon be annihilated, except so far as they are barely necessary
to the organization of the general government. The powers of the general
legislature extend to every case that is of the least importance—there is
nothing valuable to human nature, nothing dear to freemen, but what is
within its power. It has authority to make laws which will affect the lives,
the liberty, and property of every man in the United States; nor can the
constitution or laws of any state, in any way prevent or impede the full
and complete execution of every power given. The legislative power is
competent to lay taxes, duties, imposts, and excises;—there is no limitation

to this power, unless it be said that the clause* which directs the use to which those taxes, and duties shall be applied, may be said to be a limitation: but this is no restriction of the power at all, for by this clause they are to be applied to pay the debts and provide for the common defence and general welfare of the United States; but the legislature have authority to contract debts at their discretion; they are the sole judges of what is necessary to provide for the common defence, and they only are to determine what is for the general welfare; this power therefore is neither more nor less, than a power to lay and collect taxes, imposts, and excises, at their pleasure; not only the power to lay taxes unlimited, as to the amount they may require, but it is perfect and absolute to raise them in any mode they please. No state legislature, or any power in the state governments, have any more to do in carrying this into effect, than the authority of one state has to do with that of another. In the business therefore of laying and collecting taxes, the idea of confederation is totally lost, and that of one entire republic is embraced. It is proper here to remark, that the authority to lay and collect taxes is the most important of any power that can be granted; it connects with it almost all other powers, or at least will in process of time draw all other after it; it is the great mean of protection, security, and defence, in a good government, and the great engine of oppression and tyranny in a bad one. This cannot fail of being the case, if we consider the contracted limits which are set by this constitution, to the late governments, on this article of raising money. No state can emit paper money—lay any duties, or imposts, on imports, or exports, but by consent of the Congress; and then the net produce shall be for the benefit of the United States: the only mean therefore left, for any state to support its government and discharge its debts, is by direct taxation; and the United States have also power to lay and collect taxes, in any way they please. Every one who has thought on the subject, must be convinced that but small sums of money can be collected in any country, by direct taxes, when the fœderal government begins to exercise the right of taxation in all its parts, the legislatures of the several states will find it impossible to raise monies to support their governments. Without money they cannot be supported, and they must dwindle away, and, as before observed, their powers absorbed in that of the general government.

It might be here shewn, that the power in the federal legislative, to raise and support armies at pleasure, as well in peace as in war, and their controul over the militia, tend, not only to a consolidation of the government, but the destruction of liberty.—I shall not, however, dwell upon

*Article I, section 8, clause i.

these, as a few observations upon the judicial power of this government, in addition to the preceding, will fully evince the truth of the position.

The judicial power of the United States is to be vested in a supreme court, and in such inferior courts as Congress may from time to time ordain and establish. The powers of these courts are very extensive; their jurisdiction comprehends all civil causes, except such as arise between citizens of the same state; and it extends to all cases in law and equity arising under the constitution. One inferior court must be established, I presume, in each state, at least, with the necessary executive officers appendant thereto. It is easy to see, that in the common course of things, these courts will eclipse the dignity, and take away from the respectability, of the state courts. These courts will be, in themselves, totally independent of the states, deriving their authority from the United States, and receiving from them fixed salaries; and in the course of human events it is to be expected, that they will swallow up all the powers of the courts in the respective states.

How far the clause in the 8th section of the 1st article may operate to do away all idea of confederated states, and to effect an entire consolidation of the whole into one general government, it is impossible to say. The powers given by this article are very general and comprehensive, and it may receive a construction to justify the passing almost any law. A power to make all laws, which shall be *necessary and proper*, for carrying into execution, all powers vested by the constitution in the government of the United States, or any department or officer thereof, is a power very comprehensive and definite, and may, for ought I know, be exercised in such manner as entirely to abolish the state legislatures. Suppose the legislature of a state should pass a law to raise money to support their government and pay the state debt, may the Congress repeal this law, because it may prevent the collection of a tax which they may think proper and necessary to lay, to provide for the general welfare of the United States? For all laws made, in pursuance of this constitution, are the supreme law of the land, and the judges in every state shall be bound thereby, any thing in the constitution or laws of the different states to the contrary notwithstanding.—By such a law, the government of a particular state might be overturned at one stroke, and thereby be deprived of every means of its support.

It is not meant, by stating this case, to insinuate that the constitution would warrant a law of this kind; or unnecessarily to alarm the fears of the people, by suggesting, that the federal legislature would be more likely to pass the limits assigned them by the constitution, than that of an individual state, further than they are less responsible to the people. But what is meant is, that the legislature of the United States are vested with the great and uncontroulable powers, of laying and collecting taxes, duties, imposts, and excises; of regulating trade, raising and supporting armies, organizing, arming, and disciplining the militia, instituting courts, and other general powers. And are by this clause invested with the power of making all laws, *proper and necessary*, for carrying all these into execution; and they may so exercise this power as entirely to annihilate all the state governments, and reduce this country to one single government. And if they may do it, it is pretty certain they will; for it will be found that the power retained by individual states, small as it is, will be a clog upon the wheels of the government of the United States; the latter therefore will be naturally inclined to remove it out of the way. Besides, it is a truth confirmed by the unerring experience of ages, that every man, and every body of men, invested with power, are ever disposed to increase it, and to acquire a superiority over every thing that stands in their way. This disposition, which is implanted in human nature, will operate in the federal legislature to lessen and ultimately to subvert the state authority, and having such advantages, will most certainly succeed, if the federal government succeeds at all. It must be very evident then, that what this constitution wants of being a complete consolidation of the several parts of the union into one complete government, possessed of perfect legislative, judicial, and executive powers, to all intents and purposes, it will necessarily acquire in its exercise and operation.

Let us now proceed to enquire, as I at first proposed, whether it be best the thirteen United States should be reduced to one great republic, or not? It is here taken for granted, that all agree in this, that whatever government we adopt, it ought to be a free one; that it should be so framed as to secure the liberty of the citizens of America, and such an one as to admit of a full, fair, and equal representation of the people. The question then will be, whether a government thus constituted, and founded on such principles, is practicable, and can be exercised over the whole United States, reduced into one state?

If respect is to be paid to the opinion of the greatest and wisest men who have ever thought or wrote on the science of government, we shall be constrained to conclude, that a free republic cannot succeed over a country of such immense extent, containing such a number of inhabitants, and these encreasing in such rapid progression as that of the whole United States. Among the many illustrious authorities which might be produced to this point, I shall content myself with quoting only two. The one is the baron de Montesquieu, spirit of laws,* chap. xvi. vol. i. "It is natural

---

*Charles Louis de Secondat, Baron de Montesquieu, *The Spirit of Laws* (2 vols., Geneva, 1748). By 1773 five English editions had been printed. Montesquieu was quoted often in the debate over ratification of the Constitution, by Federalists and Antifederalists alike.

to a republic to have only a small territory, otherwise it cannot long subsist. In a large republic there are men of large fortunes, and consequently of less moderation; there are trusts too great to be placed in any single subject; he has interest of his own; he soon begins to think that he may be happy, great and glorious, by oppressing his fellow citizens; and that he may raise himself to grandeur on the ruins of his country. In a large republic, the public good is sacrified to a thousand views; it is subordinate to exceptions, and depends on accidents. In a small one, the interest of the public is easier perceived, better understood, and more within the reach of every citizen; abuses are of less extent, and of course are less protected." Of the same opinion is the marquis Beccarari.

History furnishes no example of a free republic, any thing like the extent of the United States. The Grecian republics were of small extent; so also was that of the Romans. Both of these, it is true, in process of time, extended their conquests over large territories of country; and the consequence was, that their governments were changed from that of free governments to those of the most tyrannical that ever existed in the world.

Not only the opinion of the greatest men, and the experience of mankind, are against the idea of an extensive republic, but a variety of reasons may be drawn from the reason and nature of things, against it. In every government, the will of the sovereign is the law. In despotic governments, the supreme authority being lodged in one, his will is law, and can be as easily expressed to a large extensive territory as to a small one. In a pure democracy the people are the sovereign, and their will is declared by themselves; for this purpose they must all come together to deliberate, and decide. This kind of government cannot be exercised, therefore, over a country of any considerable extent; it must be confined to a single city, or at least limited to such bounds as that the people can conveniently assemble, be able to debate, understand the subject submitted to them, and declare their opinion concerning it.

In a free republic, although all laws are derived from the consent of the people, yet the people do not declare their consent by themselves in person, but by representatives, chosen by them, who are supposed to know the minds of their constituents, and to be possessed of integrity to declare this mind.

In every free government, the people must give their assent to the laws by which they are governed. This is the true criterion between a free government and an arbitrary one. The former are ruled by the will of the whole, expressed in any manner they may agree upon; the latter by the will of one, or a few. If the people are to give their assent to the laws, by persons chosen and appointed by them, the manner of the choice and the number chosen, must be such, as to possess, be disposed, and consequently qualified to declare the sentiments of the people; for if they do not know, or are not disposed to speak the sentiments of the people, the people do not govern, but the sovereignty is in a few. Now, in a large extended country, it is impossible to have a representation, possessing the sentiments, and of integrity, to declare the minds of the people, without having it so numerous and unwieldly, as to be subject in great measure to the inconveniency of a democratic government.

The territory of the United States is of vast extent; it now contains near three millions of souls, and is capable of containing much more than ten times that number. Is it practicable for a country, so large and so numerous as they will soon become, to elect a representation, that will speak their sentiments, without their becoming so numerous as to be incapable of transacting public business? It certainly is not.

In a republic, the manners, sentiments, and interests of the people should be similar. If this be not the case, there will be a constant clashing of opinions; and the representatives of one part will be continually striving against those of the other. This will retard the operations of government, and prevent such conclusions as will promote the public good. If we apply this remark to the condition of the United States, we shall be convinced that it forbids that we should be one government. The United States includes a variety of climates. The productions of the different parts of the union are very variant, and their interests, of consequence, diverse. Their manners and habits differ as much as their climates and productions; and their sentiments are by no means coincident. The laws and customs of the several states are, in many respects, very diverse, and in some opposite; each would be in favor of its own interests and customs, and, of consequence, a legislature, formed of representatives from the respective parts, would not only be too numerous to act with any care or decision, but would be composed of such heterogenous and discordant principles, as would constantly be contending with each other.

The laws cannot be executed in a republic, of an extent equal to that of the Unites States, with promptitude.

The magistrates in every government must be supported in the execution of the laws, either by an armed force, maintained at the public expence for that purpose; or by the people turning out to aid the magistrate upon his command, in case of resistance.

In despotic governments, as well as in all the monarchies of Europe, standing armies are kept up to execute the commands of the prince or the magistrate, and are employed for this purpose when occasion requires: But they have always proved the destruction of liberty, and is abhorrent to the spirit of a free republic. In England, where they depend upon the parliament for their annual support, they have always been complained of as oppressive and unconstitutional, and are seldom employed in executing of the laws; never except on extraordinary occasions, and then under the direction of a civil magistrate.

A free republic will never keep a standing army to execute its laws. It must depend upon the support of its citizens. But when a government is to receive its support from the aid of the citizens, it must be so constructed as to have the confidence, respect, and affection of the people. Men who, upon the call of the magistrate, offer themselves to execute the laws, are influenced to do it either by affection to the government, or from fear; where a standing army is at hand to punish offenders, every man is actuated by the latter principle, and therefore, when the magistrate calls, will obey: but, where this is not the case, the government must rest for its support upon the confidence and respect which the people have for their government and laws. The body of the people being attached, the government will always be sufficient to support and execute its laws, and to operate upon the fears of any faction which may be opposed to it, not only to prevent an opposition to the execution of the laws themselves, but also to compel the most of them to aid the magistrate; but the people will not be likely to have such confidence in their rulers, in a republic so extensive as the United States, as necessary for these purposes. The confidence which the people have in their rulers, in a free republic, arises from their knowing them, from their being responsible to them for their conduct, and from the power they have of displacing them when they misbehave: but in a republic of the extent of this continent, the people in general would be acquainted with very few of their rulers: the people at large would know little of their proceedings, and it would be extremely difficult to change them. The people in Georgia and New-Hampshire would not know one another's mind, and therefore could not act in concert to enable them to effect a general change of representatives. The different parts of so extensive a country could not possibly be made acquainted with the conduct of their representatives, nor be informed of the reasons upon which measures were founded. The consequence will be, they will have no confidence in their legislature, suspect them of ambitious views, be jealous of every measure they adopt, and will not support the laws they pass. Hence the government will be nerveless and inefficient, and no way will be left to render it otherwise, but by establishing an armed force to execute the laws at the point of the bayonet—a government of all others the most to be dreaded.

In a republic of such vast extent as the United-States, the legislature cannot attend to the various concerns and wants of its different parts. It cannot be sufficiently numerous to be acquainted with the local condition and wants of the different districts, and if it could, it is impossible it should have sufficient time to attend to and provide for all the variety of cases of this nature, that would be continually arising.

In so extensive a republic, the great officers of government would soon become above the controul of the people, and abuse their power to the purpose of aggrandizing themselves, and oppressing them. The trust committed to the executive offices, in a country of the extent of the United-States, must be various and of magnitude. The command of all the troops and navy of the republic, the appointment of officers, the power of pardoning offences, the collecting of all the public revenues, and the power of expending them, with a number of other powers, must be lodged and exercised in every state, in the hands of a few. When these are attended with great honor and emolument, as they always will be in large states, so as greatly to interest men to pursue them, and to be proper objects for ambitious and designing men, such men will be ever restless in their pursuit after them. They will use the power, when they have acquired it, to the purposes of gratifying their own interest and ambition, and it is scarcely possible, in a very large republic, to call them to account for their misconduct, or to prevent their abuse of power.

These are some of the reasons by which it appears, that a free republic cannot long subsist over a country of the great extent of these states. If then this new constitution is calculated to consolidate the thirteen states into one, as it evidently is, it ought not to be adopted.

Though I am of opinion, that it is a sufficient objection to this government, to reject it, that it creates the whole union into one government, under the form of a republic, yet if this objection was obviated, there are exceptions to it, which are so material and fundamental, that they ought to determine every man, who is a friend to the liberty and happiness of mankind, not to adopt it. I beg the candid and dispassionate attention of my countrymen while I state these objections—they are such as have obtruded themselves upon my mind upon a careful attention to the matter, and such as I sincerely believe are well founded. There are many objections, of small moment, of which I shall take no notice—perfection is not to be expected in any thing that is the production of man—and if I did not in my conscience believe that this scheme was defective in the fundamental principles—in the foundation upon which a free and equal government must rest—I would hold my peace.

CATO III
New York Journal, 25 October 1787*

To the CITIZENS of the STATE of NEW-YORK.

In the close of my last introductory address, I told you, that my object in future would be to take up this new form of national government, to compare it with the experience and opinions of the most sensible and approved political authors, and to show you that its principles, and the exercise of them will be dangerous to your liberty and happiness.

Although I am conscious that this is an arduous undertaking, yet I will perform it to the best of my ability.

The freedom, equality, and independence which you enjoyed by nature, induced you to consent to a political power. The same principles led you to examine the errors and vices of a British superintendence, to divest yourselves of it, and to reassume a new political shape. It is acknowledged that there are defects in this, and another is tendered to you for acceptance; the great question then, that arises on this new political principle, is, whether it will answer the ends for which it is said to be offered to you, and for which all men engage in political society, to wit, the mutual preservation of their lives, liberties, and estates.

The recital, or premises on which this new form of government is erected, declares a consolidation or union of all the thirteen parts, or states, into one great whole, under the firm of the United States, for all the various and important purposes therein set forth.—But whoever seriously considers the immense extent of territory comprehended within the limits of the United States, together with the variety of its climates, productions, and commerce, the difference of extent, and number of inhabitants in all; the dissimilitude of interest, morals, and policies, in almost every one, will receive it as an intuitive truth, that a consolidated republican form of government therein, can never *form a perfect union, establish justice, insure domestic tranquility, promote the general welfare, and secure the blessings of liberty to you and your posterity*, for to these objects it must be directed: this unkindred legislature therefore, composed of interests opposite and dissimilar in their nature, will in its exercise, emphatically be, like a house divided against itself.

The governments of Europe have taken their limits and form from adventitious circumstances, and nothing can be argued on the motive of agreement from them; but these adventitious political principles, have

*This is the third of seven essays signed "Cato" that appeared in the *New York Journal* between 27 September 1787 and 3 January 1788. The author is not known, but contemporaries attributed it to Governor George Clinton. This essay was reprinted in the New York *Daily Advertiser*, 27 October; and the *Albany Gazette*, 8 November.

nevertheless produced effects that have attracted the attention of philosophy, which has established axioms in the science of politics therefrom, as irrefragable as any in Euclid. It is natural, says Montesquieu, *to a republic to have only a small territory, otherwise it cannot long subsist: in a large one, there are men of large fortunes, and consequently of less moderation; there are too great deposits to intrust in the hands of a single subject, an ambitious person soon becomes sensible that he may be happy, great, and glorious by oppressing his fellow citizens, and that he might raise himself to grandeur, on the ruins of his country. In large republics, the public good is sacrificed to a thousand views; in a small one the interest of the public is easily perceived, better understood, and more within the reach of every citizen; abuses have a less extent, and of course are less protected*—he also shews you, that the duration of the republic of Sparta, was owing to its having continued with the same extent of territory after all its wars; and that the ambition of Athens and Lacedemon to command and direct the union, lost them their liberties, and gave them a monarchy.

From this picture, what can you promise yourselves, on the score of consolidation of the United States, into one government—impracticability in the just exercise of it—your freedom insecure—even this form of government limited in its continuance—the employments of your country disposed of to the opulent, to whose contumely you will continually be an object—you must risque much, by indispensibly placing trusts of the greatest magnitude, into the hands of individuals, whose ambition for power, and agrandisement, will oppress and grind you—where, from the vast extent of your territory, and the complication of interests, the science of government will become intricate and perplexed, and too misterious for you to understand, and observe; and by which you are to be conducted into a monarchy, either limited or despotic; the latter, Mr. Locke remarks, *is a government derived from neither nature, nor compact.**

Political liberty, the great Montesquieu again observes, *consists in security, or at least in the opinion we have of security*; and this *security* therefore, or the *opinion*, is best obtained in moderate governments, where the mildness of the laws, and the equality of the manners, beget a confidence in the people, which produces this security, or the opinion. This moderation in governments, depends in a great measure on their limits, connected with their political distribution.

---

*In his *Second Treatise of Government* (1690), John Locke (1632–1704) stated that ". . . despotic power is an absolute, arbitrary power one man has over another to take his life whenever he pleases. This is a power which neither nature gives—for it has made no such distinction between one man and another—nor compact can convey, for man, not having such an arbitrary power over his own life, cannot give another man such a power over it. . . ."

The extent of many of the states in the Union, is at this time, almost too great for the superintendence of a republican form of government, and must one day or other, revolve into more vigorous ones, or by separation be reduced into smaller, and more useful, as well as moderate ones. You have already observed the feeble efforts of Massachusetts against their insurgents;* with what difficulty did they quell that insurrection; and is not the province of Maine at this moment, on the eve of separation from her. The reason of these things is, that for the security of the *property* of the community, in which expressive term Mr. Lock makes life, liberty, and estate, to consist—the wheels of a free republic are necessarily slow in their operation; hence in large free republics, the evil sometimes is not only begun, but almost completed, before they are in a situation to turn the current into a contrary progression: the extremes are also too remote from the usual seat of government, and the laws therefore too feeble to afford protection to all its parts, and insure *domestic tranquility* without the aid of another principle. If, therefore, this state, and that of N. Carolina, had an army under their controul, they never would have lost Vermont, and Frankland,† nor the state of Massachusetts suffer an insurrection, or the dismemberment of her fairest district, but the exercise of a principle which would have prevented these things, if we may believe the experience of ages, would have ended in the destruction of their liberties.

Will this consolidated republic, if established, in its exercise beget such confidence and compliance, among the citizens of these states, as to do without the aid of a standing army—I deny that it will.—The malcontents in each state, who will not be a few, nor the least important, will be exciting factions against it—the fear of a dismemberment of some of its parts, and the necessity to enforce the execution of revenue laws (a fruitful source of oppression) on the extremes and in the other districts of the government, will incidentally, and necessarily require a permanent force, to be kept on foot—will not political security, and even the opinion of it, be extinguished? can mildness and moderation exist in a government, where the primary incident in its exercise must be force? will not violence destroy confidence, and can equality subsist, where the extent, policy, and practice of it, will naturally lead to make odious distinctions among citizens?

The people, who may compose this national legislature from the southern states, in which, from the mildness of the climate, the fertility of the soil, and the value of its productions, wealth is rapidly acquired,

*A reference to Shays's Rebellion in the fall and winter of 1786–87.
†Vermont was seeking its independence from New York and the State of Franklin (modern Tennessee) from North Carolina.

and where the same causes naturally lead to luxury, dissipation, and a passion for aristocratic distinctions; where slavery is encouraged, and liberty of course, less respected, and protected; who know not what it is to acquire property by their own toil, nor to œconomise with the savings of industry—will these men therefore be as tenacious of the liberties and interests of the more northern states, where freedom, independence, industry, equality, and frugality, are natural to the climate and soil, as men who are your own citizens, legislating in your own state, under your inspection, and whose manners, and fortunes, bear a more equal resemblance to your own?

It may be suggested, in answer to this, that whoever is a citizen of one state, is a citizen of each, and that therefore he will be as interested in the happiness and interest of all, as the one he is delegated from; but the argument is fallacious, and, whoever has attended to the history of mankind, and the principles which bind them together as parents, citizens, or men, will readily perceive it. These principles are, in their exercise, like a pebble cast on the calm surface of a river, the circles begin in the center, and are small, active, and forcible, but as they depart from that point, they lose their force, and vanish into calmness.

The strongest principle of union resides within our domestic walls. The ties of the parent exceed that of any other; as we depart from home, the next general principle of union is amongst citizens of the same state, where acquaintance, habits, and fortunes, nourish affection, and attachment; enlarge the circle still further, &, as citizens of different states, though we acknowledge the same national denomination, we lose the ties of acquaintance, habits, and fortunes, and thus, by degrees, we lessen in our attachments, till, at length, we no more than acknowledge a sameness of species. Is it therefore, from certainty like this, reasonable to believe, that inhabitants of Georgia, or New-Hampshire, will have the same obligations towards you as your own, and preside over your lives, liberties, and property, with the same care and attachment? Intuitive reason, answers in the negative.

In the course of my examination of the principles of consolidation of the states into one general government, many other reasons against it have occurred, but I flatter myself, from those herein offered to your consideration, I have convinced you that it is both presumptious and impracticable consistent with your safety. To detain you with further remarks, would be useless—I shall however, continue in my following numbers, to anilise this new government, pursuant to my promise.

AN OLD WHIG IV
Philadelphia *Independent Gazetteer*, 27 October 1787 (excerpt)*

It is beyond a doubt that the new federal constitution, if adopted, will in a great measure destroy, if it do not totally annihilate, the separate governments of the several states. We shall, in effect, become one great Republic.—Every measure of any importance, will be Continental.—What will be the consequence of this? One thing is evident—that no Republic of so great a magnitude, ever did, or ever can exist. But a few years elapsed, from the time in which ancient Rome extended her dominions beyond the bounds of Italy, until the downfal of her Republic; and all political writers agree, that a Republican government can exist only in a narrow territory: but a confederacy of different Republics has, in many instances, existed and flourished for a long time together—The celebrated *Helvetian* league, which exists at this moment in full vigor, and with unimpaired strength, whilst its origin may be traced to the confines of antiquity, is one, among many examples on this head; and at the same time furnishes an eminent proof of how much less importance it is, that the constituent parts of a confederacy of Republics may be rightly framed than it is, that the confederacy itself should be rightly organized;—for hardly any two of the Swiss cantons have the same form of government, and they are almost equally divided in their religious principles, which have so often rent asunder the firmest establishments. A confederacy of Republics must be the establishment in America, or we must cease altogether to retain the Republican form of government. From the moment we become one great Republic, either in form or substance, the period is very shortly removed, when we shall sink first into monarchy, and then into despotism.—If there were no other fault in the proposed constitution, it must sink by its own weight. The continent of North-America can no more be governed by one Republic, than the fabled Atlas could support the heavens. Is it not worthy a few months labour, to attempt the rescuing this country from the despotism, which at this moment holds the best and fairest regions of the earth in thraldom and wretchedness?—To attempt the forming a plan of confederation, which may enable us at once to support our continental union with vigor and efficacy, and to maintain the rights of the separate

*This is the fourth of eight essays signed "An Old Whig" that appeared in the Philadelphia *Independent Gazetteer* between 12 October 1787 and 6 February 1788. The author is not known, but there was speculation that a group of Pennsylvania Antifederalists—George Bryan, John Smilie, James Hutchinson, and others—might have jointly written the series. Another contemporary guessed that it was Bryan alone. This essay was reprinted in the Philadelphia *Freeman's Journal*, 31 October; *New York Morning Post*, 3 November; Baltimore *Maryland Gazette*, 6 November; *Massachusetts Gazette*, 27 November; and *New York Journal*, 8 December. It was also printed as a broadside in Philadelphia.

states and the invaluable liberty of the subject? These ideas of political felicity, to some people, may seem like the visions of an Utopian fancy; and I am persuaded that some amongst us have as little disposition to realize them, as they have to recollect the principles, which inspired us in our revolt from Great-Britain. But there is at least, this consolation in aiming at excellence, that, if we do not obtain our object, we can make considerable progress towards it.—The science of politics has very seldom had fair play. So much of passion, interest and temporary prospects of gain are mixed in the pursuit, that a government has been much oftener established, with a view to the particular advantages or necessities of a few individuals, than to the permanent good of society. If the men, who, at different times, have been entrusted to form plans of government for the world, had been really actuated by no other views than a regard to the public good, the condition of human nature in all ages would have been widely different, from that which has been exhibited to us in history. In this country perhaps we are possessed of more than our share of political virtue. If we will exercise a little patience, and bestow our best endeavours on the business, I do not think it impossible, that we may yet form a federal constitution, much superior to any form of government, which has ever existed in the world;—but, whenever this important work shall be accomplished, I venture to pronounce, that it will not be done without a *careful attention to the framing of a bill of rights.**

Federalist

JAMES WILSON
Speech in Pennsylvania Convention, 24 November 1787†

The extent of country for which the New Constitution was required, produced another difficulty in the business of the Fœderal Convention. It is the opinion of some celebrated writers that to a small territory, the

---

*For the continuation, see the Bill of Rights section, below.

†*The Substance of a Speech Delivered by James Wilson, Esq. Explanatory of the General Principles of the Proposed Federal Constitution* ... (Philadelphia, 1787), 5. James Wilson, a lawyer in Philadelphia, was an important member of the Constitutional Convention and represented Philadelphia in the state ratifying Convention, which met from 20 November to 15 December 1787. Two summaries of this speech were reprinted in twenty-five newspapers. A pamphlet version was printed in Philadelphia on 28 November. (The text of the speech printed here is taken from this pamphlet.) Eleven newspapers from New Hampshire to New York reprinted this pamphlet version by 7 January 1788. The speech was also included in Thomas Lloyd's one-volume edition of the Pennsylvania Convention debates printed in Philadelphia on 7 February 1788.

democratical, to a midling territory, (as Montesquieu has termed it) the monarchical, and, to an extensive territory, the despotic form of government, is best adapted. Regarding then, the wide and almost unbounded jurisdiction of the United States, at first view, the hand of despotism seemed necessary to controul, connect, and protect it; and hence the chief embarrasment arose. For, we knew that, although our Constituents would chearfully submit to the legislative restraints of a free government, they would spurn at every attempt to shackle them with despotic power.

In this dilemma, a Fœderal Republic naturally presented itself to our observation, as a species of government which secured all the internal advantages of a republic, at the same time that it maintained the external dignity and force of a monarchy. The definition of this form of government may be found in Montesquieu, who says, I believe, that it consists in assembling distinct societies, which are consolidated into a new body, capable of being encreased by the addition of other members;—an expanding quality peculiarly fitted to the circumstances of America.

But, while a Fœderal Republic, removed one difficulty, it introduced another, since there existed not any precedent to assist our deliberations; for, though there are many single governments, both ancient and modern, the history and principles of which are faithfully preserved, and well understood, a perfect confederation of independent states is a system hitherto unknown. The Swiss Cantons, which have often been mentioned in that light, cannot properly be deemed a Fœderal Republic, but merely a system of United States. The United Netherlands are also an assemblage of states; yet, as their proceedings are not the result of their combined decisions, but of the decisions of each state individually, their association is evidently wanting in that quality which is essential to constitute a Fœderal Republic. With respect to the Germanic Body, its members are of so disproportionate a size, their separate governments and jurisdictions so different in nature and extent, the general purpose and operation of their union so indefinite and uncertain, and the exterior power of the House of Austria so prevalent, that little information could be obtained or expected from that quarter. Turning then to ancient history, we find the Achæan and Lycian leagues, and the Amphyctionic council bearing a superficial resemblance to a Fœderal Republic; but of all these, the accounts which have been transmitted to us, are too vague and imperfect to supply a tolerable theory, and they are so destitute of that minute detail from which practical knowledge may be derived, that they must now be considered rather as subjects of curiosity, than of use or information.

PUBLIUS: THE FEDERALIST 39 (JAMES MADISON)
New York *Independent Journal*, 16 January 1788*

To the People of the State of New-York.

The last paper having concluded the observations which were meant to introduce a candid survey of the plan of government reported by the convention, we now proceed to the execution of that part of our undertaking. The first question that offers itself is, whether the general form and aspect of the government be strictly republican? It is evident that no other form would be reconcileable with the genius of the people of America; with the fundamental principles of the revolution; or with that honorable determination, which animates every votary of freedom, to rest all our political experiments on the capacity of mankind for self-government. If the plan of the Convention therefore be found to depart from the republican character, its advocates must abandon it as no longer defensible.

What then are the distinctive characters of the republican form? Were an answer to this question to be sought, not by recurring to principles, but in the application of the term by political writers, to the constitutions of different States, no satisfactory one would ever be found. Holland, in which no particle of the supreme authority is derived from the people, has passed almost universally under the denomination of a republic. The same title has been bestowed on Venice, where absolute power over the great body of the people, is exercised in the most absolute manner, by a small body of hereditary nobles. Poland, which is a mixture of aristocracy and of monarchy in their worst forms, has been dignified with the same appellation. The government of England, which has one republican branch only, combined with a hereditery aristocracy and monarchy, has with equal impropriety been frequently placed on the list of republics. These examples, which are nearly as dissimilar to each other as to a genuine republic, shew the extreme inaccuracy with which the term has been used in political disquisitions.

If we resort for a criterion, to the different principles on which different forms of government are established, we may define a republic to be, or at least may bestow that name on, a government which derives all its powers directly or indirectly from the great body of the people; and is administered by persons holding their offices during pleasure, for a limited period, or during good behaviour. It is *essential* to such a gov-

*This is one of eighty-five essays entitled *The Federalist* and signed by "Publius" that first appeared in newspapers in New York City and in a two-volume edition between 27 October 1787 and 28 May 1788. The authors were Alexander Hamilton, James Madison, and John Jay. This essay, by James Madison, was also printed in the New York *Daily Advertiser* on 16 January. It was reprinted in the *New York Packet*, 18 January, and the *New York Journal*, 30 January.

ernment, that it be derived from the great body of the society, not from an inconsiderable proportion, or a favored class of it; otherwise a handful of tyrannical nobles, exercising their oppressions by a delegation of their powers, might aspire to the rank of republicans, and claim for their government the honorable title of republic. It is *sufficient* for such a government, that the persons administering it be appointed, either directly or indirectly, by the people; and that they hold their appointments by either of the tenures just specified; otherwise every government in the United States, as well as every other popular government that has been or can be well organized or well executed, would be degraded from the republican character. According to the Constitution of every State in the Union, some or other of the officers of government are appointed indirectly only by the people. According to most of them the chief magistrate himself is so appointed.* And according to one, this mode of appointment is extended to one of the co-ordinate branches of the legislature. According to all the Constitutions also, the tenure of the highest offices is extended to a definite period, and in many instances, both within the legislative and executive departments, to a period of years. According to the provisions of most of the constitutions, again, as well as according to the most respectable and received opinions on the subject, the members of the judiciary department are to retain their offices by the firm tenure of good behaviour.

On comparing the Constitution planned by the Convention, with the standard here fixed, we perceive at once that it is in the most rigid sense conformable to it. The House of Representatives, like that of one branch at least of all the State Legislatures, is elected immediately by the great body of the people. The Senate, like the present Congress, and the Senate of Maryland, derives its appointment indirectly from the people.† The President is indirectly derived from the choice of the people, according to the example in most of the States. Even the judges, with all other officers of the Union, will, as in the several States, be the choice, though a remote choice, of the people themselves. The duration of the appointments is equally conformable to the republican standard, and to the model of the State Constitutions. The House of Representatives is periodically elective as in all the States: and for the period of two years as in the State of South-Carolina. The Senate is elective for the period of six years; which is but one year more than the period of the Senate of Maryland; and but two more than of the Senates of New-York and Virginia. The President is to continue in office for the period of four years;

---

*The executive was elected by the people in five states; the legislature elected the executive in eight states.

†In Maryland, senators were chosen by electors who were elected by the people.

as in New-York and Delaware, the chief magistrate is elected for three years, and in South-Carolina for two years. In the other States the election is annual. In several of the States however, no constitutional provision is made for the impeachment of the Chief Magistrate. And in Delaware and Virginia, he is not impeachable till out of office. The President of the United States is impeachable at any time during his continuance in office. The tenure by which the Judges are to hold their places, is, as it unquestionably ought to be, that of good behaviour. The tenure of the ministerial offices generally will be a subject of legal regulation, conformably to the reason of the case, and the example of the State Constitutions.

Could any further proof be required of the republican complextion of this system, the most decisive one might be found in its absolute prohibition of titles of nobility, both under the Federal and the State Governments; and in its express guarantee of the republican form to each of the latter.

But it was not sufficient, say the adversaries of the proposed Constitution, for the convention to adhere to the republican form. They ought, with equal care, to have preserved the *federal* form, which regards the union as a *confederacy* of sovereign States; instead of which, they have framed a *national* government, which regards the union as a *consolidation* of the States. And it is asked by what authority this bold and radical innovation was undertaken. The handle which has been made of this objection requires, that it should be examined with some precision.

Without enquiring into the accuracy of the distinction on which the objection is founded, it will be necessary to a just estimate of its force, first to ascertain the real character of the government in question; secondly, to enquire how far the Convention were authorised to propose such a government; and thirdly, how far the duty they owed to their country, could supply any defect of regular authority.

First. In order to ascertain the real character of the government it may be considered in relation to the foundation on which it is to be established; to the sources from which its ordinary powers are to be drawn; to the operation of those powers; to the extent of them; and to the authority by which future changes in the government are to be introduced.

On examining the first relation, it appears on one hand that the Constitution is to be founded on the assent and ratification of the people of America, given by deputies elected for the special purpose; but on the other that this assent and ratification is to be given by the people, not as individuals composing one entire nation; but as composing the distinct and independent States to which they respectively belong. It is to be the assent and ratification of the several States, derived from the supreme authority in each State, the authority of the people themselves. The act therefore establishing the Constitution, will not be a *national* but a *federal* act.

That it will be a federal and not a national act, as these terms are understood by the objectors, the act of the people as forming so many independent States, not as forming one aggregate nation, is obvious from this single consideration that it is to result neither from the decision of a *majority* of the people of the Union, nor from that of a *majority* of the States. It must result from the *unanimous* assent of the several States that are parties to it, differing no other wise from their ordinary assent than in its being expressed, not by the legislative authority, but by that of the people themselves. Were the people regarded in this transaction as forming one nation, the will of the majority of the whole people of the United States, would bind the minority; in the same manner as the majority in each State must bind the minority; and the will of the majority must be determined either by a comparison of the individual votes; or by considering the will of a majority of the States, as evidence of the will of a majority of the people of the United States. Neither of these rules has been adopted. Each State in ratifying the Constitution, is considered as a sovereign body independent of all others, and only to be bound by its own voluntary act. In this relation then the new Constitution will, if established, be a *federal* and not a *national* Constitution.

The next relation is to the sources from which the ordinary powers of government are to be derived. The house of representatives will derive its powers from the people of America, and the people will be represented in the same proportion, and on the same principle, as they are in the Legislature of a particular State. So far the Government is *national* not *federal*. The Senate on the other hand will derive its powers from the States, as political and co-equal societies; and these will be represented on the principle of equality in the Senate, as they now are in the existing Congress. So far the government is *federal*, not *national*. The executive power will be derived from a very compound source. The immediate election of the President is to be made by the States in their political characters. The votes allotted to them, are in a compound ratio, which considers them partly as distinct and co-equal societies; partly as unequal members of the same society. The eventual election, again is to be made by that branch of the Legislature which consists of the national representatives; but in this particular act, they are to be thrown into the form of individual delegations from so many distinct and co-equal bodies politic. From this aspect of the Government, it appears to be of a mixed character presenting at least as many *federal* as *national* features.

The difference between a federal and national Government as it relates to the *operation of the Government* is ⟨by the adversaries of the plan of the convention⟩* supposed to consist in this, that in the former, the powers operate on the political bodies composing the confederacy, in their political capacities: In the latter, on the individual citizens, composing the nation, in their individual capacities. On trying the Constitution by this criterion, it falls under the *national*, not the *federal* character; though perhaps not so compleatly, as has been understood. In several cases and particularly in the trial of controversies to which States may be parties, they must be viewed and proceeded against in their collective and political capacities only. So far the national countenance of the Government on this side seems so to be disfigured by a few federal features. But this blemish is perhaps unavoidable in any plan; and the operation of the Government on the people in their individual capacities, in its ordinary and most essential proceedings, may† on the whole designate it in this relation a *national* Government.

But if the Government be national with regard to the *operation* of its powers, it changes its aspect again when we contemplate it in relation to the *extent* of its powers. The idea of a national Government involves in it, not only an authority over the individual citizens; but an indefinite supremacy over all persons and things, so far as they are objects of lawful Government. Among a people consolidated into one nation, this supremacy is compleatly vested in the national Legislature. Among communities united for particular purposes, it is vested partly in the general, and partly in the municipal Legislatures. In the former case, all local authorities are subordinate to the supreme; and may be controuled, directed or abolished by it at pleasure. In the latter the local or municipal authorities form distinct and independent portions of the supremacy, no more subject within their respective spheres to the general authority, than the general authority is subject to them, within its own sphere. In this relation then the proposed Government cannot be deemed a *national* one; since its jurisdiction extends to certain enumerated objects only, and leaves to the several States a residuary and inviolable sovereignty over all other objects. It is true that in controversies relating to the boundary between the two jurisdictions, the tribunal which is ultimately to decide, is to be established under the general Government. But this does not change the principle of the case. The decision is to be impartially made, according to the rules of the Constitution; and all the usual and most effectual precautions are taken to secure this impartiality. Some such tribunal is clearly essential to prevent an appeal to the sword, and a dissolution of the compact; and that it ought

---

*The material in angle brackets was added in the book version.
†In the book version, "may" was deleted and replaced by "will in the sense of its opponents."

to be established under the general, rather than under the local Governments; or to speak more properly, that it could be safely established under the first alone, is a position not likely to be combated.

If we try the Constitution by its last relation, to the authority by which amendments are to be made, we find it neither wholly *national*, nor wholly *federal*. Were it wholly national, the supreme and ultimate authority would reside in the *majority* of the people of the Union; and this authority would be competent at all times, like that of a majority of every national society, to alter or abolish its established Government. Were it wholly federal on the other head, the concurrence of each State in the Union would be essential to every alteration that would be binding on all. The mode provided by the plan of the Convention is not founded on either of these principles. In requiring more than a majority, and particularly, in computing the proportion by *States*, not by *citizens*, it departs from the *national*, and advances towards the *federal* character: In rendering the concurrence of less than the whole number of States sufficient, it loses again the *federal*, and partakes of the *national* character.

The proposed Constitution therefore ⟨even when tested by the rules laid down by its antagonists⟩* is in strictness neither a national nor a federal constitution; but a composition of both. In its foundation, it is federal, not national; in the sources from which the ordinary powers of the Government are drawn, it is partly federal, and partly national: in the operation of these powers, it is national, not federal: In the extent of them again, it is federal, not national: And finally, in the authoritative mode of introducing amendments, it is neither wholly federal, nor wholly national.

PUBLIUS: THE FEDERALIST 10 (JAMES MADISON)
New York *Daily Advertiser*, 22 November 1787†

To the People of the State of New-York.

Among the numerous advantages promised by a well constructed Union, none deserves to be more accurately developed than its tendency to break and control the violence of faction. The friend of popular governments, never finds himself so much alarmed for their character and fate, as when he contemplates their propensity to this dangerous vice. He

---

*The material in angle brackets was added in the book version.

†This essay was the first in *The Federalist* series written by James Madison. He had expressed similar ideas in his notes, "Vices of the Political System," written in early 1787, in speeches in the Constitutional Convention on 6 and 26 June, and in a letter to Thomas Jefferson, 24 October. The essay was reprinted in the *New York Packet*, 23 November; New York *Independent Journal*, 24 November; *Pennsylvania Gazette*, 2 January 1788; and the *Hudson Weekly Gazette*, 10 January.

will not fail therefore to set a due value on any plan which, without violating the principles to which he is attached, provides a proper cure for it. The instability, injustice and confusion introduced into the public councils, have in truth been the mortal diseases under which popular governments have every where perished; as they continue to be the favorite and fruitful topics from which the adversaries to liberty derive their most specious declamations. The valuable improvements made by the American Constitutions on the popular models, both ancient and modern, cannot certainly be too much admired; but it would be an unwarrantable partiality, to contend that they have as effectually obviated the danger on this side as was wished and expected. Complaints are every where heard from our most considerate and virtuous citizens, equally the friends of public and private faith, and of public and personal liberty; that our governments are too unstable; that the public good is disregarded in the conflicts of rival parties; and that measures are too often decided, not according to the rules of justice, and the rights of the minor party; but by the superior force of an interested and over-bearing majority. However anxiously we may wish that these complaints had no foundation, the evidence of known facts will not permit us to deny that they are in some degree true. It will be found indeed, on a candid review of our situation, that some of the distresses under which we labor, have been erroneously charged on the operation of our governments; but it will be found, at the same time, that other causes will not alone account for many of our heaviest misfortunes; and particularly, for that prevailing and increasing distrust of public engagements, and alarm for private rights, which are echoed from one end of the continent to the other. These must be chiefly, if not wholly, effects of the unsteadiness and injustice, with which a factious spirit has tainted our public administration.

By a faction I understand a number of citizens, whether amounting to a majority or minority of the whole, who are united and actuated by some common impulse of passion, or of interest, adverse to the rights of other citizens, or to the permanent and aggregate interests of the community.

There are two methods of curing the mischiefs of faction: the one, by removing its causes; the other, by controling its effects.

There are again two methods of removing the causes of faction: the one by destroying the liberty which is essential to its existence; the other, by giving to every citizen the same opinions, the same passions, and the same interests.

It could never be more truly said than of the first remedy, that it is worse than the disease. Liberty is to faction, what air is to fire, an aliment without which it instantly expires. But it could not be a less folly to abolish liberty, which is essential to political life, because it nourishes faction, than it would be to wish the annihilation of air, which is essential to animal life, because it imparts to fire its destructive agency.

The second expedient is as impracticable, as the first would be unwise. As long as the reason of man continues fallible, and he is at liberty to exercise it, different opinions will be formed. As long as the connection subsists between his reason and his self-love, his opinions and his passions will have a reciprocal influence on each other; and the former will be objects to which the latter will attach themselves. The diversity in the faculties of men from which the rights of property originate, is not less an insuperable obstacle to a uniformity of interests. The protection of these faculties is the first object of Government. From the protection of different and unequal faculties of acquiring property, the possession of different degrees and kinds of property immediately results: and from the influence of these on the sentiments and views of the respective proprietors, ensues a division of the society into different interests and parties.

The latent causes of faction are thus sown in the nature of man; and we see them every where brought into different degrees of activity, according to the different circumstances of civil society. A zeal for different opinions concerning religion, concerning Government, and many other points, as well of speculation as of practice; an attachment to different leaders ambitiously contending for pre-eminence and power; or to persons of other descriptions whose fortunes have been interesting to the human passions, have in turn divided mankind into parties, inflamed them with mutual animosity, and rendered them much more disposed to vex and oppress each other, than to co-operate for their common good. So strong is this propensity of mankind to fall into mutual animosities, that where no substantial occasion presents itself, the most frivolous and fanciful distinctions have been sufficient to kindle their unfriendly passions, and excite their most violent conflicts. But the most common and durable source of factions, has been the various and unequal distribution of property. Those who hold, and those who are without property, have ever formed distinct interests in society. Those who are creditors, and those who are debtors, fall under a like discrimination. A landed interest, a manufacturing interest, a mercantile interest, a monied interest, with many lesser interests, grow up of necessity in civilized nations, and divide them into different classes, actuated by different sentiments and views. The regulation of these various and interfering interests forms the principal task of modern Legislation, and involves the spirit of party and faction in the necessary and ordinary operations of Government.

No man is allowed to be a judge in his own cause; because his interest would certainly bias his judgment, and, not improbably, corrupt his integrity. With equal, nay with greater reason, a body of men, are unfit to be both judges and parties, at the same time; yet, what are many of the most important acts of legislation, but so many judicial determinations, not indeed concerning the rights of single persons, but concerning the rights of large bodies of citizens; and what are the different classes of legislators, but advocates and parties to the causes which they determine? Is a law proposed concerning private debts? It is a question to which the creditors are parties on one side, and the debtors on the other. Justice ought to hold the balance between them. Yet the parties are and must be themselves the judges; and the most numerous party, or, in other words, the most powerful faction must be expected to prevail. Shall domestic manufactures be encouraged, and in what degree, by restrictions on foreign manufactures? are questions which would be differently decided by the landed and the manufacturing classes; and probably by neither, with a sole regard to justice and the public good. The apportionment of taxes on the various descriptions of property, is an act which seems to require the most exact impartiality; yet there is perhaps no legislative act in which greater opportunity and temptation are given to a predominant party, to trample on the rules of justice. Every shilling with which they over-burden the inferior number, is a shilling saved to their own pockets.

It is in vain to say, that enlightened statesmen will be able to adjust these clashing interests, and render them all subservient to the public good. Enlightened statesmen will not always be at the helm: Nor, in many cases, can such an adjustment be made at all, without taking into view indirect and remote considerations, which will rarely prevail over the immediate interest which one party may find in disregarding the rights of another, or the good of the whole.

The inference to which we are brought, is, that the *causes* of faction cannot be removed; and that relief is only to be sought in the means of controling its *effects*.

If a faction consists of less than a majority, relief is supplied by the republican principle, which enables the majority to defeat its sinister views by regular vote: It may clog the administration, it may convulse the society; but it will be unable to execute and mask its violence under the forms of the constitution. When a majority is included in a faction, the form of popular government on the other hand enables it to sacrifice to its ruling passion or interest, both the public good and the rights of other citizens. To secure the public good, and private rights, against the danger of such a faction, and at the same time to preserve the spirit and the form of popular government, is then the great object to which our enquiries are directed: Let me add that it is the great desideratum, by which alone this form of government can be rescued from the opprobrium under which it has so long labored, and be recommended to the esteem and adoption of mankind.

By what means is this object attainable? Evidently by one of two only. Either the existence of the same passion or interest in a majority at the same time, must be prevented; or the majority, having such co-existent passion or interest, must be rendered, by their number and local situation, unable to concert and carry into effect schemes of oppression. If the impulse and the opportunity be suffered to coincide, we well know that neither moral nor religious motives can be relied on as an adequate control. They are not found to be such on the injustice and violence of individuals, and lose their efficacy in proportion to the number combined together; that is, in proportion as their efficacy becomes needful.

From this view of the subject, it may be concluded, that a pure Democracy, by which I mean, a Society, consisting of a small number of citizens, who assemble and administer the Government in person, can admit of no cure for the mischiefs of faction. A common passion or interest will, in almost every case, be felt by a majority of the whole; a communication and concert results from the form of Government itself; and there is nothing to check the inducements to sacrifice the weaker party, or an obnoxious individual. Hence it is, that such Democracies have ever been spectacles of turbulence and contention; have ever been found incompatible with personal security, or the rights of property; and have in general been as short in their lives, as they have been violent in their deaths. Theoretic politicians, who have patronized this species of Government, have erroneously supposed, that by reducing mankind to a perfect equality in their political rights, they would, at the same time, be perfectly equalized and assimilated in their possessions, their opinions, and their passions.

A Republic, by which I mean a Government in which the scheme of representation takes place, opens a different prospect, and promises the cure for which we are seeking. Let us examine the points in which it varies from pure Democracy, and we shall comprehend both the nature of the cure, and the efficacy which it must derive from the Union.

The two great points of difference between a Democracy and a Republic are, first, the delegation of the Government, in the latter, to a small number of citizens elected by the rest: secondly, the greater number of citizens, and greater sphere of country, over which the latter may be extended.

The effect of the first difference is, on the one hand to refine and enlarge the public views, by passing them through the medium of a chosen body of citizens, whose wisdom may best discern the true interest of their country, and whose patriotism and love of justice, will be least likely to sacrifice it to temporary or partial considerations. Under such a regulation, it may well happen that the public voice pronounced by the representatives of the people, will be more consonant to the public good, than if pronounced by the people themselves convened for the purpose. On the other hand, the effect may be inverted. Men of factious tempers, of local prejudices, or of sinister designs, may by intrigue, by corruption or by other means, first obtain the suffrages, and then betray the interests of the people. The question resulting is, whether small or extensive Republics are most favorable to the election of proper guardians of the public weal; and it is clearly decided in favor of the latter by two obvious considerations.

In the first place it is to be remarked that however small the Republic may be, the Representatives must be raised to a certain number, in order to guard against the cabals of a few; and that however large it may be, they must be limited to a certain number, in order to guard against the confusion of a multitude. Hence the number of Representatives in the two cases, not being in proportion to that of the Constituents, and being proportionally greatest in the small Republic, it follows, that if the proportion of fit characters, be not less, in the large than in the small Republic, the former will present a greater option, and consequently a greater probability of a fit choice.

In the next place, as each Representative will be chosen by a greater number of citizens in the large than in the small Republic, it will be more difficult for unworthy candidates to practise with success the vicious arts, by which elections are too often carried; and the suffrages of the people being more free, will be more likely to centre on men who possess the most attractive merit, and the most diffusive and established characters.

It must be confessed, that in this, as in most other cases, there is a mean, on both sides of which inconveniencies will be found to lie. By enlarging too much the number of electors, you render the representative too little acquainted with all their local circumstances and lesser interests; as by reducing it too much, you render him unduly attached to these, and too little fit to comprehend and pursue great and national objects. The Federal Constitution forms a happy combination in this respect; the great and aggregate interests being referred to the national, the local and particular, to the state legislatures.

The other point of difference is, the greater number of citizens and extent of territory which may be brought within the compass of Republican, than of Democratic Government; and it is this circumstance principally which renders factious combinations less to be dreaded in the former, than in the latter. The smaller the society, the fewer probably will be the distinct parties and interests composing it; the fewer the distinct parties and interests, the more frequently will a majority be found of the same party; and the smaller the number of individuals composing a majority, and the smaller the compass within which they are placed, the more easily will they concert and execute their plans of oppression. Extend the sphere, and you take in a greater variety of parties and interests; you make it less probable that a majority of the whole will have a common motive to invade the rights of other citizens; or if such a common motive exists, it will be more difficult for all who feel it to discover their own strength, and to act in unison with each other. Besides other impediments, it may be remarked, that where there is a consciousness of unjust or dishonorable purposes, communication is always checked by distrust, in proportion to the number whose concurrence is necessary.

Hence it clearly appears, that the same advantage, which a Republic has over a Democracy, in controling the effects of faction, is enjoyed by a large over a small Republic—is enjoyed by the Union over the States composing it. Does this advantage consist in the substitution of Representatives, whose enlightened views and virtuous sentiments render them superior to local prejudices, and to schemes of injustice? It will not be denied, that the Representation of the Union will be most likely to possess these requisite endowments. Does it consist in the greater security afforded by a greater variety of parties, against the event of any one party being able to outnumber and oppress the rest? In an equal degree does the encreased variety of parties, comprised within the Union, encrease this security. Does it, in fine, consist in the greater obstacles opposed to the concert and accomplishment of the secret wishes of an unjust and interested majority? Here, again, the extent of the Union gives it the most palpable advantage.

The influence of factious leaders may kindle a flame within their particular States, but will be unable to spread a general conflagration through the other States: a religious sect, may degenerate into a political faction in a part of the Confederacy; but the variety of sects dispersed over the entire face of it, must secure the national Councils against any danger from that source: a rage for paper money, for an abolition of debts, for an equal division of property, or for any other improper or wicked project, will be less apt to pervade the whole body of the Union, than a particular member of it; in the same proportion as such a malady is more likely to taint a particular county or district, than an entire State.

In the extent and proper structure of the Union, therefore, we behold a Republican remedy for the diseases most incident to Republican Government. And according to the degree of pleasure and pride, we feel in being Republicans, ought to be our zeal in cherishing the spirit, and supporting the character of Federalists.

EDMUND RANDOLPH
Speech in Virginia Ratifying Convention, 6 June 1788 (excerpt)*

I therefore conclude, that the Confederation is too defective to deserve correction. Let us take farewell of it, with reverential respect, as an old benefactor. It is gone, whether this House says so, or not. It is gone, Sir, by its own weakness. I am afraid I have tired the patience of this House; but I trust you will pardon me, as I was urged by the importunity of the Gentleman [Patrick Henry], in calling for the reasons of laying the ground-work of this plan. It is objected by the Honorable Gentleman over the way (Mr. *George Mason*) that a republican Government is impracticable in an extensive territory, and the extent of the United States is urged as a reason for the rejection of this Constitution. Let us consider the definition of a republican Government, as laid down by a man who is highly esteemed. Montesquieu, so celebrated among politicians, says, "That a republican Government is that in which the body, or only a part of the people, is possessed of the supreme power; a monarchical, that in which a single person governs by fixed and established laws; a despotic Government, that in which a single person, without law, and without rule, directs every thing by his own will and caprice." This author has not distinguished a republican Government from a monarchy, by the extent of its boundaries, but by the nature of its principles. He, in another place, contradistinguishes it, as a government of laws, in opposition to others which he denominates a government of men. The empire or Government of laws, according to that phrase, is that in which the laws are made with the free will of the people; hence then, if laws be made by the assent of the people, the Government may be deemed free. When laws are made with integrity, and executed with wisdom, the question is, whether a great extent of country will tend to abridge the liberty of the people. If defensive force be necessary in proportion to the extent of country, I conceive that in a judiciously constructed Government, be the country ever so extensive, its inhabitants will be proportionably numerous and able to defend it. Extent of country, in my conception, ought to be no bar to the adoption of a good Government. No extent on earth seems to me too great, provided the laws be wisely made and executed. The prin-

Debates and Other Proceedings of the Convention of Virginia... (3 vols., Petersburg, Va., 1788–89), I, 93–94. Edmund Randolph, Governor of Virginia, had played an important role in the Constitutional Convention. He introduced the Virginia Plan on 29 May and spoke in favor of a strong national government. But in the end, he insisted on giving the state ratifying conventions the power to propose amendments that would be considered by a second general convention. When the Constitutional Convention rejected this idea, Randolph refused to sign the Constitution. In the Virginia Convention, however, Randolph defended the Constitution and supported ratification without prior amendments.

ciples of representation and responsibility, may pervade a large as well as
a small territory; and tyranny is as easily introduced into a small as into
a great district. If it be answered, that some of the most illustrious and
distinguished authors, are of a contrary opinion, I reply, that authority
has no weight with me till I am convinced—that not the dignity of names,
but the force of reasoning gains my assent.

FRANCIS CORBIN
Speech in Virginia Ratifying Convention, 7 June 1788 (excerpt)*

A superintending coercive power is absolutely indispensible. This
does not exist under the present articles of Confederation. To vest it with
such a power, on its present construction, without any alteration, would
be extremely dangerous, and might lead to civil war. Gentlemen must,
before this, have been convinced of the necessity of an alteration. Our
state-vessel has sprung a-leak—We must embark in a new bottom, or sink
into perdition. The Honorable Gentleman [Patrick Henry] has objected
to the Constitution, on the old worn out idea, that a republican Government is best calculated for a small territory. If a republic, Sir, cannot be
accommodated to an extensive country, let me ask, how small must a
country be to suit the genius of republicanism? In what particular extent
of country can a republican Government exist? If contracted into as small
a compass as you please, it must labour under many disadvantages. Too
small an extent will render a republic weak, vulnerable, and contemptible.—Liberty, in such a petty State, must be on a precarious footing;—its
existence must depend on the philanthropy and good nature of its neighbours. Too large an extent, it is said, will produce confusion and tyranny.
What has been so often deprecated will be removed by this plan. The
extent of the United States cannot render this Government oppressive.
The powers of the General Government are only of a general nature; and
their object is to protect, defend, and strengthen the United States: But
the internal administration of Government is left to the State Legislatures,
who exclusively retain such powers as will give the States the advantages
of small republics, without the danger commonly attendant on the weakness of such Governments. There are controversies even about the name
of this Government. It is denominated by some a Federal, by others, a

*Debates and Other Proceedings of the Convention of Virginia... (3 vols., Petersburg, Va.,
1788–89), I, 114–16. Francis Corbin was a member of the Virginia House of Delegates from 1784
to 1794. In October 1787, he introduced the resolutions in the House calling for the state Convention.

Consolidated Government. The definition given of it by my honorable friend (Mr. *Madison*) is, in my opinion, accurate. Let me, however, call it by another name, a Representative Federal Republic, as contradistinguished from a Confederacy. The former is more wisely constructed than the latter—It places the remedy in the hands which *feel* the disorder—The other places the remedy in those hands which *cause* the disorder. The evils that are most complained of in such Governments (and with justice) are faction, dissension, and consequent subjection of the minority, to the caprice and arbitrary decisions of the majority, who, instead of consulting the interest of the whole community collectively, attend sometimes to partial and local advantages. To avoid this evil, is perhaps the great *desiderata* of republican wisdom; it may be termed the Philosopher's stone. Yet, Sir, this evil will be avoided by this Constitution: Faction will be removed by the system now under consideration, because all the causes which are generally productive of faction are removed. This evil does not take its flight entirely: For were jealousies and divisions entirely at an end, it might produce such lethargy, as would ultimately terminate in the destruction of liberty; to the preservation of which, watchfulness is absolutely necessary. It is transferred from the State Legislatures to Congress, where it will be more easily controuled. Faction will decrease in proportion to the diminution of counsellors. It is much easier to controul it in small, than in large bodies. Our State Legislature consists of upwards of 160, which is a greater number than Congress will consist of at first. Will not more concord and unanimity exist in one, than in thirteen such bodies? Faction will more probably decrease, or be entirely removed, if the interest of a nation be entirely concentrated, than if entirely diversified. If thirteen men agree, there will be no faction. Yet if of opposite, and of heterogeneous dispositions, it is impossible that a majority of such clashing minds can ever concur to oppress the minority. It is impossible that this Government, which will make us one people, will have a tendency to assimilate our situations; and is admirably calculated to produce harmony and unanimity, can ever admit of an oppressive combination, by one part of the Union against the other. A Confederate Government is of all others best calculated for an extensive country. Its component individual Governments, administer and afford all the local conveniences, that the most compact Governments can do; and the strength and energy of the confederacy may be equal to those of any Government. A Government of this kind may extend to all the Western world: Nay, I may say, *ad infinitum*. But it is needless to dwell any longer on this subject, for the objection that an extensive territory is repugnant to a republican Government, applies against this and every State in the Union, except Delaware and Rhode-Island. Were the objection well founded, a republican Government could exist in none of the States except those two. Such an argument goes to the dissolution of the Union, and its absurdity is demonstrated by our own experience.

EDMUND RANDOLPH
Speech in Virginia Ratifying Convention, 10 June 1788 (excerpt)*

After having acknowledged the evil tendency of separate confederacies, he [Patrick Henry] recurs to this, that this country is too extensive for this system. If there be an Executive dependent for its election on the people; a judiciary which will administer the laws with justice, no extent of country can be too great for a republic. Where is there a precedent to prove that this country is too extensive for a Government of this kind? America cannot find a precedent to prove this. Theoretic writers have adopted a position, that extensive territories will not admit of a Republican Government. These positions were laid down before the science of Government was as well understood as it is now. Where would America look for a precedent to warrant her adoption of that position. If you go to Europe before arts and sciences had arrived at their present perfection, no example worthy of imitation can be found. The history of England from the reign of Henry the 7th; of Spain, since that of Charles the 5th; and of France, since that of Francis the 1st, prove, that they have greatly improved in the science of politics since that time. Representation, the source of American liberty, and English liberty, was a thing not understood in its full extent till very lately. The position I have spoken of was founded upon an ignorance of the principles of representation. Its force must be now done away, as this principle is so well understood. If laws are to be made by the people themselves, in their individual capacities, it is evident, that they cannot conveniently assemble together for this purpose, but in a very limited sphere; but if the business of legislation be transacted by Representatives, chosen periodically by the people, it is obvious that it may be done in any extent of country. The experience of this Commonwealth, and of the United States, proves this assertion.

*Debates and Other Proceedings of the Convention of Virginia . . . (3 vols., Petersburg, Va., 1788–89), I, 7–8.

2

The House of Representatives

DURING THE REVOLUTION *all of the American states established republican forms of government where the people chose representatives to attend state legislatures. The lower houses of the legislatures, generally the centers of power in the state governments, were often large and represented most segments of society.*

Delegates to the Confederation Congress were usually elected by the state legislatures. (In Connecticut and Rhode Island the people elected their congressional delegates directly.) Each state could elect two to seven delegates, but generally states sent no more than three delegates to Congress at any one time. Thus Congress was usually composed of fewer than forty delegates—more commonly under thirty. The unicameral Confederation Congress voted by state—not by delegate—and each state had one vote. Delaware, the smallest state in the Union, therefore, had as much power in Confederation affairs as Virginia, the largest, wealthiest state. Delegates to the Constitutional Convention from the three large states—Virginia, Massachusetts, and Pennsylvania—opposed this method of representation and suffrage in Congress.

The Constitution called for a bicameral Congress composed of a House of Representatives and a Senate. Representation in the House was to be based on population, while the states were to continue to remain equal in the Senate. Representatives would be apportioned among the states based on a census taken every ten years with no more than one representative for every 30,000 people. No state, however small its population, was to be deprived of at least one repre-

sentative. Per capita voting in both houses of Congress replaced the Confederation's state voting.

Small-state Antifederalists opposed the inequality of state representation in the House. They maintained that the states were distinct political units and ought to be so represented. Obviously Antifederalists in large states did not share this view.

Opponents of the Constitution charged that the House of Representatives was too small to represent adequately all segments of American society. The Constitution provided that the first U.S. House of Representatives would be composed of 65 members. Even tiny Rhode Island had more assemblymen than that. Consequently, Antifederalists wanted safeguards built into the Constitution guaranteeing regular increases in the number of representatives as the country's population increased.

Antifederalists also attacked the biennial elections of Representatives. Delegates to the Confederation Congress had one-year terms as did most state legislators. Two-year terms seemed another step to remove representatives from the control of the people, especially since the Confederation's mandatory rotation in office and the right of state legislatures to recall their congressmen were abandoned by the new Constitution.

The Constitution was also criticized for not giving the House of Representatives a role in treaty-making. Since treaties were part of the supreme law of the land, Antifederalists charged that treaties could arbitrarily affect the lives of all Americans without direct input from the immediate representatives of the people. Furthermore, money bills—traditionally the sole prerogative of the lower houses of legislatures—could now be amended by the Senate.

Federalists answered these criticisms forcefully. For the first time, they said, the people would be represented proportionately by their numbers. The House of Representatives would indeed grow as the nation enlarged, but this increase would have to be controlled so that the House could function properly. The two-year term of office was also necessary to assure Representatives of a certain degree of continuity. One-year terms would mean that Representatives from the more distant states would spend most of their time travelling back and forth to Congress and running for reelection rather than serving in office. Furthermore, it would require more time for Representatives to familiarize themselves with the complexities of national issues.

Federalists also argued that, although the House of Representatives had no direct involvement in treaty-making, it still had influence over treaties through its control over the appropriations of funds. In addition, the House's power to impeach officeholders who violated their trusts gave the House considerable power in all governmental affairs.

Antifederalist

LUTHER MARTIN'S GENUINE INFORMATION
Baltimore *Maryland Gazette*, 1 January 1788 (excerpt)*

The Jersey propositions being thus rejected, the convention took up those reported by the committee, and proceeded to debate them by paragraphs—It was now that they who disapproved the report found it necessary to make a *warm* and *decided opposition*, which took place upon the discussion of the seventh resolution, which related to the *inequality* of representation in the *first* branch.—Those who advocated this inequality, urged, that when the articles of confederation were formed, it was *only* from *necessity* and *expediency* that the States were admitted *each* to have an *equal vote;* but that our situation was *now altered*, and therefore those States who considered it contrary to their interest, would *no longer abide* by it. They said no State ought to wish to have influence in government, except in proportion to what it contributes to it; that if it contributes but little, it ought to have but a small vote; that taxation and representation ought always to go together; that if one State had *sixteen times as many inhabitants* as another, or was *sixteen times as wealthy*, it ought to have *sixteen times as many votes;* that an inhabitant of Pennsylvania ought to have as much weight and consequence as an inhabitant of Jersey or Delaware; that it was contrary to the feelings of the human mind—what the *large States* would *never* submit to; that the *large States* would have *great objects* in view, in which they would never permit the *smaller States* to thwart them; that *equality of suffrage* was the rotten part of the constitution, and that this was a happy time to get clear of it. In fine, that it was the

---

*Luther Martin, the attorney general of Maryland, attended the Constitutional Convention from 9 June until its recess on 26 July. He returned on 13 August and left on 4 September. Martin favored strengthened powers for the central government without, however, undermining the general position of the states. Soon, however, Martin judged that the Convention had gone too far in creating a national government. He then became one of the most outspoken critics of the Constitution both within the Convention and later in the public debate over ratification.

On 23 November the Maryland House of Delegates requested the state's delegates to the Constitutional Convention to report. Martin attended the House on 29 November and described events in the Convention. He then expanded his speech and submitted it to the Baltimore *Maryland Gazette* which published it in twelve installments from 28 December 1787 to 8 February 1788. On 12 April the entire account was printed as a pamphlet in Philadelphia.

In this essay Martin begins by stating that the small states' proposal (the New Jersey Propositions) was rejected on 19 June and strenuous debate ensued over the large-state plan (the Virginia Plan). This essay was reprinted in the *Pennsylvania Packet*, 12 January; *New York Journal*, 18 January; *Pennsylvania Herald*, 19 January; Philadelphia *Independent Gazetteer*, 21 January; Boston *American Herald*, 11 February; *State Gazette of South Carolina*, 14, 17, 21 April. Lengthy excerpts appeared in an Antifederalist essay by "A Republican Federalist," Philadelphia *Freeman's Journal*, 16 January.

poison which contaminated our whole system, and the source of all the evils we experienced.

This, Sir, is the substance of the arguments, if arguments they can be called, which were used in favour of *inequality of suffrage.*—Those, who advocated the *equality of suffrage*, took the matter up on the original principles of government—They urged that all men considered in a state of nature, before any government formed, are equally free and independent, no one having any right or authority to exercise power over another, and this *without any regard to difference in personal strength, understanding, or wealth*—That when such individuals enter into government, they have *each* a right to an *equal voice* in its first formation, and afterwards have *each* a right to an *equal vote* in every matter which relates to their government— That if it could be done conveniently, they have a right to exercise it in person—Where it cannot be done in person but for convenience, representatives are appointed to act for them, *every person* has a *right* to an *equal vote* in choosing that representative who is entrusted to do for the whole, that which the whole, if they could assemble, might do in person, and in the transacting of which each would have an equal voice—That if we were to admit, because a man was *more wise, more strong,* or *more wealthy*, he should be entitled to *more votes* than another, it would be *inconsistent with the freedom and liberty* of *that other*, and would reduce him to *slavery*—Suppose, for instance, ten individuals in a state of nature, about to enter into government, *nine* of whom are *equally wise, equally strong*, and *equally wealthy*, the *tenth* is *ten times as wise*, ten times as *strong* or ten times as *rich;* if for this reason he is to have *ten votes* for *each vote of either of the others*, the *nine* might as well have *no vote at all*, since though the *whole nine* might assent to a measure, yet the *vote of the tenth* would *countervail*, and *set aside all their votes*—If this *tenth* approved of what *they* wished to adopt, it would be well, but if he disapproved, he could prevent it, and in the same manner he could carry into execution *any measure he wished contrary to the opinion of all the others, he* having *ten votes*, and the *other* all together *but nine*—It is evident, that on these principles, *the nine* would have *no will nor discretion of their own*, but must be *totally dependent* on the *will* and *discretion* of the *tenth*, to *him they* would be as *absolutely slaves* as *any negro* is to his *master.*—If *he* did not attempt to carry into execution any measures injurious to the *other nine*, it could only be said that *they* had a *good master*, they would not be the *less slaves*, because *they* would be *totally dependent* on the *will* of *another*, and not on *their own will*—They might not *feel their chains*, but they would notwithstanding *wear them*, and whenever their *master* pleased he might draw them so tight as to gall them to the bone. Hence it was urged the *inequality of representation*, or giving to one man more votes than another on account of his wealth, &c. was *altogether inconsistent with the principles of liberty*, and in the *same proportion as it should be adopted*, in favour of *one* or *more*, in *that proportion are the others inslaved*—It was urged that though every individual should have an equal voice in the government, yet, even then superiour wealth, strength or understanding, would give great and undue advantages to those who possessed them. That wealth attracts respect and attention; superior strength would cause the weaker and more feeble to be cautious how they offended, and to put up with small injuries rather than to engage in an unequal contest—In like manner superior understanding would give its possessor many opportunities of profiting at the expence of the more ignorant.—Having thus established these principles with respect to the *rights* of *individuals* in a *state of nature*, and what is due to *each* on entering into government, principles established by every writer on liberty, they proceeded to shew that *States*, when *once formed*, are considered *with respect* to *each other as individuals* in a state of nature—That, like individuals, each *State* is considered *equally free* and *equally independent*, the *one* having no right to exercise authority over the *other*, though more *strong, more wealthy*, or *abounding with more inhabitants*—That when a number of *States* unite themselves under a *federal government*, the *same principles apply* to *them* as when a *number* of *individual men* unite themselves under a *State government*—That every argument which shews *one man* ought not to have *more votes* than *another*, because he is *wiser, stronger* or *wealthier*, proves that *one State* ought not to have *more votes* than *another*, because it is *stronger, richer, or more populous*—And that by *giving one State*, or *one or two States more votes* than the *others*, the *others* thereby are *enslaved to such State or States*, having the *greater number of votes*, in the *same manner* as in the case before put of *individuals* where *one* has *more votes than the others*—That the reason why each individual man in forming a State government should have an equal vote is, because each individual before he enters into government is *equally free* and *independent*—So *each State*, when *States enter* into a *federal government*, are entitled to an *equal vote*, because before they entered into such federal government, *each State* was *equally free* and *equally independent*—That *adequate* representation of *men formed into a State government*, consists in *each man* having an *equal voice* either personally, or if by representatives, that he should have an equal voice in choosing the representative—So adequate representation of *States* in a *federal government*, consists in *each State* having an *equal voice* either in person or by its representative in every thing which relates to the federal government—That this *adequacy of representation* is *more important* in a *federal*, than in a *State* government, because the members of a State government, the *district* of which is *not very large*, have generally such a *common interest*, that laws can scarcely be made by *one* part *oppressive* to the *others*, without *their suffering in common;* but the *different States* composing an *extensive federal empire*, widely distant, *one* from the *other*, may have *interests so totally distinct*, that the *one* part might be greatly *benefited* by what would be *destructive* to the *other*.

They were not satisfied by resting it on principles; they also appealed to history—They shewed that in the amphyctionic confederation of the Grecian cities, *each city* however *different* in *wealth, strength,* and other *circumstances*, sent the same *number* of deputies, and had *each* an *equal voice* in every thing that related to the common concerns of Greece. It was shewn that in the seven provinces of the United Netherlands, and the confederated Cantons of Switzerland, *each Canton* and *each province* have an *equal vote*, although there are as great distinctions of wealth, strength, population, and extent of territory among those provinces and *those Cantons*, as among *these States*. It was said, that the maxim that taxation and representation ought to go together, was true so far, that no person ought to be *taxed* who is not *represented*, but not in the extent insisted upon, to wit, that the *quantum* of *taxation* and *representation* ought to be the *same;* on the contrary, the *quantum* of *representation* depends upon the quantum of *freedom*, and therefore *all*, whether *individual States*, or individual *men*, who are *equally free*, have a right to *equal representation—* That to those who insist that he who pays the greatest share of taxes, ought to have the greatest number of votes; it is a sufficient answer to say, that *this rule* would be *destructive* of the *liberty* of the *others*, and would render *them slaves* to the *more rich* and *wealthy—*That if one man pays *more taxes* than another, it is because he has *more wealth* to be protected by government, and he receives greater benefits from the government—So if one State pays more to the federal government, it is because as a State, she enjoys greater blessings from it; she has more wealth protected by it, or a greater number of inhabitants, whose rights are secured, and who share its advantages.

GEORGE MASON
Speech in Virginia Ratifying Convention, 4 June 1788 (excerpt)*

With respect to the representation so much applauded, I cannot think it such a full and free one as it is represented; but I must candidly acknowledge, that this defect results from the very nature of the Govern-

*Debates and Other Proceedings of the Convention of Virginia . . . (3 vols., Petersburg, Va., 1788–89), I, 45–46.

ment. It would be impossible to have a full and adequate representation in the General Government; it would be too expensive and too unweildy: We are then under the necessity of having this a very inadequate representation: Is this general representation to be compared with the real, actual, substantial representation of the State Legislatures? It cannot bear a comparison. To make representation real and actual, the number of Representatives ought to be adequate; they ought to mix with the people, think as they think, feel as they feel, ought to be perfectly amenable to them, and thoroughly acquainted with their interest and condition: Now these great ingredients are, either not at all, or in so small a degree, to be found in our Federal Representatives, that we have no real, actual, substantial representation; but I acknowledge it results from the nature of the Government: The necessity of this inconvenience may appear a sufficient reason not to argue against it: But, Sir, it clearly shews, that we ought to give power with a sparing hand to a Government thus imperfectly constructed. To a Government, which, in the nature of things, cannot but be defective, no powers ought to be given, but such as are absolutely necessary: There is one thing in it which I conceive to be extremely dangerous. Gentlemen may talk of public virtue and confidence; we shall be told that the House of Representatives will consist of the most virtuous men on the Continent, and that in their hands we may trust our dearest rights. This, like all other assemblies, will be composed of some bad and some good men; and considering the natural lust of power so inherent in man, I fear the thirst of power will prevail to oppress the people:—What I conceive to be so dangerous, is the provision with respect to the number of Representatives: It does not expressly provide, that we shall have one for every 30,000, but that the number shall not exceed that proportion: The utmost that we can expect (and perhaps that is too much) is, that the present number shall be continued to us:—"The number of Representatives shall not exceed one for every 30,000." Now will not this be complied with, although the present number should never be increased; nay, although it should be decreased? Suppose Congress should say, that we should have one for every 200,000, will not the Constitution be complied with? For one for every 200,000 does not exceed one for every 30,000. There is a want of proportion that ought to be strictly guarded against: The worthy Gentleman [George Nicholas] tells us, we have no reason to fear; but I always fear for the rights of the people: I do not pretend to inspiration, but I think, it is apparent as the day, that the members will attend to local partial interests to prevent an augmentation of their number: I know not how they will be chosen, but whatever be the mode of choosing, our present number is but ten: And suppose our State is laid off in ten districts; those Gentlemen who shall be sent from those districts will lessen their own power and influence, in their respective districts, if they increase their number; for the greater the number of men among whom any given quantum of power is divided, the less the power of each individual. Thus they will have a local interest to prevent the increase of, and perhaps they will lessen their own number: This is evident on the face of the Constitution—so loose an expression ought to be guarded against; for Congress will be clearly within the requisition of the Constitution, although the number of Representatives should always continue what it is now, and the population of the country should increase to an immense number. Nay, they may reduce the number from 65, to one from each State, without violating the Constitution; and thus the number which is now too small, would then be infinitely too much so . . .

PATRICK HENRY
Speech in Virginia Ratifying Convention, 5 June 1788*

Consider what you are about to do before you part with this Government. Take longer time in reckoning things: revolutions like this have happened in almost every country in Europe: Similar examples are to be found in ancient Greece and ancient Rome: Instances of the people losing their liberty by their own carelessness and the ambition of a few. We are cautioned by the Honorable Gentleman who presides [Edmund Pendleton], against faction and turbulence: I acknowledge that licentiousness is dangerous, and that it ought to be provided against: I acknowledge also the new form of Government may effectually prevent it: Yet, there is another thing it will as effectually do; it will oppress and ruin the people. There are sufficient guards placed against sedition and licentiousness: For when power is given to this Government to suppress these, or, for any other purpose, the language it assumes is clear, express, and unequivocal, but when this Constitution speaks of privileges, there is an ambiguity, Sir, a fatal ambiguity;—an ambiguity which is very astonishing: In the clause under consideration, there is the strangest language that I can conceive. I mean, when it says, that there shall not be more Representatives, than one for every 30,000. Now, Sir, how easy is it to evade this privilege? "The number shall not exceed one for every 30,000." This may be satisfied by one Representative from each State. Let our numbers be ever so great, this immence continent, may, by this artful expression, be reduced to have but 13 Representatives: I confess this construction is not natural; but the

*Debates and Other Proceedings of the Convention of Virginia . . . (3 vols., Petersburg, Va., 1788–89), I, 58–74.

ambiguity of the expression lays a good ground for a quarrel. Why was it not clearly and unequivocally expressed, that they *should* be entitled to have one for every 30,000? This would have obviated all disputes; and was this difficult to be done? What is the inference? When population increases, and a State shall send Representatives in this proportion, Congress *may* remand them, because the right of having one for every 30,000 is not clearly expressed: This possibility of reducing the number to one for each State, approximates to probability by that other expression, "but each State shall at least have one Representative." Now is it not clear that from the first expression, the number might be reduced so much, that some States should have no Representative at all, were it not for the insertion of this last expression? And as this is the only restriction upon them, we may fairly conclude that they *may* restrain the number to one from each State: Perhaps the same horrors may hang over my mind again. . . . I have trespassed so long on your patience, I am really concerned that I have something yet to say. The honorable member [George Nicholas] has said that we shall be properly represented: Remember, Sir, that the number of our Representatives is but ten, whereof six is a majority. Will these men be possessed of sufficient information? A particular knowledge of particular districts will not suffice. They must be well acquainted with agriculture, commerce, and a great variety of other matters throughout the Continent: They must know not only the actual state of nations in Europe, and America, the situation of their farmers, cottagers, and mechanics, but also the relative situation and intercourse of those nations. Virginia is as large as England. Our proportion of Representatives is but ten men. In England they have 530. The House of Commons in England, numerous as they are, we are told, is bribed, and have bartered away the rights of their constituents: What then shall become of us? Will these few protect our rights? Will they be incorruptible? You say they will be better men than the English Commoners. I say they will be infinitely worse men, because they are to be chosen blindfolded: Their election (the term, as applied to their appointment, is inaccurate) will be an involuntary nomination, and not a choice.

Federalist

AN AMERICAN CITIZEN III (TENCH COXE)
Philadelphia *Independent Gazetteer*, 29 September 1787*

In pursuing the consideration of the new federal constitution, it remains now to examine the nature and powers of the house of representatives—*the immediate delegates of the people.*

Each member of this truly popular assembly will be chosen by about six thousand electors, *by the poor as well as the rich.* No decayed and venal borough will have an *unjust* share in their determinations—No old *Sarum* will send thither a representative *by the voice of a single elector*[(a)]—As we shall have no royal ministries to purchase votes, so we shall have no votes for sale. *For the suffrages of six thousand enlightened and independent Freemen are above all price*—When the encreasing population of the country shall render the body too large at the rate of one member for every thirty thousand persons, they will be returned at the greater rate of one for every forty or fifty thousand, which will render the electors still more incorruptible. For this regulation is only designed to prevent a *smaller number* than thirty thousand from having a representative. Thus we see a provision follows, that no state shall have less than one member; for if a new and greater number should hereafter be fixt on, which shall exceed the whole of the inhabitants of any state, such state, without this wholesome provision, would lose its voice in the house of representatives—A circumstance which the constitution renders *impossible.*

The people of England, whose house of commons is filled with military and civil officers and pensioners, say their liberties would be perfectly secured by triennial parliaments. *With us no placement can sit among the representatives of the people, and two years are the constitutional term of their existence.* Here again, lest wealth, powerful connexions, or even *the unwariness of the people* should place in this important trust an undeserving, unqualified or inexperienced youth, the wisdom of the convention has proposed *an absolute incapacity till the age of twenty-five.* At

[(a)] *This is the case with that British borough.*

---

*This is the third of four "American Citizen" essays written by Tench Coxe, a Philadelphia merchant and prolific Federalist essayist. The essays were published in Philadelphia between 26 September and 21 October 1787. The third essay was reprinted in seventeen newspapers from Massachusetts to South Carolina by 10 December. It was also reprinted in the Philadelphia *American Museum* (a nationally circulated magazine), in a Philadelphia broadside with the other three "American Citizen" essays, and in two Richmond, Va., pamphlet anthologies by the end of December 1787.

twenty-one a young man is made the guardian of his *own* interests, *but he cannot for a few years more be entrusted with the affairs of the nation.* He must be an inhabitant of the state that elects him, that he may be intimately acquainted with their *particular* circumstances—The house of representatives is not, *as the senate*, to have a president chosen *for them* from *without* their body, *but are to elect their speaker from their own number*— They will also appoint *all their other officers.* In great state cases, they will be *the grand inquest of the nation*, for they possess *the sole and uncontroulable power of impeachement.* They are neither *to wait the call* nor *abide the prorogations and dissolutions of a perverse or ambitious prince*, for they are to meet at least once in every year, and sit on adjournments to be agreed on between themselves and the other servants of the people. Should they differ in opinion, the president who is a temporary fellow servant and not their hereditary master, has *a mediatorial power* to adjust it for them, *but cannot prevent their constitutional meeting within the year.* They can compel the attendance of their members, that their public duty may not be *evaded* in times of difficulty or danger—The vote of each representative can be always known, as well as the proceedings of the house, *that so the people may be acquainted with the conduct of those in whom they repose so important a trust.* As was observed of the senators, they cannot make *new* offices *for themselves*, nor increase, *for their own benefit*, the emoluments of old ones, *by which the people will be exempted from needless additions to the public expences on such sordid and mercenary principles*— They are not to be restrained from *the firm and plain language*, which becomes the independent representatives of freemen, *for there is to be a perfect liberty of speech.* Without their consent *no monies can be obtained, no armies raised, no navies provided.* They *alone* can originate bills for drawing forth the revenues of the union, and *they will have a negative upon every legislative act of the other house*—So far, in short, as the sphere of federal jurisdiction extends, they will be controulable *only by the people*, and in contentions with the other branch, so far as they shall be right, *they must ever finally prevail.*

Such, my countrymen, are some of *the cautionary provisions* of the frame of government your faithful convention have submitted to your consideration—such *the foundations of peace, liberty and safety*, which have been laid by their unwearied labors—They have guarded you against *all servants* but those "whom choice and common good ordain," against *all masters* "save preserving Heaven."

PUBLIUS: THE FEDERALIST 35 (ALEXANDER HAMILTON)
New York *Independent Journal*, 5 January 1788 (excerpt)*

To the People of the State of New-York.

The idea of an actual representation of all classes of the people by persons of each class is altogether visionary. Unless it were expressly provided in the Constitution that each different occupation should send one or more members the thing would never take place in practice. Mechanics and manufacturers will always be inclined with few exceptions to give their votes to merchants in preference to persons of their own professions or trades. Those discerning citizens are well aware that the mechanic and manufacturing arts furnish the materials of mercantile enterprise and industry. Many of them indeed are immediately connected with the operations of commerce. They know that the merchant is their natural patron and friend; and they are aware that however great the confidence they may justly feel in their own good sense, their interests can be more effectually promoted by the merchant than by themselves. They are sensible that their habits in life have not been such as to give them those acquired endowments, without which in a deliberative assembly the greatest natural abilities are for the most part useless; and that the influence and weight and superior acquirements of the merchants render them more equal to a contest with any spirit which might happen to infuse itself into the public councils unfriendly to the manufacturing and trading interests. These considerations and many others that might be mentioned prove, and experience confirms it, that artisans and manufacturers will commonly be disposed to bestow their votes upon merchants and those whom they recommend. We must therefore consider merchants as the natural representatives of all these classes of the community.

With regard to the learned professions, little need be observed; they truly form no distinct interest in society; and according to their situation and talents will be indiscriminately the objects of the confidence and choice of each other and of other parts of the community.

Nothing remains but the landed interest; and this in a political view and particularly in relation to taxes I take to be perfectly united from the wealthiest landlord to the poorest tenant. No tax can be laid on land which will not affect the proprietor of millions of acres as well as the proprietor of a single acre. Every land-holder will therefore have a common interest to keep the taxes on land as low as possible; and common interest may always be reckoned upon as the surest bond of sympathy. But if we even

*Reprinted: New York *Daily Advertiser*, 7 January; *New York Packet*, 8 January; *New York Journal*, 9 January.

could suppose a distinction of interest between the opulent land-holder and middling farmer, what reason is there to conclude that the first would stand a better chance of being deputed to the national legislature than the last? If we take fact as our guide and look into our own senate and assembly we shall find that moderate proprietors of land prevail in both; nor is this less the case in the senate which consists of a smaller number than in the Assembly, which is composed of a greater number. Where the qualifications of the electors are the same, whether they have to choose a small or a large number their votes will fall upon those in whom they have most confidence; whether these happen to men of large fortunes or of moderate property or of no property at all.

It is said to be necessary that all classes of citizens should have some of their own number in the representative body, in order that their feelings and interests may be the better understood and attended to. But we have seen that this will never happen under any arrangement that leaves the votes of the people free. Where this is the case, the representative body, with too few exceptions to have any influence on the spirit of the government, will be composed of land-holders, merchants, and men of the learned professions. But where is the danger that the interests and feelings of the different classes of citizens will not be understood or attended to by these three descriptions of men? Will not the landholder know and feel whatever will promote or injure the interests of landed property? and will he not from his own interest in that species of property be sufficiently prone to resist every attempt to prejudice or incumber it? Will not the merchant understand and be disposed to cultivate as far as may be proper the interests of the mechanic and manufacturing arts to which his commerce is so nearly allied? Will not the man of the learned profession, who will feel a neutrality to the rivalships between the different branches of industry, be likely to prove an impartial arbiter between them, ready to promote either, so far as it shall appear to him conducive to the general interests of the society?

If we take into the account the momentary humors or dispositions which may happen to prevail in particular parts of the society, and to which a wise administration will never be inattentive, is the man whose situation leads to extensive inquiry and information less likely to be a competent judge of their nature, extent and foundation than one whose observation does not travel beyond the circle of his neighbours and acquaintances? Is it not natural that a man who is a candidate for the favour of the people and who is dependent on the suffrages of his fellow-citizens for the continuance of his public honors should take care to inform himself of their dispositions and inclinations and should be willing to allow them their proper degree of influence upon his conduct. This dependence, and the necessity of being bound himself and his posterity by the laws to which he gives his assent are the true, and they are strong chords of sympathy between the representative and the constituent.

PUBLIUS: THE FEDERALIST 52 (JAMES MADISON)
New York Packet, 8 February 1788*

To the People of the State of New-York.

From the more general enquiries pursued in the four last papers, I pass on to a more particular examination of the several parts of the government. I shall begin with the House of Representatives.

The first view to be taken of this part of the government, relates to the qualifications of the electors and the elected. Those of the former are to be the same with those of the electors of the most numerous branch of the State Legislatures. The definition of the right of suffrage is very justly regarded as a fundamental article of republican government. It was incumbent on the Convention therefore to define and establish this right, in the Constitution. To have left it open for the occasional regulation of the Congress, would have been improper for the reason just mentioned. To have submitted it to the legislative discretion of the States, would have been improper for the same reason; and for the additional reason, that it would have rendered too dependent on the State Governments, that branch of the Fœderal Government, which ought to be dependent on the people alone. To have reduced the different qualifications in the different States, to one uniform rule, would probably have been as dissatisfactory to some of the States, as it would have been difficult to the Convention. The provision made by the Convention appears therefore, to be the best that lay within their option. It must be satisfactory to every State; because it is conformable to the standard already established, or which may be established by the State itself. It will be safe to the United States; because, being fixed by the State Constitutions, it is not alterable by the State Governments, and it cannot be feared that the people of the States will alter this part of their Constitutions, in such a manner as to abridge the rights secured to them by the Fœderal Constitution.

The qualifications of the elected being less carefully and properly defined by the State Constitutions, and being at the same time more susceptible of uniformity, have been very properly considered and regulated by the Convention. A representative of the United States must be of the age of twenty-five years; must have been seven years a citizen of the

*Reprinted: New York *Independent Journal*, 9 February.

United States, must at the time of his election, be an inhabitant of the State he is to represent, and during the time of his service must be in no office under the United States. Under these reasonable limitations, the door of this part of the Fœderal Government, is open to merit of every description, whether native or adoptive, whether young or old, and without regard to poverty or wealth, or to any particular profession of religious faith.

The term for which the Representatives are to be elected, falls under a second view which may be taken of this branch. In order to decide on the propriety of this article, two questions must be considered; first, whether biennial elections will, in this case, be safe; secondly, whether they be necessary or useful.

First. As it is essential to liberty that the government in general, should have a common interest with the people; so it is particularly essential that the branch of it under consideration, should have an immediate dependence on, & an intimate sympathy with the people. Frequent elections are unquestionably the only policy by which this dependence and sympathy can be effectually secured. But what particular degree of frequency may be absolutely necessary for the purpose, does not appear to be susceptible of any precise calculation; and must depend on a variety of circumstances with which it may be connected. Let us consult experience, the guide that ought always to be followed, whenever it can be found.

The scheme of representation, as a substitute for a meeting of the citizens in person, being at most but very imperfectly known to ancient polity; it is in more modern times only, that we are to expect instructive examples. And even here, in order to avoid a research too vague and diffusive, it will be proper to confine ourselves to the few examples which are best known, and which bear the greatest analogy to our particular case. The first to which this character ought to be applied, is the House of Commons in Great Britain. The history of this branch of the English Constitution, anterior to the date of Magna Charta, is too obscure to yield instruction. The very existence of it has been made a question among political antiquaries. The earliest records of subsequent date prove, that Parliaments were to *sit* only, every year; not that they were to be *elected* every year. And even these annual sessions were left so much at the discretion of the monarch, that under various pretexts, very long and dangerous intermissions, were often contrived by royal ambition. To remedy this grievance, it was provided by a statute in the reign of Charles the second, that the intermissions should not be protracted beyond a period of three years. On the accession of Wil. III. when a revolution took place in the government, the subject was still more seriously resumed, and it was declared to be among the fundamental rights of the people, that Parliaments ought to be held *frequently*. By another statute which passed a few years later in the same reign, the term "frequently" which had alluded to the triennial period settled in the time of Charles II. is reduced to a precise meaning, it being expressly enacted that a new parliament shall be called within three years after the determination of the former. The last change from three to seven years is well known to have been introduced pretty early in the present century, under an alarm for the Hanoverian succession.* From these facts it appears, that the greatest frequency of elections which has been deemed necessary in that kingdom, for binding the representatives to their constituents, does not exceed a triennial return of them. And if we may argue from the degree of liberty retained even under septennial elections, and all the other vicious ingredients in the parliamentary constitution, we cannot doubt that a reduction of the period from seven to three years, with the other necessary reforms, would so far extend the influence of the people over their representatives, as to satisfy us, that biennial elections under the fœderal system, cannot possibly be dangerous to the requisite dependence of the house of representatives on their constituents.

Elections in Ireland till of late were regulated entirely by the discretion of the crown, and were seldom repeated except on the accession of a new Prince, or some other contingent event. The parliament which commenced with George II. was continued throughout his whole reign, a period of about thirty-five years. The only dependence of the representatives on the people consisted, in the right of the latter to supply occasional vacancies, by the election of new members, and in the chance of some event which might produce a general new election. The ability also of the Irish parliament, to maintain the rights of their constituents, so far as the disposition might exist, was extremely shackled by the controul of the crown over the subjects of their deliberation. Of late these shackles, if I mistake not, have been broken; and octennial parliaments have besides been established.† What effect may be produced by this partial reform, must be left to further experience. The example of Ireland, from

---

*In 1664 Parliament enacted the Triennial Act providing for "the assembling and holding of parliaments once in three years at the least." The Declaration of Rights of 1689 declared that parliaments should be "held frequently," and in 1694 Parliament passed another Triennial Act stipulating "that from henceforth a parliament shall be holden once in three years at the least." The Septennial Act of 1716 stated that parliaments "shall . . . have continuance for seven years and no longer."

†In 1768 the Irish Parliament provided that general elections be held every eight years. Before the passage of this Octennial Act, Irish parliaments did not dissolve regularly, and general elections could be required only upon the death of the British monarch (J.C. Beckett, *The Making of Modern Ireland*, 1603–1923 [New York, 1973], 162, 200–1).

this view of it, can throw but little light on the subject. As far as we can draw any conclusion from it, it must be, that if the people of that country have been able, under all these disadvantages, to retain any liberty whatever, the advantage of biennial elections would secure to them every degree of liberty which might depend on a due connection between their representatives and themselves.

Let us bring our enquiries nearer home. The example of these States when British colonies claims particular attention; at the same time that it is so well known, as to require little to be said on it. The principle of representation, in one branch of the Legislature at least, was established in all of them. But the periods of election were different. They varied from one to seven years. Have we any reason to infer from the spirit and conduct of the representatives of the people, prior to the revolution, that biennial elections would have been dangerous to the public liberties? The spirit which every where displayed itself at the commencement of the struggle; and which vanquished the obstacles to independence, is the best of proofs that a sufficient portion of liberty had been every where enjoyed to inspire both a sense of its worth, and a zeal for its proper enlargement. This remark holds good as well with regard to the then colonies, whose elections were least frequent, as to those whose elections were most frequent. Virginia was the colony which stood first in resisting the parliamentary usurpations of Great-Britain: it was the first also in espousing by public act, the resolution of independence. In Virginia nevertheless, if I have not been misinformed, elections under the former government were septennial. This particular example is brought into view, not as a proof of any peculiar merit, for the priority in those instances, was probably accidental; and still less of any advantage in *septennial* elections, for when compared with a greater frequency they are inadmissible: but merely as a proof, and I conceive it to be a very substantial proof, that the liberties of the people can be in no danger from *biennial* elections.

The conclusion resulting from these examples will be not a little strengthened by recollecting three circumstances. The first is that the Fœderal Legislature will possess a part only of that supreme legislative authority which is vested completely in the British parliament, and which with a few exceptions was exercised by the colonial Assemblies and the Irish Legislature. It is a received and well founded maxim, that, where no other circumstances affect the case, the greater the power is, the shorter ought to be its duration; and, conversely, the smaller the power, the more safely may its duration be protracted. In the second place, it has, on another occasion, been shewn that the Fœderal Legislature will not only be restrained by its dependence on the people as other legislative bodies are; but that it will be moreover watched and controuled by the several collateral Legislatures, which other legislative bodies are not. And in the third place, no comparison can be made between the means that will be possessed by the more permanent branches of the Fœderal Government for seducing, if they should be disposed to seduce, the House of Representatives from their duty to the people; and the means of influence over the popular branch, possessed by the other branches of the governments above cited. With less power therefore to abuse, the Fœderal Representatives, can be less tempted on one side, and will be doubly watched on the other.

PUBLIUS: THE FEDERALIST 53 (JAMES MADISON)
New York *Independent Journal*, 9 February 1788*

To the People of the State of New-York.

I shall here perhaps be reminded of a current observation, "that where annual elections end, tyranny begins." If it be true as has often been remarked, that sayings which become proverbial, are generally founded in reason, it is not less true that when once established, they are often applied to cases to which the reason of them does not extend. I need not look for a proof beyond the case before us. What is the reason on which this proverbial observation is founded? No man will subject himself to the ridicule of pretending that any natural connection subsists between the sun or the seasons, and the period within which human virtue can bear the temptations of power. Happily for mankind, liberty is not in this respect confined to any single point of time; but lies within extremes, which afford sufficient latitude for all the variations which may be required by the various situations and circumstances of civil society. The election of magistrates might be, if it were found expedient, as in some instances it actually has been, daily, weekly, or monthly, as well as annual; and if circumstances may require a deviation from the rule on one side, why not also on the other side. Turning our attention to the periods established among ourselves, for the election of the most numerous branches of the state legislatures, we find them by no means coinciding any more in this instance, than in the elections of other civil magistrates. In Connecticut and Rhode-Island, the periods are half-yearly. In the other states, South-Carolina excepted, they are annual. In South-Carolina, they are biennial; as is proposed in the federal government. Here is a difference, as four to one, between the longest and shortest periods; and yet it would be not easy to shew that Connecticut or Rhode-Island is better governed, or enjoys a greater share of rational liberty than South-Carolina; or that either

*Reprinted: *New York Packet*, 12 February.

the one or the other of these states are distinguished in these respects, and by these causes, from the states whose elections are different from both.

In searching for the grounds of this doctrine, I can discover but one, and that is wholly inapplicable to our case. The important distinction so well understood in America between a constitution established by the people, and unalterable by the government; and a law established by the government, and alterable by the government, seems to have been little understood and less observed in any other country. Wherever the supreme power of legislation has resided, has been supposed to reside also, a full power to change the form of the government. Even in Great-Britain, where the principles of political and civil liberty have been most discussed; and where we hear most of the rights of the constitution, it is maintained that the authority of the parliament is transcendent and uncontroulable, as well with regard to the constitution, as the ordinary objects of legislative provision. They have accordingly, in several instances, actually changed, by legislative acts, some of the most fundamental articles of the government. They have in particular, on several occasions, changed the periods of election; and on the last occasion, not only introduced septennial, in place of triennial, elections; but by the same act continued themselves in place four years beyond the term for which they were elected by the people. An attention to these dangerous practices has produced a very natural alarm in the votaries of free government, of which frequency of elections is the corner stone; and has led them to seek for some security to liberty against the danger to which it is exposed. Where no constitution paramount to the government, either existed or could be obtained, no constitutional security similar to that established in the United States, was to be attempted. Some other security therefore was to be sought for; and what better security would the case admit, than that of selecting and appealing to some simple and familiar portion of time, as a standard for measuring the danger of innovations, for fixing the national sentiment, and for uniting the patriotic exertions. The most simple and familiar portion of time, applicable to the subject, was that of a year; and hence the doctrine has been inculcated by a laudable zeal to erect some barrier against the gradual innovations of an unlimited government, that the advance towards tyranny was to be calculated by the distance of departure from the fixed point of annual elections. But what necessity can there be of applying this expedient to a government, limited as the federal government will be, by the authority of a paramount constitution? Or who will pretend that the liberties of the people of America will not be more secure under biennial elections, unalterably fixed by such a constitution, than those of any other nation would be, where elections were annual or even more frequent, but subject to alterations by the ordinary power of the government?

The second question stated is, whether biennial elections be necessary or useful? The propriety of answering this question in the affirmative will appear from several very obvious considerations.

No man can be a competent legislator who does not add to an upright intention and a sound judgment, a certain degree of knowledge of the subjects on which he is to legislate. A part of this knowledge may be acquired by means of information which lie within the compass of men in private as well as public stations. Another part can only be attained, or at least thoroughly attained, by actual experience in the station which requires the use of it. The period of service ought therefore in all such cases to bear some proportion to the extent of practical knowledge, requisite to the due performance of the service. The period of legislative service established in most of the states for the more numerous branch is, as we have seen, one year. The question then may be put into this simple form; does the period of two years bear no greater proportion to the knowledge requisite for federal legislation, than one year does to the knowledge requisite for state legislation? The very statement of the question in this form, suggests the answer that ought to be given to it.

In a single state the requisite knowledge, relates to the existing laws which are uniform throughout the state, and with which all the citizens are more or less conversant; and to the general affairs of the state, which lie within a small compass, are not very diversified, and occupy much of the attention and conversation of every class of people. The great theatre of the United States presents a very different scene. The laws are so far from being uniform, that they vary in every state; whilst the public affairs of the union are spread throughout a very extensive region, and are extremely diversified by the local affairs connected with them, and can with difficulty be correctly learnt in any other place, than in the central councils, to which a knowledge of them will be brought by the representatives of every part of the empire. Yet some knowledge of the affairs, and even of the laws of all the states, ought to be possessed by the members from each of the states. How can foreign trade be properly regulated by uniform laws, without some acquaintance with the commerce: the ports, the usages, and the regulations, of the different states. How can the trade between the different states be duly regulated without some knowledge of their relative situations in these and other points? How can taxes be judiciously imposed, and effectually collected, if they be not accommodated to the different laws and local circumstances relating to these objects in the different states? How can uniform regulations for the militia be duly provided without a similar knowledge of many internal circumstances by which the states are distinguished from each other? These are the principal objects of federal legislation, and suggest most forceably, the extensive information which the representatives ought to acquire. The other inferior objects will require a proportional degree of information with regard to them.

It is true that all these difficulties will by degrees be very much diminished. The most laborious task will be the proper inauguration of the government, and the primeval formation of a federal code. Improvements on the first draught will every year become both easier and fewer. Past transactions of the government will be a ready and accurate source of information to new members. The affairs of the union will become more and more objects of curiosity and conversation among the citizens at large. And the increased intercourse among those of different states will contribute not a little to diffuse a mutual knowledge of their affairs, as this again will contribute to a general assimilation of their manners and laws. But with all these abatements the business of federal legislation must continue so far to exceed both in novelty and difficulty, the legislative business of a single state as to justify the longer period of service assigned to those who are to transact it.

A branch of knowledge which belongs to the acquirements of a federal representative, and which has not been mentioned, is that of foreign affairs. In regulating our own commerce he ought to be not only acquainted with the treaties between the United States and other nations, but also with the commercial policy and laws of other nations. He ought not be altogether ignorant of the law of nations, for that as far it is a proper object of municipal legislation is submitted to the federal government. And although the house of representatives is not immediately to participate in foreign negotiations and arrangements, yet from the necessary connection between the several branches of public affairs, those particular branches will frequently deserve attention in the ordinary course of legislation, and will sometimes demand particular legislative sanction and cooperation. Some portion of this knowledge may no doubt be acquired in a man's closet; but some of it also can only be derived from the public sources of information; and all of it will be acquired to best effect by a practical attention to the subject during the period of actual service in the legislature.

There are other considerations of less importance perhaps, but which are not unworthy of notice. The distance which many of the representatives will be obliged to travel, and the arrangements rendered necessary by that circumstance, might be much more serious objections with fit men to this service if limited to a single year than if extended to two years. No argument can be drawn on this subject from the case of the delegates to the existing Congress. They are elected annually it is true; but their re-election is considered by the legislative assemblies almost as a matter of course. The election of the representatives by the people would not be governed by the same principle.

A few of the members, as happens in all such assemblies, will possess superior talents, will by frequent re-elections, become members of long standing; will be thoroughly masters of the public business, and perhaps not unwilling to avail themselves of those advantages. The greater the proportion of new members, and the less the information of the bulk of the members, the more apt will they be to fall into the snares that may be laid for them. This remark is no less applicable to the relation which will subsist between the house of representatives and the senate.

It is an inconveniency mingled with the advantages of our frequent elections, even in single states where they are large and hold but one legislative session in the year, that spurious elections cannot be investigated and annulled in time for the decision to have its due effect. If a return can be obtained, no matter by what unlawful means, the irregular member, who takes his seat of course, is sure of holding it a sufficient time, to answer his purposes. Hence a very pernicious encouragement is given to the use of unlawful means for obtaining irregular returns. Were elections for the federal legislature to be annual, this practice might become a very serious abuse, particularly in the more distant states. Each house is, as it necessarily must be, the judge of the elections, qualifications and returns of its members, and whatever improvements may be suggested by experience for simplifying and accelerating the process in disputed cases. So great a portion of a year would unavoidably elapse, before an illegitimate member could be dispossessed of his seat, that the prospect of such an event, would be little check to unfair and illicit means of obtaining a seat.

All these considerations taken together warrant us in affirming that biennial elections will be as useful to the affairs of the public, as we have seen that they will be safe to the liberties of the people.

PUBLIUS: THE FEDERALIST 55 (JAMES MADISON)
New York *Independent Journal*, 13 February 1788*

To the People of the State of New-York.

The number of which the House of Representatives is to consist, forms another, and a very interesting point of view under which this

*Reprinted: *New York Packet*, 15 February.

branch of the federal legislature may be contemplated. Scarce any article indeed in the whole constitution seems to be rendered more worthy of attention, by the weight of character and the apparent force of argument, with which it has been assailed. The charges exhibited against it are, first, that so small a number of representatives will be an unsafe depositary of the public interests; secondly, that they will not possess a proper knowledge of the local circumstances of their numerous constituents; thirdly, that they will be taken from that class of citizens which will sympathize least with the feelings of the mass of the people, and be most likely to aim at a permanent elevation of the few on the depression of the many; fourthly, that defective as the number will be in the first instance, it will be more and more disproportionate, by the increase of the people, and the obstacles which will prevent a correspondent increase of the representatives.

In general it may be remarked on this subject, that no political problem is less susceptible of a precise solution, than that which relates to the number most convenient for a representative legislature: Nor is there any point on which the policy of the several states is more at variance; whether we compare their legislative assemblies directly with each other, or consider the proportions which they respectively bear to the number of their constituents. Passing over the difference between the smallest and largest states, as Delaware, whose most numerous branch consists of twenty-one representatives, and Massachusetts, where it amounts to between three and four hundred; a very considerable difference is observable among states nearly equal in population. The number of representatives in Pennsylvania is not more than one-fifth of that in the state last mentioned. New-York, whose population is to that of South-Carolina as six to five, has little more than one third of the number of representatives. As great a disparity prevails between the states of Georgia and Delaware, or Rhode-Island. In Pennsylvania the representatives do not bear a greater proportion to their constituents than of one for every four or five thousand. In Rhode-Island, they bear a proportion of at least one for every thousand. And according to the constitution of Georgia, the proportion may be carried to one for every ten electors; and must unavoidably far exceed the proportion in any of the other States.

Another general remark to be made is, that the ratio between the representatives and the people, ought not to be the same where the latter are very numerous, as where they are very few. Were the representatives in Virginia to be regulated by the standard in Rhode-Island, they would at this time amount to between four and five hundred; and twenty or thirty years hence, to a thousand. On the other hand, the ratio of Pennsylvania, if applied to the state of Delaware, would reduce the Representative as-

sembly of the latter to seven or eight members. Nothing can be more
fallacious than to found our political calculations on arithmetical principles. Sixty or seventy men, may be more properly trusted with a given
degree of power than six or seven. But it does not follow, that six or
seven hundred would be proportionally a better depository. And if we
carry on the supposition to six or seven thousand, the whole reasoning
ought to be reversed. The truth is, that in all cases a certain number at
least seems to be necessary to secure the benefits of free consultation and
discussion, and to guard against too easy a combination for improper
purposes: As on the other hand, the number ought at most to be kept
within a certain limit, in order to avoid the confusion and intemperance
of a multitude. In all very numerous assemblies, of whatever characters
composed, passion never fails to wrest the sceptre from reason. Had every
Athenian citizen been a Socrates; every Athenian assembly would still have
been a mob.

It is necessary also to recollect here the observations which were
applied to the case of biennial elections. For the same reason that the
limited powers of the Congress and the controul of the state legislatures,
justify less frequent elections than the public safety might otherwise require; the members of the Congress need be less numerous than if they
possessed the whole power of legislation, and were under no other than
the ordinary restraints of other legislative bodies.

With these general ideas in our minds, let us weigh the objections
which have been stated against the number of members proposed for the
House of Representatives. It is said in the first place, that so small a number
cannot be safely trusted with so much power.

The number of which this branch of the legislature is to consist at
the outset of the government, will be sixty five. Within three years a
census is to be taken, when the number may be augmented to one for
every thirty thousand inhabitants; and within every successive period of
ten years, the census is to be renewed, and augmentations may continue
to be made under the above limitation. It will not be thought an extravagant
conjecture, that the first census, will, at the rate of one for every thirty
thousand raise the number of representatives to at least one hundred.
Estimating the negroes in the proportion of three fifths, it can scarcely
be doubted that the population of the United States will by that time, if
it does not already, amount to three millions. At the expiration of twenty
five years, according to the computed rate of increase, the number of
representatives will amount to two hundred; and of fifty years, to four
hundred. This is a number which I presume will put an end to all fears
arising from the smallness of the body. I take for granted here what I
shall in answering the fourth objection hereafter shew, that the number

of representatives will be augmented from time to time in the manner provided by the constitution. On a contrary supposition, I should admit the objection to have very great weight indeed.

The true question to be decided then is whether the smallness of the number, as a temporary regulation, be dangerous to the public liberty: Whether sixty five members for a few years, and a hundred or two hundred for a few more, be a safe depositary for a limited and well guarded power of legislating for the United States? I must own that I could not give a negative answer to this question, without first obliterating every impression which I have received with regard to the present genius of the people of America, the spirit, which actuates the state legislatures, and the principles which are incorporated with the political character of every class of citizens. I am unable to conceive that the people of America in their present temper, or under any circumstances which can speedily happen, will chuse, and every second year repeat the choice of sixty five or an hundred men, who would be disposed to form and pursue a scheme of tyranny or treachery. I am unable to conceive that the state legislatures which must feel so many motives to watch, and which possess so many means of counteracting the federal legislature, would fail either to detect or to defeat a conspiracy of the latter against the liberties of their common constituents. I am equally unable to conceive that there are at this time, or can be in any short time, in the United States any sixty five or an hundred men capable of recommending themselves to the choice of the people at large, who would either desire or dare within the short space of two years, to betray the solemn trust committed to them. What change of circumstances time and a fuller population of our country may produce, requires a prophetic spirit to declare, which makes no part of my pretensions. But judging from the circumstances now before us, and from the probable state of them within a moderate period of time, I must pronounce that the liberties of America can not be unsafe in the number of hands proposed by the federal constitution.

From what quarter can the danger proceed? Are we afraid of foreign gold? If foreign gold could so easily corrupt our federal rulers, and enable them to ensnare and betray their constituents, how has it happened that we are at this time a free and independent nation? The Congress which conducted us through the revolution were a less numerous body than their successors will be; they were not chosen by nor responsible to their fellow citizens at large; though appointed from year to year, and recallable at pleasure, they were generally continued for three years; and prior to the ratification of the federal articles, for a still longer term; they held their consultations always under the veil of secrecy; they had the sole transaction of our affairs with foreign nations; through the whole course of the war, they had the fate of their country more in their hands, than it is to be hoped will ever be the case with our future representatives; and from the greatness of the prize at stake and the eagerness of the party which lost it, it may well be supposed, that the use of other means than force would not have been scrupled: yet we know by happy experience that the public trust was not betrayed; nor has the purity of our public councils in this particular ever suffered even from the whispers of calumny.

Is the danger apprehended from the other branches of the federal government? But where are the means to be found by the President or the Senate, or both? Their emoluments of office it is to be presumed will not, and without a previous corruption of the house of representatives cannot, more than suffice for very different purposes: Their private fortunes, as they must all be American citizens, cannot possibly be sources of danger. The only means then which they can possess, will be in the dispensation of appointments. Is it here that suspicion rests her charge? Sometimes we are told that this fund of corruption is to be exhausted by the President in subduing the virtue of the Senate. Now the fidelity of the other house is to be the victim. The improbability of such a mercenary and perfidious combination of the several members of government standing on as different foundations as republican principles will well admit, and at the same time accountable to the society over which they are placed, ought alone to quiet this apprehension. But fortunately the constitution has provided a still further safeguard. The members of the Congress are rendered ineligible to any civil offices that may be created or of which the emoluments may be increased, during the term of their election. No offices therefore can be dealt out to the existing members, but such as may become vacant by ordinary casualties; and to suppose that these would be sufficient to purchase the guardians of the people, selected by the people themselves, is to renounce every rule by which events ought to be calculated, and to substitute an indiscriminate and unbounded jealousy, with which all reasoning must be vain. The sincere friends of liberty who give themselves up to the extravagancies of this passion are not aware of the injury they do their own cause. As there is a degree of depravity in mankind which requires a certain degree of circumspection and distrust: So there are other qualities in human nature, which justify a certain portion of esteem and confidence. Republican government presupposes the existence of these qualities in a higher degree than any other form. Were the pictures which have been drawn by the political jealousy of some among us, faithful likenesses of the human character, the inference would be that there is not sufficient virtue among men for self government; and that nothing less than the chains of despotism can restrain them from destroying and devouring one another.

PUBLIUS: THE FEDERALIST 56 (JAMES MADISON)
New York *Independent Journal*, 16 February 1788*

To the People of the State of New-York.

The *second* charge against the House of Representatives is, that it will be too small to possess a due knowledge of the interests of its constituents.

As this objection evidently proceeds from a comparison of the proposed number of representatives, with the great extent of the United States, the number of their inhabitants, and the diversity of their interests, without taking into view at the same time the circumstances which will distinguish the Congress from other legislative bodies, the best answer that can be given to it, will be a brief explanation of these peculiarities.

It is a sound and important principle that the representative ought to be acquainted with the interests and circumstances of his constituents. But this principle can extend no farther than to those circumstances and interests, to which the authority and care of the representative relate. An ignorance of a variety of minute and particular objects, which do not lie within the compass of legislation, is consistent with every attribute necessary to a due performance of the legislative trust. In determining the extent of information required in the exercise of a particular authority, recourse then must be had to the objects within the purview of that authority.

What are to be the objects of federal legislation? Those which are of most importance, and which seem most to require local knowledge, are commerce, taxation, and the militia.

A proper regulation of commerce requires much information, as has been elsewhere remarked; but as far as this information relates to the laws and local situation of each individual state, a very few representatives would be very sufficient vehicles of it to the federal councils.

Taxation will consist, in great measure, of duties which will be involved in the regulation of commerce. So far the preceeding remark is applicable to this object. As far as it may consist of internal collections, a more diffusive knowledge of the circumstances of the state may be necessary. But will not this also be possessed in sufficient degree by a very few intelligent men diffusively elected within the state. Divide the largest state into ten or twelve districts, and it will be found that there will be no peculiar local interest in either, which will not be within the knowledge of the representative of the district. Besides this source of information, the laws of the state framed by representatives from every part of it, will be almost of themselves a sufficient guide. In every state there have been made, and must continue to be made, regulations on this subject, which will in many cases leave little more to be done by the federal legislature, than to review the different laws, and reduce them into one general act. A skilful individual in his closet, with all the local codes before him, might compile a law on some subjects of taxation for the whole union, without any aid from oral information; and it may be expected, that whenever internal taxes may be necessary, and particularly in cases requiring uniformity throughout the states, the more simple objects will be preferred. To be fully sensible of the facility which will be given to this branch of federal legislation, by the assistance of the state codes, we need only suppose for a moment, that this or any other state were divided into a number of parts, each having and exercising within itself a power of local legislation. Is it not evident that a degree of local information and preparatory labour would be found in the several volumes of their proceedings, which would very much shorten the labours of the general legislature, and render a much smaller number of members sufficient for it? The federal councils will derive great advantage from another circumstance. The representatives of each state will not only bring with them a considerable knowledge of its laws, and a local knowledge of their respective districts; but will probably in all cases have been members, and may even at the very time be members of the state legislature, where all the local information and interests of the state are assembled, and from whence they may easily be conveyed by a very few hands into the legislature of the United States.

The observations made on the subject of taxation apply with greater force to the case of the militia. For however different the rules of discipline may be in different states; They are the same throughout each particular state; and depend on circumstances which can differ but little in different parts of the same state.*

The attentive reader will discern that the reasoning here used to prove the sufficiency of a moderate number of representatives, does not in any respect contradict what was urged on another occasion with regard to the extensive information which the representatives ought to possess, and the time that might be necessary for acquiring it. This information, so far as it may relate to local objects, is rendered necessary and difficult,

---

*This paragraph was replaced in the book edition with the following paragraph: "With regard to the regulation of the militia, there are scarcely any circumstances in reference to which local knowledge can be said to be necessary. The general face of the country, whether mountainous or level, most fit for the operations of infantry or cavalry, is almost the only consideration of this nature that can occur. The art of war teaches general principles of organization, movement, and discipline, which apply universally."

not by a difference of laws and local circumstances within a single state; but of those among different states. Taking each state by itself, its laws are the same, and its interests but little diversified. A few men therefore will possess all the knowledge requisite for a proper representation of them. Were the interests and affairs of each individual state, perfectly simple and uniform, a knowledge of them in one part would involve a knowledge of them in every other, and the whole state might be competently represented, by a single member taken from any part of it. On a comparison of the different states together, we find a great dissimilarity in their laws, and in many other circumstances connected with the objects of federal legislation, with all of which the federal representatives ought to have some acquaintance. Whilst a few representatives therefore from each state may bring with them a due knowledge of their own state, every representative will have much information to acquire concerning all the other states. The changes of time, as was formerly remarked, on the comparative situation of the different states, will have an assimilating effect. The effect of time on the internal affairs of the states taken singly, will be just the contrary. At present some of the states are little more than a society of husbandmen. Few of them have made much progress in those branches of industry, which give a variety and complexity to the affairs of a nation. These however will in all of them be the fruits of a more advanced population; and will require on the part of each state a fuller representation. The foresight of the Convention has accordingly taken care that the progress of population may be accompanied with a proper increase of the representative branch of the government.

The experience of Great Britain which presents to mankind so many political lessons, both of the monitory and exemplary kind, and which has been frequently consulted in the course of these enquiries, corroborates the result of the reflections which we have just made. The number of inhabitants in the two kingdoms of England and Scotland, cannot be stated at less than eight millions. The representatives of these eight millions in the House of Commons, amount to five hundred fifty eight. Of this number one ninth are elected by three hundred and sixty four persons, and one half by five thousand seven hundred and twenty three persons.[a] It cannot be supposed that the half thus elected, and who do not even reside among the people at large, can add any thing either to the security of the people against the government; or to the knowledge of their circumstances and interests, in the legislative councils. On the contrary it is notorious that

[a]Burgh's polit. disquis. [James Burgh, *Political Disquisitions: or, An Enquiry into Public Errors, Defects, and Abuses . . .* (3 vols., London, 1774–1775), I, 45, 48.]

they are more frequently the representatives and instruments of the executive magistrate, than the guardians and advocates of the popular rights. They might therefore with great propriety be considered as something more than a mere deduction from the real representatives of the nation. We will however consider them, in this light alone, and will not extend the deduction, to a considerable number of others, who do not reside among their constituents, are very faintly connected with them, and have very little particular knowledge of their affairs. With all these concessions two hundred and seventy nine persons only will be the depository of the safety, interest and happiness of eight millions; that is to say: There will be one representative only to maintain the rights and explain the situation *of twenty eight thousand six hundred and seventy* constituents, in an assembly exposed to the whole force of executive influence, and extending its authority to every object of legislation within a nation whose affairs are in the highest degree diversified and complicated. Yet it is very certain not only that a valuable portion of freedom has been preserved under all these circumstances, but that the defects in the British code are chargeable in a very small proportion, on the ignorance of the legislature concerning the circumstances of the people. Allowing to this case the weight which is due to it: And comparing it with that of the House of Representatives as above explained, it seems to give the fullest assurance that a representative for every *thirty thousand inhabitants* will render the latter both a safe and competent guardian of the interests which will be confided to it.

3

———————◆———————

The Senate

Dᴜʀɪɴɢ ᴛʜᴇ ᴄᴏɴꜰᴇᴅᴇʀᴀᴛɪᴏɴ ᴘᴇʀɪᴏᴅ *most of the states had bicameral legislatures. Only Pennsylvania and Georgia had single-house assemblies. The Confederation Congress was also but one house. The shortcomings of these few unicameral legislatures were so apparent that there was virtually no debate in the Constitutional Convention over the establishment of a bicameral Congress. There was, however, considerable debate over representation in each house.*

Early in the Convention it was agreed that the House of Representatives should be apportioned among the states on the basis of population. Large-state delegates wanted the representation in the Senate based upon the same principle, but small-state delegates wanted the states to be equally represented in the Senate. Eventually a compromise determined that the Senate would in fact be composed of two senators from every state while the House of Representatives would be apportioned by population. In both houses of Congress, voting would be by individual— not by states.

During the debate over ratification, Antifederalists from the large states attacked the equality of the states in the Senate as oppressive to their populations. If Delaware, with less than ten percent of Virginia's population, had the same representation as the Old Dominion, how could anyone imagine that Virginians were properly represented?

Antifederalists also denounced the aristocratic nature of the Senate. Senators were to be elected by their state legislatures for six-year terms. Neither mandatory rotation in office nor recall was provided for by the Constitution. Thus, once Senators got in office, it was feared they might be reelected perpetually, serving for life.

The combination of the Senate and President in appointments and treaty-making was denounced as a violation of the principle of separation of powers. How could the Senate be expected to impeach corrupt officeholders after confirming their appointments? Who would be held responsible for unwise treaties? The shared responsibility of the Senate and Presidency meant, in essence, that there would be no responsibility for malfeasance in office. A privy council, Antifederalists argued, would more adequately serve as advisor to the President.

Antifederalists also decried the placement of the Vice President of the United States as president of the Senate with the power to cast the deciding vote when the Senate deadlocked. Not only did this placement violate the separation of powers principle, but it gave one state an extra vote in the Senate. The Senate, Antifederalists argued, should elect its own presiding officer from among its members.

Federalists justified the equality of the states in the Senate on the basis of expediency. Without this concession to the small states, agreement in the Constitutional Convention would have been unobtainable. Furthermore, the different constituency of the Senate, coupled with the six-year term with one-third of the Senators being elected every two years, promised greater stability for Congress.

The Senate's role in advising the President on appointments and treaties was justified in several ways. The Senate, with its six-year term, it was suggested, would be the repository of much wisdom and experience, both of which should be made available to the President. A privy council would be expensive, would add another layer onto the government, and would not necessarily be an improvement on the Senate as a means of advising the President.

To counter the charge of the Senate's aristocratic nature, Federalists pointed out that the Senate could do nothing by itself. In passing legislation, the Senate needed the agreement of the House of Representatives. In treaty-making and appointments, the Senate acted in conjunction with, and most probably in response to, the actions of the President. If Senators violated their trust, they would not be reelected by their state legislatures.

Antifederalist

FEDERAL FARMER
c. 8 November 1787 (excerpt)*

The house of representatives is on the plan of consolidation, but the senate is entirely on the federal plan; and Delaware will have as much constitutional influence in the senate, as the largest state in the union; and in this senate are lodged legislative, executive and judicial powers: Ten states in this union urge that they are small states, nine of which were present in the convention.—They were interested in collecting large powers into the hands of the senate, in which each state still will have its equal share of power. I suppose it was impracticable for the three large states, as they were called, to get the senate formed on any other principles:—but this only proves, that we cannot form one general government on equal and just principles—and proves, that we ought not to lodge in it such extensive powers before we are convinced of the practicability of organizing it on just and equal principles. The senate will consist of two members from each state, chosen by the state legislature, every sixth year. The clause referred to, respecting the elections of representatives, empowers the general legislature to regulate the elections of senators also, "except as to the places of chusing senators."†—There is, therefore, but little more security in the elections than in those of representatives:— Fourteen senators make a quorum for business, and a majority of the senators present give the vote of the senate, except in giving judgment upon an impeachment, or in making treaties, or in expelling a member, when two thirds of the senators present must agree.—The members of the legislature are not excluded from being elected to any military offices, or any civil offices, except those created, or the emoluments of which shall be increased by themselves: two-thirds of the members present, of either house, may expel a member at pleasure.—The senate is an independent branch of the legislature, a court for trying impeachments, and also a part of the executive, having a negative in the making of all treaties, and in appointing almost all officers.

The vice-president is not a very important, if not an unnecessary part of the system—he may be a part of the senate at one period, and act as the supreme executive magistrate at another—The election of this officer, as well as of the president of the United States seems to be properly

---

*The *Letters from the Federal Farmer* was a forty-page pamphlet published in New York City around 8 November. It was one of the most significant Antifederalist publications, going through "four editions" with several thousand copies sold. The authorship is uncertain.
†Article I, section 4.

secured; but when we examine the powers of the president, and the forms of the executive, shall perceive that the general government, in this part, will have a strong tendency to aristocracy, or the government of the few. The executive is, in fact, the president and senate in all transactions of any importance; the president is connected with, or tied to the senate; he may always act with the senate, never can effectually counteract its views: The president can appoint no officer, civil or military, who shall not be agreeable to the senate; and the presumption is, that the will of so important a body will not be very easily controuled, and that it will exercise its powers with great address.

CINCINNATUS IV (ARTHUR LEE): TO JAMES WILSON, ESQUIRE
New York Journal, 22 November 1787 (excerpt)*

I come now, sir, to the most exceptionable part of the Constitution— the senate. In this, as in every other part, you are in the line of your profession, and on that ground assure your fellow citizens, that—"perhaps there never was a charge made with less reason, than that which predicts the institution of a baneful aristocracy in the Fœderal Senate." And yet your conscience smote you, sir, at the beginning, and compelled you to prefix a "perhaps" to this strange assertion. The senate, you say, branches into two characters—the one legislative and the other executive. This phraseology is quaint, and the position does not state the whole truth. I am very sorry, sir, to be so often obliged to reprehend the suppression of information at the moment that you stood forth to instruct your fellow citizens, in what they were supposed not to understand. In this character, you should have abandoned your professional line, and told them, not only the truth, but the whole truth. The whole truth then is, that the same body, called the senate, is vested with—legislative—executive—and judicial powers. The two first you acknowledge; the last is conveyed in these words, sec. 3d. The senate shall have the sole power to try all impeachments. On this point then we are to come to issue—whether a senate so constituted is likely to produce a baneful aristocracy, which will swallow up the democratic rights and liberties of the nation.

To judge on this question, it is proper to examine minutely into the constitution and powers of the senate; and we shall then see with what

*This is the fourth of six "Cincinnatus" essays addressed to James Wilson published in the *New York Journal* from 1 November to 6 December 1787. The essays were written by Arthur Lee of Virginia who was a member of the three-man Confederation Board of Treasury. The entire essay was reprinted in the Philadelphia *Freeman's Journal* on 30 January. The first four paragraphs printed here were reprinted in the *Salem Mercury* on 11 December 1787.

anxious and subtle cunning it is calculated for the proposed purpose. 1st. It is removed from the people, being chosen by the legislatures—and exactly in the ratio of their removal from the people, do aristocratic principles constantly infect the minds of man. 2d. They endure, two thirds for four, and one-third for six years, and in proportion to the duration of power, the aristocratic exercise of it, and attempts to extend it, are invariably observed to increase. 3d. From the union of the executive with the legislative functions, they must necessarily be longer together, or rather constantly assembled; and in proportion to their continuance together, will they be able to form effectual schemes for extending their own power, and reducing that of the democratic branch. If any one would wish to see this more fully illustrated, let him turn to the history of the Decemviri in Rome. 4th. Their advice and consent being necessary to the appointment of all the great officers of state, both at home and abroad, will enable them to win over any opponents to their measures in the house of representatives, and give them the influence which, we see, accompanies this power in England; and which, from the nature of man, must follow it every where. 5th. The sole power of impeachment being vested in them, they have it in their power to controul the representative in this high democratic right; to screen from punishment, or rather from conviction, all high offenders, being their creatures, and to keep in awe all opponents to their power in high office. 6th. The union established between them and the vice president, who is made one of the corps, and will therefore be highly animated with the aristocratic spirit of it, furnishes them a powerful shield against popular suspicion and enquiry, he being the second man in the United States who stands highest in the confidence and estimation of the people. And lastly, the right of altering or amending moneybills, is a high additional power given them as a branch of the legislature, which their analogous branch, in the English parliament, could never obtain, because it has been guarded by the representatives of the people there, with the most strenuous solicitude as one of the vital principles of democratic liberty.

Is a body so vested with means to soften & seduce—so armed with power to screen or to condemn—so fortified against suspicion and enquiry—so largely trusted with legislative powers—so independent of and removed from the people—so tempted to abuse and extend these powers— is this a body which freemen ought ever to create, or which freemen can ever endure? Or is it not a monster in the political creation, which we ought to regard with horror? Shall we thus forge our own fetters? Shall we set up the idol, before which we shall soon be obliged, however, reluctantly to bow? Shall we consent to see a proud aristocracy erect his domineering crest in triumph over our prostrate liberties?

But we shall yet see more clearly, how highly favored this senate has been, by taking a similar view of the representative body. This body is the true representative of the democratic part of the system; the shield and defence of the people. This body should have weight from its members, and the high controul which it should alone possess. We can form no idea of the necessary number in this untried system, to give due weight to the democratic part, but from the example of England. Had it not been intended to humble this branch, it would have been fixed, at least, at their standard. We are to have one representative for every thirty thousand—they have nearly one for ten thousand souls. Their number is about six millions; their representatives five hundred and fifteen. When we are six millions, we shall have only two hundred representatives. In point of number therefore and the weight derived from it, the representative proposed by the constitution is remarkable feeble. It is farther weakened by the senate being allowed not only to reject, but to alter and amend money-bills. Its transcendent and incommunicable power of impeachment—that high source of its dignity and controul—in which alone the majesty of the people feels his sceptre, and bears aloft his fasces—is rendered ineffectual, by its being triable before its rival branch, the senate, the patron and prompter of the measures against which it is to sit in judgment. It is therefore most manifest, that from the very nature of the constitution the right of impeachment apparently given, is really rendered ineffectual. And this is contrived with so much art, that to discover it you must bring together various and distant parts of the constitution, or it will not strike the examiner, that the same body that advises the executive measures of government which are usually the subject of impeachment, are the sole judges on such impeachments. They must therefore be both party and judge, and must condemn those who have executed what they advised. Could such a monstrous absurdity have escaped men who were not determined, at all events, to vest all power in this aristocratic body? Is it not plain, that the senate is to be exalted by the humiliation of the democracy. A democracy which, thus bereft of its powers, and shorn of its strength; will stand a melancholy monument of popular impotence.

Hitherto I have examined your senate by its intrinsic and its comparative powers. Let us next examine, how far the principles of its constitution are compatible with what our own constitutions lay down, and what the best writers on the subject have determined to be essential to free and good government.

In every state constitution, with a very trifling exception in that of Massachusetts, the legislative and executive powers are vested in different and independent bodies.—Will any one believe, that it is because we are become wiser, that in twelve years we are to overthrow every system which reason and experience taught us was right. Or is it, that a few men, forming a plan at Philadelphia subversive of all former principles, then posting to Congress, and passing it there, and next dispersing themselves in the several states to propagate their errors, and, if they can, get chosen into the state conventions; are actuated by motives of interest and bad ambition? I should be very unwilling to believe the latter, and yet it is utterly incomprehensible, how such a systematic violation of all that has been deemed wise and right, from which no other result can be expected, but the establishment of a baneful aristocracy, could have been recommended to a free and enlightened people.

"Lorsque dans la meme personne, says Montesquieu, ou dans le meme corps de magistrature, la puissance legislative est re-unie a la puissance executive; il n'y a point de liberte; parce qu'on peut craindre que le meme monarque, ou le meme Senat ne fasse des loix tyranniques, pour les executer tyranniquement." "When the legislative and executive powers are united in the same person, or in the same corps, there can be no liberty. Because, it may be feared, that the same monarch or senate will make tyrannical laws, that they may execute them tyrannically." I am aware that this great man is speaking of a senate being the whole legislative; whereas the one before us is but a branch of the proposed legislature. But still the reason applies, inasmuch as the legislative power of the senate will enable it to negative all bills that are meant to controul the executive, and from being secure of preventing any abridgment, they can watch every pliant hour of the representative body to promote an enlargement of the executive powers. One thing at least is certain, that by making this branch of the legislature participant in the executive, you not only prevent the legislature from being a check upon the executive, but you inevitably prevent its being checked or controuled by the other branch.

To the authority of Montesquieu, I shall add that of Mr. de Lolme; whose disquisition on government, is allowed to be deep, solid, and ingenious. "Il ne suffisoit pas, says he, d'oter aux legislateurs l'execution des loix, par consequent, l'exemption qui en est la suite immediate; il falloit encore, leur oter ce qui eut produit les memes effects—l'espoir de jamais se l'attribuer—It is not only necessary to take from the legislature the executive power which would exempt them from the laws; but they should not have even a hope of being ever able to arrogate to themselves that power." To remove this hope from their expectation, it would have been proper, not only to have previously laid down, in a declaration of rights, that these powers should be forever separate and incommunicable; but the frame of the proposed constitution, should have had that separation religiously in view, through all its parts. It is manifest this was not the object of its framers, but, that on the contrary there is a studied mixture of them in the senate as necessary to erect it into that potent aristocracy which it must infallibly produce. In pursuit of this darling object, than which no greater calamity can be brought upon the people, another egregious error in constitutional principles is committed. I mean that of dividing the executive powers, between the senate and the president. Unless more harmony and less ambition should exist between these two executives than ever yet existed between men in power, or than can exist while human nature is as it is: this absurd division must be productive of constant contentions for the lead, must clog the execution of government to a mischievous, and sometimes to a disgraceful degree, and if they should unhappily harmonize in the same objects of ambition, their number and their combined power, would preclude all fear of that responsibility, which is one of the great securities of good, and restraints on bad governments. Upon these principles M. de Lolme has foreseen that "the effect of a division of the executive power is the establishment of absolute power in one of continual contention"; he therefore lays it down, as a general rule "pour q'un etat soit tranquille il faut que le pouvoir executif y soit reùnie"—for the tranquillity of the state it is necessary that the executive power should be in one. I will add, that this singlehood of the executive, is indispensably necessary to effective execution as well as to the responsibility and rectitude of him to whom it is entrusted.

By this time I hope it is evident from reason and authority, that in the constitution of the senate there is much cunning and little wisdom; that we have much to fear from it, and little to hope, and then it must necessarily produce a baneful aristocracy, by which the democratic rights of the people will be overwhelmed.

It was probably upon this principle that a member of the convention, of high and unexceeded reputation for wisdom and integrity, is said to have emphatically declared, that *he would sooner lose his right hand, than put his name to such a Constitution.**

LUTHER MARTIN'S GENUINE INFORMATION
Baltimore *Maryland Gazette*, 8 January 1788 (excerpt)†

[An Account of Events in the Constitutional Convention]

It was further said, that in a *federal* government over States *equally* free, sovereign and independent, *every State* ought to have an equal share

---

*The reference is to George Mason, a Virginia delegate to the Constitutional Convention.

†Reprinted: *Pennsylvania Packet*, 1 February; Philadelphia *Independent Gazetteer*, 9 February; *New York Journal*, 20, 22, 25 February; and the *State Gazette of South Carolina*, 28 April, 1 May.

in *making* the *federal laws* or *regulations*—in *deciding* upon them, and in *carrying them into execution, neither* of which was the case in *this* system, but the *reverse*, the States not having an *equal voice* in the *legislature*, nor in the *appointment* of the *executive*, the *judges*, and the *other officers of government*—It was insisted, that in the *whole* system there was but *one federal* feature—the appointment of the senators by the States in their sovereign capacity, that is by their legislatures, and the equality of suffrage in that branch; but it was said that *this feature* was only *federal* in *appearance*.

To prove *this*, and that the Senate *as constituted* could not be a *security* for the *protection* and *preservation* of the *State governments*, and that the *senators* could not be justly considered the *representatives* of the *States* as *States*, it was observed, that upon *just principles* of *representation*, the *representative* ought to *speak* the sentiments of his *constituents*, and ought to *vote* in the *same manner* that his *constituents* would do (as far as he can judge) provided his constituents were acting in *person*, and had the same knowledge and information with himself; and therefore that the *representative* ought to be *dependant* on his *constituents*, and *answerable* to them— that the connection between the *representative* and the *represented*, ought to be as *near* and as *close* as *possible;* according to these principles, Mr. Speaker, in this State it is provided by *its constitution*, that the representatives in Congress, shall be chosen *annually*, shall be *paid* by the *State*, and shall be subject to *recall* even within the year; so *cautiously* has our *constitution* guarded against an *abuse* of the trust reposed in our representatives in the federal government; whereas by the *third* and *sixth* sections of the *first* article of this new system, the senators are to be chosen for *six* years instead of being chosen *annually;* instead of being paid by *their States* who send them, *they* in conjunction with the other branch, are to *pay themselves* out of the treasury of the United States; and are not liable to be *recalled* during the period for which they are chosen—Thus, Sir, for *six years* the *senators* are rendered totally and absolutely *independent* of *their States*, of *whom* they ought to be the *representatives*, without *any bond* or *tie* between them—During *that time* they may join in measures *ruinous* and *destructive* to *their States*, even such as should *totally annihilate* their *State governments*, and their States *cannot recall* them, *nor exercise any controul over them.* Another consideration, Mr. Speaker, it was thought ought to have *great weight* to prove that the *smaller* States cannot *depend* on the *senate* for the *preservation* of *their rights*, either against *large* and *ambitious States*, or against an *ambitious, aspiring President.*—The senate, Sir, is so constituted, that they are not only to compose one branch of the legislature, but by the second section of the second article, they are to *compose a privy council for the President;* hence it will be necessary, that they should be, in a great measure, a *permanent* body, *constantly residing* at the seat of government. *Seventy* years is estimated for the life of a man; it can hardly be supposed, that a senator, especially from the States remote from the seat of empire, will accept of an appointment which must *estrange* him for *six years from his State*, without giving up to a great degree his prospects in his *own State*. If he has a family, he will take his family with him to the place where the government shall be fixed, *that* will become his *home*, and there is every reason to expect that his *future* views and prospects will *centre* in the *favours* and *emoluments* either of the *general government*, or of the government of *that State* where the seat of empire is established:—In *either* case, he is *lost* to his *own State*. If he places his future prospects in the favours and emoluments of the *general government*, he will become the *dependant* and *creature* of the *President*, as the system *enables* a senator to be *appointed to offices*, and without the *nomination* of the *President, no appointment can take place*; as *such*, he will favour the wishes of the President, and concur in his measures, who, if he has no *ambitious views of his own* to gratify, may be *too favourable* to the *ambitious views* of the *large States*, who will have an *undue share* in his *original appointment*, and *on whom* he will be *more dependant* afterwards than on the States which are smaller. If the senator places his future prospects in that *State* where the seat of empire is fixed; from that time he will be in every question wherein its particular interest may be concerned the *representative* of *that State*, not of *his own*.

Federalist

AN AMERICAN CITIZEN II (TENCH COXE)
Philadelphia *Independent Gazetteer*, 28 September 1787*

We have seen that the late honorable Convention, in designating the nature of the chief executive office of the United States, *have deprived it of all the dangerous appendages of royalty*, and provided for *the frequent expiration of its limited powers*—As our President bears *no resemblance to a King*, so we shall see the Senate have *no similitude to nobles*.

First then not being hereditary, their *collective* knowledge, wisdom and virtue are not precarious, *for by these qualities alone are they to obtain*

---

*This essay was reprinted in nineteen newspapers from New Hampshire to South Carolina. It was also reprinted in the Philadelphia *American Museum*, in a Philadelphia broadside with the other three essays in the series, and in two Richmond, Va., pamphlet anthologies by the end of December 1787.

their offices; and they will have none of the *peculiar* follies and vices of those men, *who possess power merely because their fathers held it before them*, for they will be educated (under equal advantages and with equal prospects) among and on a footing with the other sons of a free people—If we recollect the characters, who have, at various periods, filled the seats of Congress, we shall find this expectation *perfectly reasonable*. Many *young* men of genius and *many characters of more matured abilities, without fortunes*, have been honored with that trust. *Wealth has had but few representatives there, and those have been generally possessed of respectable personal qualifications*. There have also been many instances of persons, not eminently endowed with mental qualities, who have been sent thither *from a reliance on their virtues, public and private*—As the Senators *are still to be elected by the legislatures of the states*, there can be no doubt of *equal safety and propriety* in their future appointment, especially as no further pecuniary qualification is required by the constitution.

They can hold *no other office* civil or military under the United States, nor can they join *in making provisions for themselves*, either by creating new places or encreasing the emoluments of old ones. As their sons are not to succeed them, they will not be induced to aim at an increase of perpetuity of their powers, at the expence of the liberties of the people of which those sons will be a part. They possess *a much smaller share of the judicial power* than the upper house in Britain, for they are not, as there, the highest court in civil affairs. Impeachments *alone* are the cases cognizable before them, and in what other place could matters of that nature be so properly and safely determined? The judges of the federal courts will owe their appointments to the president and senate, therefore may not feel so perfectly free *from favor, affection and influence*, as the upper house, who receive their power from the people, through their state representatives, and are immediately responsible to those assemblies, and finally to the nation at large—Thus we see when a daring or dangerous offender is brought to the bar of public justice, the people *who alone can impeach him by their immediate representatives*, will cause him to be tried, *not by judges appointed in the heat of the occasion*, but by two thirds of *a select body, chosen a long time before, for various purposes by the collected wisdom of their state legislatures*. From a pretence or affection of extraordinary purity and excellence of character *their word of honor* is the sanction, under which these high courts in other countries, have given their sentence—but with us, like the other judges of the union, like the rest of the people *of which they are never to forget they are a part* it is required, that they be on oath.

No ambitious, undeserving or unexperienced *youth* can acquire a seat in this house by means of the most enormous wealth or most powerful connections, *till thirty years have ripened his abilities and fully discovered his merits to his country*—a more rational ground of preference surely than mere property.

The senate though more independent of the people as to *the free exercise of their judgement and abilities*, than the house of representatives, by the longer term of their office, must be older and more experienced men and the public treasures, *the sinews of the state*, cannot be called forth by their original motion. They may *restrain the profusion or errors* of the house of representatives, *but they cannot take the necessary measures to raise a national revenue.*

The people, through the electors, *prescribe* them such a president as shall be *best qualified to controul them.*

They can only, by conviction on impeachment, *remove and incapacitate a dangerous officer*, but the punishment of him as a criminal *remains within the province of the courts of law to be conducted under all the ordinary forms and precautions*, which exceedingly diminishes the importance of their judicial powers. They are *detached*, as much as possible, from *local* prejudices in favour of their respective states, by having *a separate and independent vote*, for the sensible and conscientious use of which, every member will find *his person, honor and character* seriously bound—He cannot shelter himself, *under a vote in behalf of his state*, among his immediate colleagues. As there are only *two*, he cannot be voluntarily or involuntarily governed *by the majority of the deputation*—He will be obliged, by wholsome provisions, *to attend his public duty*, and thus in great national questions *must give a vote* of the honesty of which, he will find it necessary to convince his constituents.

The senate *must always receive the exceptions of the president* against any of their legislative acts, which, without *serious deliberation and sufficient reasons*, they will seldom disregard. They will also feel a considerable check *from the constitutional powers of the state legislatures*, whose rights they will not be disposed to infringe, since they are the bodies *to which they owe their existence*, and are moreover to remain *the immediate guardians of the people.*

And lastly the senate will feel *the mighty check of the house of representatives*—a body *so pure in its election*, so intimately connected, by its interests and feelings, *with the people at large*, so guarded against *corruption and influence*—so much, from its nature, *above all apprehensions*, that it *must ever be able to maintain the high ground assigned to it by the federal constitution.*

PUBLIUS: THE FEDERALIST 62 (JAMES MADISON)
New York *Independent Journal*, 27 February 1788*

To the People of the State of New-York.

Having examined the constitution of the house of representatives, and answered such of the objections against it as seemed to merit notice, I enter next on the examination of the senate. The heads into which this member of the government may be considered, are—I. the qualifications of senators—II. the appointment of them by the state legislatures—III. the equality of representation in the senate—IV. the number of senators, and the term for which they are to be elected—V. the powers vested in the senate.

I. The qualifications proposed for senators, as distinguished from those of representatives, consist in a more advanced age, and a longer period of citizenship. A senator must be thirty years of age at least; as a representative, must be twenty-five. And the former must have been a citizen nine years; as seven years are required for the latter. The propriety of these distinctions is explained by the nature of the senatorial trust; which requiring greater extent of information and stability of character, requires at the same time that the senator should have reached a period of life most likely to supply these advantages; and which participating immediately in transactions with foreign nations, ought to be exercised by none who are not thoroughly weaned from the prepossessions and habits incident to foreign birth and education. The term of nine years appears to be a prudent mediocrity between a total exclusion of adopted citizens, whose merit and talents may claim a share in the public confidence; and an indiscriminate and hasty admission of them, which might create a channel for foreign influence on the national councils.

II. It is equally unnecessary to dilate on the appointment of senators by the state legislatures. Among the various modes which might have been devised for constituting this branch of the government, that which has been proposed by the convention is probably the most congenial with the public opinion. It is recommended by the double advantage of favouring a select appointment, and of giving to the state governments such an agency in the formation of the federal government, as must secure the authority of the former; and may form a convenient link between the two systems.

III. The equality of representation in the senate is another point, which, being evidently the result of compromise between the opposite pretensions of the large and the small states, does not call for much discussion. If indeed it be right that among a people thoroughly incorporated

*Reprinted: *New York Packet*, 29 February.

into one nation, every district ought to have a *proportional* share in the government; and that among independent and sovereign states bound together by simple league, the parties however unequal in size, ought to have an *equal* share in the common councils, it does not appear to be without some reason, that in a compound republic partaking both of the national and federal character, the government ought to be founded on a mixture of the principles of proportional and equal representation. But it is superfluous to try by the standard of theory, a part of the constitution which is allowed on all hands to be the result not of theory, but "of a spirit of amity, and that mutual deference and concession which the peculiarity of our political situation rendered indispensable."* A common government with powers equal to its objects, is called for by the voice, and still more loudly by the political situation of America. A government founded on principles more consonant to the wishes of the larger states, is not likely to be obtained from the smaller states. The only option then for the former lies between the proposed government and a government still more objectionable. Under this alternative the advice of prudence must be, to embrace the lesser evil; and instead of indulging a fruitless anticipation of the possible mischiefs which may ensue, to contemplate rather the advantageous consequences which may qualify the sacrifice.

In this spirit it may be remarked, that the equal vote allowed to each state, is at once a constitutional recognition of the portion of sovereignty remaining in the individual states, and an instrument for preserving that residuary sovereignty. So far the equality ought to be no less acceptable to the large than to the small states; since they are not less solicitous to guard by every possible expedient against an improper consolidation of the states into one simple republic.

Another advantage accruing from this ingredient in the constitution of the senate, is the additional impediment it must prove against improper acts of legislation. No law or resolution can now be passed without the concurrence first of a majority of the people, and then of a majority of the states. It must be acknowledged that this complicated check on legislation may in some instances be injurious as well as beneficial; and that the peculiar defence which it involves in favour of the smaller states would be more rational, if any interests common to them, and distinct from those of the other states, would otherwise be exposed to peculiar danger. But as the larger states will always be able by their power over the supplies to defeat unreasonable exertions of this prerogative of the lesser states; and as the facility and excess of law-making seem to be the diseases to

*Quoted from the letter of President of the Constitutional Convention George Washington to the President of Congress, 17 September 1787.

which our governments are most liable, it is not impossible that this part of the constitution may be more convenient in practice than it appears to many in contemplation.

IV. The number of senators and the duration of their appointment come next to be considered. In order to form an accurate judgment on both these points, it will be proper to enquire into the purposes which are to be answered by a senate; and in order to ascertain these it will be necessary to review the inconveniencies which a republic must suffer from the want of such an institution.

First. It is a misfortune incident to republican government, though in a less degree than to other governments, that those who administer it, may forget their obligations to their constituents, and prove unfaithful to their important trust. In this point of view, a senate, as a second branch of the legislative assembly, distinct from, and dividing the power with, a first, must be in all cases a salutary check on the government. It doubles the security to the people, by requiring the concurrence of two distinct bodies in schemes of usurpation or perfidy, where the ambition or corruption of one, would otherwise be sufficient. This is a precaution founded on such clear principles, and now so well understood in the United States, that it would be more than superfluous to enlarge on it. I will barely remark that as the improbability of sinister combinations will be in proportion to the dissimilarity in the genius of the two bodies; it must be politic to distinguish them from each other by every circumstance which will consist with a due harmony in all proper measures, and with the genuine principles of republican government.

Secondly. The necessity of a senate is not less indicated by the propensity of all single and numerous assemblies, to yield to the impulse of sudden and violent passions, and to be seduced by factious leaders, into intemperate and pernicious resolutions. Examples on this subject might be cited without number; and from proceedings within the United States, as well as from the history of other nations. But a position that will not be contradicted need not be proved. All that need be remarked is that a body which is to correct this infirmity ought itself be free from it, and consequently ought to be less numerous. It ought moreover to possess great firmness, and consequently ought to hold its authority by a tenure of considerable duration.

Thirdly. Another defect to be supplied by a senate lies in a want of due acquaintance with the objects and principles of legislation. It is not possible that an assembly of men called for the most part from pursuits of a private nature, continued in appointment for a short time, and led by no permanent motive to devote the intervals of public occupation to a study of the laws, the affairs and the comprehensive interests of their country, should, if left wholly to themselves, escape a variety of important errors in the exercise of their legislative trust. It may be affirmed, on the best grounds, that no small share of the present embarrassments of America is to be charged on the blunders of our governments; and that these have proceeded from the heads rather than the hearts of most of the authors of them. What indeed are all the repealing, explaining and amending laws, which fill and disgrace our voluminous codes, but so many monuments of deficient wisdom; so many impeachments exhibited by each succeeding, against each preceding session; so many admonitions to the people of the value of those aids which may be expected from a well constituted senate?

A good government implies two things; first, fidelity to the object of government, which is the happiness of the people; secondly, a knowledge of the means by which that object can be best attained. Some governments are deficient in both these qualities: Most governments are deficient in the first. I scruple not to assert that in the American governments, too little attention has been paid to the last. The federal constitution avoids this error; and what merits particular notice, it provides for the last in a mode which increases the security for the first.

Fourthly. The mutability in the public councils, arising from a rapid succession of new members, however qualified they may be, points out in the strongest manner, the necessity of some stable institution in the government. Every new election in the states, is found to change one half of the representatives. From this change of men must proceed a change of opinions; and from a change of opinions, a change of measures. But a continual change even of good measures is inconsistent with every rule of prudence, and every prospect of success. The remark is verified in private life, and becomes more just as well as more important, in national transactions.

To trace the mischievous effects of a mutable government would fill a volume. I will hint a few only, each of which will be perceived to be a source of innumerable others.

In the first place it forfeits the respect and confidence of other nations, and all the advantages connected with national character. An individual who is observed to be inconstant to his plans, or perhaps to carry on his affairs without any plan at all, is marked at once by all prudent people as a speedy victim to his own unsteadiness and folly. His more friendly neighbours may pity him; but all will decline to connect their fortunes with his; and not a few will seize the opportunity of making their fortunes out of his. One nation is to another what one individual is to another; with this melancholy distinction perhaps, that the former with fewer of the benevolent emotions than the latter, are under fewer restraints also from taking undue advantage of the indiscretions of each other. Every nation consequently whose affairs betray a want of wisdom and stability, may calculate on every loss which can be sustained from the more systematic policy of its wiser neighbours. But the best instruction on this subject is unhappily conveyed to America by the example of her own situation. She finds that she is held in no respect by her friends; that she is the derision of her enemies; and that she is a prey to every nation which has an interest in speculating on her fluctuating councils and embarrassed affairs.

The internal effects of a mutable policy are still more calamitous. It poisons the blessings of liberty itself. It will be of little avail to the people that the laws are made by men of their own choice, if the laws be so voluminous that they cannot be read, or so incoherent that they cannot be understood; if they be repealed or revised before they are promulged, or undergo such incessant changes that no man who knows what the law is to day can guess what it will be to morrow. Law is defined to be a rule of action; but how can that be a rule, which is little known and less fixed?

Another effect of public instability is the unreasonable advantage it gives to the sagacious, the enterprising and the moneyed few, over the industrious and uninformed mass of the people. Every new regulation concerning commerce or revenue; or in any manner affecting the value of the different species of property, presents a new harvest to those who watch the change, and can trace its consequences; a harvest reared not by themselves but by the toils and cares of the great body of their fellow citizens. This is a state of things in which it may be said with some truth that laws are made for the *few* not for the *many*.

In another point of view great injury results from an unstable government. The want of confidence in the public councils damps every useful undertaking; the success and profit of which may depend on a continuance of existing arrangements. What prudent merchant will hazard his fortunes in any new branch of commerce, when he knows not but that his plans may be rendered unlawful before they can be executed? What farmer or manufacturer will lay himself out for the encouragement given to any particular cultivation or establishment, when he can have no assurance that his preparatory labors and advances will not render him a victim to an inconstant government? In a word no great improvement or laudable enterprise, can go forward, which requires the auspices of a steady system of national policy.

But the most deplorable effect of all is that diminution of attachment and revenue [reverence] which steals into the hearts of the people, towards a political system which betrays so many marks of infirmity, and disappoints so many of their flattering hopes. No government any more than an individual will long be respected, without being truly respectable, nor be truly respectable without possessing a certain portion of order and stability.

4

The President

THE CONSTITUTIONAL CONVENTION *had more difficulty drafting provisions for the election and responsibilities of the President than for any other part of the Constitution. Americans had considerable experience with executives—they had lived under the British king, who had power to veto colonial acts of legislation even before they went into effect. The Articles of Confederation provided for no separate executive, but the Confederation Congress did elect its own president who served more or less as the Speaker of Congress. The states under the Articles each had a governor or president, most of whom were relatively weak in comparison to their state assemblies. Perhaps the governors of New York and Massachusetts served as the best models for the Constitutional Convention in shaping the image of the new American President.*

Soon after it convened, the Constitutional Convention agreed to have a single executive as opposed to the triple executive favored by a handful of delegates who feared the reinstitution of the monarchy. Greater disagreement persisted on the manner of electing the President. Some delegates wanted a President elected by Congress for a long term but ineligible for reelection. Others favored direct election by the people for short terms and with no restrictions on the number of consecutive terms. A compromise eventually provided that the President would be elected for a four-year term by electors chosen in a manner prescribed by the state legislatures. No restrictions were placed on the President's eligibility to be reelected.

During the debate over the ratification of the Constitution, Antifederalists charged that the President would become a king—in fact, he would be the worst kind of a king: an elected one. Cabals and intrigues would surely develop over the reelection of the incumbent. Some even charged that the orderly transfer of power from a defeated incumbent was too much to expect, especially since the President had complete control over the country's military and the states' militia when called up for federal service.

Antifederalists also charged that the Constitution was defective in that it violated the commonly held belief that the three branches of government ought to be separate. The mixture of power and responsibility over appointments to office and treaty-making bothered many Americans. Would the Senate really exercise authority in the appointment of officers or would the President's power to nominate be tantamount to the power to appoint? Who would be responsible if corrupt individuals were appointed—the President, the Senate or both? And could it be expected that Senators who had confirmed officeholders would convict those same individuals on impeachment?

Similar fears were expressed over the treaty-making power. The Constitution declared that treaties should be the supreme law of the land. Yet, the House of Representatives, elected directly by the people, played no role in the drafting or adoption of treaties. Only the President and the Senate had responsibility in this important area that could affect the lives of every American.

Several critics of the Constitution suggested that the dangerous connection between the President and the Senate could be eliminated by substituting a privy council for the Senate. This council, which had precedents in both the British and American state governments, would advise the President on both appointments and treaty-making. If privy councillors gave faulty advice, they could be held accountable.

Antifederalists charged that the President would have too much influence over legislation through his veto power over acts of Congress and that the President's pardoning power was dangerous. He could conspire with others in treasonable activities and guarantee his co-conspirators pardons if their activities were discovered.

Federalists praised the Presidency. They pointed to the weakness of the Confederation and state governments with their almost powerless executives. America needed a separate President with executive powers to enforce federal laws and conduct foreign policy. Federalists contrasted the President with the British monarch. The former had limited power checked by two other branches of government, while the latter had almost limitless power. Some state executives even had greater power in certain areas than the President.

The President, it was argued, would be accountable to both the people and Congress. If he failed to satisfy the people, he would not be reelected; if he committed crimes, he could be impeached by Congress. Furthermore, everyone realized that George Washington would be elected the first President. This great man had already once voluntarily given up total power in 1783, preferring a rural retirement; he could be expected to follow a similar course of action after he set the new government under the Constitution in motion. Washington's example would be followed by his successors.

Antifederalist

AN OLD WHIG V
Philadelphia *Independent Gazetteer*, 1 November 1787 (excerpt)*

If we pass over the consideration of this subject so essential to the preservation of our liberties, and turn our eyes to the *form* of the government which the Convention have proposed to us, I apprehend that changing the prospect will not wholly alleviate our fears.—A few words on this head, will close the present letter. In the first place the office of President of the United States appears to me to be clothed with such powers as are dangerous. To be the fountain of all honors in the United States, commander in chief of the army, navy and militia, with the power of making treaties and of granting pardons, and to be vested with an authority to put a negative upon all laws, unless two thirds of both houses shall persist in enacting it, and put their names down upon calling the yeas and nays for that purpose, is in reality to be a KING as much *a King as the King of Great Britain*, and a King too of the worst kind;—an elective King.—If such powers as these are to be trusted in the hands of any man, they ought for the sake of preserving the peace of the community at once to be made hereditary.—Much as I abhor kingly government, yet I venture to pronounce where kings are admitted to rule they should most certainly be vested with hereditary power. The election of a King whether it be in America or Poland, will be a scene of horror and confusion; and I am perfectly serious when I declare that, as a friend to my country, I shall despair of any happiness in the United States until this office is either reduced to a lower pitch of power or made perpetual and hereditary.— When I say that our future President will be as much a king as the king of Great-Britain, I only ask of my readers to look into the constitution of that country, and then tell me what important prerogative the King of Great-Britain is entitled to, which does not also belong to the President during his continuance in office.—The King of Great-Britain it is true can create nobility which our President cannot; but our President will have the power of making all the *great men*, which comes to the same thing.—

---

*Reprinted: *New York Morning Post*, 10 November, and *New York Journal*, 11 December. It was also printed as a broadside in Philadelphia.

All the difference is that we shall be embroiled in contention about the choice of the man, whilst they are at peace under the security of an hereditary succession.—To be tumbled headlong from the pinnacle of greatness and be reduced to a shadow of departed royalty is a shock almost too great for human nature to endure. It will cost a man many struggles to resign such eminent powers, and ere long, we shall find, some one who will be very unwilling to part with them.—Let us suppose this man to be a favorite with his army, and that they are unwilling to part with their beloved commander in chief; or to make the thing familiar, let us suppose, a future President and commander in chief adored by his army and the militia to as great a degree as our late illustrious commander in chief; and we have only to suppose one thing more, that this man is without the virtue, the moderation and love of liberty which possessed the mind of our late general, and this country will be involved at once in war and tyranny. So far is it from its being improbable that the man who shall hereafter be in a situation to make the attempt to perpetuate his own power, should want [i.e., lack] the virtues of General Washington; that it is perhaps a chance of one hundred millions to one that the next age will not furnish an example of so disinterested a use of great power. We may also suppose, without trespassing upon the bounds of probability, that this man may not have the means of supporting in private life the dignity of his former station; that like Cæsar, he may be at once ambitious and poor, and deeply involved in debt.—Such a man would die a thousand deaths rather than sink from the heights of splendor and power into obscurity and wretchedness. We are certainly about giving our president too much or too little; and in the course of less than twenty years we shall find that we have given him enough to enable him to take all. It would be infinitely more prudent to give him at once as much as would content him, so that we might be able to retain the rest in peace; for if once power is seized by violence not the least fragment of liberty will survive the shock. I would therefore advise my countrymen seriously to ask themselves this question;—Whether they are prepared TO RECEIVE A KING? If they are to say at once, and make the kingly office hereditary; to frame a constitution that should set bounds to his power, and, as far as possible secure the liberty of the subject. If we are not prepared to *receive a king*, let us call another convention to revise the proposed constitution, and form it anew on the principles of a confederacy of free republics; but by no means, under pretence of a republic, to lay the foundation for a military government, which is the worst of all tyrannies.

LUTHER MARTIN: GENUINE INFORMATION
Baltimore *Maryland Gazette*, 29 January 1788*

[An account of events in the Constitutional Convention.]

The *second article*, relates to the executive—his mode of election—his powers—and the length of time he should continue in office.

On these subjects, there was a great diversity of sentiment—Many of the members were desirous that the president should be elected for seven years, and not to be eligible a second time—others proposed that he should not be absolutely ineligible, but that he should not be capable of being chosen a second time, until the expiration of a certain number of years—The supporter of the above propositions, went upon the idea that the best security for liberty was a limited duration and a rotation of office in the chief executive department.

There was a party who attempted to have the president appointed during good behaviour, without any limitation as to time, and not being able to succeed in that attempt, they then endeavoured to have him re-eligible without any restraint.—It was objected that the choice of a president to continue in office during good behaviour, would be at once rendering our system an elective monarchy—and, that if the president was to be re-eligible without any interval of disqualification, it would amount nearly to the same thing, since with the powers that the president is to enjoy, and the interest and influence with which they will be attended, he will be almost absolutely certain of being re-elected from time to time, as long as he lives—As the propositions were reported by the committee of the whole house, the president was to be chosen for seven years, and not to be eligible at any time after—In the same manner the proposition was agreed to in convention, and so was it reported by the committee of detail, although a variety of attempts were made to alter that part of the system by those who were of a contrary opinion, in which they repeatedly failed; but, Sir, by never losing sight of their object, and choosing a proper time for their purpose, they succeeded at length in obtaining the alteration, which was not made until within the last twelve days before the convention adjourned.†

---

*Reprinted: *Pennsylvania Packet*, 8 February; Philadelphia *Independent Gazetteer*, 13 February; *New York Journal*, 14, 15, 17 March; Boston *American Herald*, 10 April (excerpt); *State Gazette of South Carolina*, 19, 22 May (excerpt).

†On 31 August a committee of eleven, one delegate from each state present, was appointed to consider those parts of the Constitution or parts of reports that had been postponed. On 4 September, the day Luther Martin left the Convention, the committee proposed a four-year term for the President with no restriction on reelection. This proposal was debated, amended, and adopted between 4 and 6 September (Farrand, II, 481, 497–502, 511–29).

As the propositions were agreed to by the committee of the whole house, the president was to be appointed by the national legislature, and as it was reported by the committee of detail, the choice was to be made by ballot in such a manner, that the States should have an equal voice in the appointment of this officer, as they, of right, ought to have; but those who wished as far as possible to establish a *national* instead of a *federal* government, made repeated attempts to have the president chosen by the people at large; on this the sense of the convention was taken, I think not less than three times while I was there, and as often rejected;* but within the last fortnight of their session, they obtained the alteration in the manner it now stands, by which the large States have a very undue influence in the appointment of the president.—There is no case where the States will have an equal voice in the appointment of the president, except where two persons shall have each an equal number of votes, and those a majority of the whole number of electors, a case very unlikely to happen, or where no person has a majority of the votes; in these instances the house of representatives are to choose by ballot, each State having an equal voice, but they are confined in the last instance to the five who have the greatest number of votes, which gives the largest States a very unequal chance of having the president chose under their nomination.

As to the vice-president, that great officer of government, who is in case of death, resignation, removal or inability of the president, to supply his place, and be vested with his powers, and who is officially to be the president of the senate, there is no provision by which a majority of the voices of the electors are necessary for his appointment, but after it is decided who is chosen president, that person who has the next greatest number of votes of the electors, is declared to be legally elected to the vice-presidency, so that by this system it is very possible, and not improbable, that he may be appointed by the electors of a *single large State;* and a very undue influence in the senate is given to that State of which the vice-president is a citizen, since in every question where the senate is divided that State will have two votes, the president having on those occasions a casting voice.—Every part of the system which relates to the vice-president, as well as the present mode of electing the president, was introduced and agreed upon after I left Philadelphia.

Objections were made to that part of this article, by which the president is appointed commander in chief of the army and navy of the United States, and of the militia of the several States, and it was wished to be so far restrained, that he should not command in person; but this

---

*The election of the President by the people was first considered on 1 June. It was later rejected on 17 July and 24 August (Farrand, I, 68, 69; II, 32, 402).

could not be obtained.*—The power given to the president of granting reprieves and pardons, was also thought extremely dangerous, and as such opposed—The president thereby has the power of pardoning those who are guilty of treason, as well as of other offences; it was said that no treason was so likely to take place as that in which the president himself might be engaged—the attempt to assume to himself powers not given by the constitution, and establish himself in regal authority—in which attempt a provision is made for him to secure from punishment the creatures of his ambition, the associates and abettors of his treasonable practices, by granting them pardons should they be defeated in their attempts to subvert the constitution.

To that part of this article also, which gives the president a right to *nominate*, and with the consent of the senate to appoint all the officers, civil and military, of the United States, there were considerable opposition—it was said that the person who *nominates*, will always in reality *appoint*, and that this was giving the president a power and influence which together with the other powers, bestowed upon him, would place him above all restraint and controul. In fine, it was urged, that the president as here constituted, was a king in every thing but the name—that though he was to be chosen but for a limited time, yet at the expiration of that time if he is not re-elected, it will depend entirely upon his own moderation whether he will resign that authority with which he has once been invested—that from his having the appointment of all the variety of officers in every part of the civil department for the union, who will be very numerous—in them and their connexions, relations, friends and dependants, he will have a formidable host devoted to his interest, and ready to support his ambitious views.—That the army and navy, which may be encreased without restraint as to numbers, the officers of which from the highest to the lowest, are all to be appointed by him and dependant on his will and pleasure, and commanded by him in person, will, of course, be subservient to his wishes, and ready to execute his commands; in addition to which, the militia also are entirely subjected to his orders— That these circumstances, combined together, will enable him, when he pleases, to become a king in *name*, as well as in substance, and establish himself in office not only for his own life, but even if he chooses, to have that authority perpetuated to his family.

It was further observed, that the only appearance of responsibility in the president, which the system holds up to our view, is the provision

---

*The New Jersey Amendments to the Articles of Confederation, proposed on 15 June, provided that the federal executive, as commander in chief, should not "on any occasion take command of any troops, so as personally to conduct any enterprise as General, or in other capacity" (Farrand, I, 244).

for impeachment; but that when we reflect that he cannot be impeached but by the house of delegates, and that the members of this house are rendered dependant upon, and unduly under the influence of the president, by being appointable to offices of which he has the sole nomination, so that without his favour and approbation, they cannot obtain them, there is little reason to believe that a majority will ever concur in impeaching the president, let his conduct be ever so reprehensible, especially too, as the final event of that impeachment will depend upon a different body, and the members of the house of delegates will be certain, should the decision be ultimately in favour of the president, to become thereby the objects of his displeasure, and to bar to themselves every avenue to the emoluments of government.

Should he, contrary to probability, be impeached, he is afterwards to be tried and adjudged by the senate, and without the concurrence of two-thirds of the members who shall be present, he cannot be convicted— This senate being constituted a privy council to the president, it is probable many of its leading and influential members may have advised or concurred in the very measures for which he may be impeached; the members of the senate also are by the system, placed as unduly under the influence of, and dependent upon the president, as the members of the other branch, since they also are appointable to offices, and cannot obtain them but through the favour of the president—There will be great, important and valuable offices under this government, should it take place, more than sufficient to enable him to hold out the expectation of one of them to *each* to the senators—Under these circumstances, will any person conceive it to be difficult for the president always to secure to himself more than one-third of that body? Or, can it reasonably be believed, that a criminal will be convicted who is constitutionally empowered to bribe his judges, at the head of whom is to preside on those occasions the chief justice, which officer in his original appointment, must be *nominated* by the president, and will therefore, probably, be appointed not so much for his eminence in legal knowledge and for his integrity, as from favouritism and influence, since the president knowing that in case of impeachment the chief justice is to preside at his trial, will naturally wish to fill that office with a person of whose voice and influence he shall consider himself secure.—These are reasons to induce a belief that there will be but little probability of the president ever being either impeached or convicted; but it was also urged, that vested with the powers which the system gives him and with the influence attendant upon those powers, to him it would be but of little consequence whether he was impeached or convicted, since he will be able to set both at defiance.—These considerations occasioned a part of the convention to give a negative to this part of the system establishing the executive as it is now offered for our acceptance.

Antifederalist and Federalist

VIRGINIA RATIFYING CONVENTION
Debates on the Presidency, 17–18 June 1788*

17 JUNE 1788

Mr. *George Mason*,—Mr. Chairman.—There is not a more important article in the Constitution than this. The great fundamental principle of responsibility in republicanism is here saped. The President is elected without rotation.—It may be said that a new election may remove him, and place another in his stead. If we judge from the experience of all other countries, and even our own, we may conclude, that as the President of the United States may be re-elected, so he will. How is it in every Government where rotation is not required? Is there a single instance of a great man not being re-elected? Our Governor is obliged to return after a given period, to a private station. It is so in most of the States.† This President will be elected time after time—He will be continued in office for life.—If we wish to change him, the great powers in Europe will not allow us.

The Honorable Gentleman my colleague in the late Federal Convention [Edmund Randolph], mentions with applause those parts of which he had expressed his approbation; but when he comes to those parts of which he had expressed his disapprobation, he says not a word. If I am mistaken, let me be put right. I shall not make use of his name, but in the course of this investigation, I shall use the arguments of that Gentleman against it.

Will not the great powers of Europe, as France and Great-Britain, be interested in having a friend in the President of the United States; and will they not be more interested in his election, than in that of the King of Poland? The people of Poland have a right to displace their King. But do they ever do it? No. Prussia and Russia, and other European powers, would not suffer it. This clause will open a door to the dangers and

*Debates and Other Proceedings of the Convention of Virginia... (3 vols., Petersburg, Va., 1788–89), III, 67–78.

†Pennsylvania, Maryland, Virginia, North Carolina, South Carolina and Georgia all had provisions in their state constitutions prohibiting governors from succeeding themselves in office.

misfortunes which the people of Poland undergo. The powers of Europe will interpose, and we shall have a civil war in the bowels of our country, and be subject to all the horrors and calamities of an elective Monarchy. This very executive officer, may, by consent of Congress, receive a stated pension from European Potentates. This is an idea not altogether new in America. It is not many years ago, since the revolution, that a foreign power offered emoluments to persons holding offices under our Government. It will moreover be difficult to know, whether he receives emoluments from foreign powers or not. The Electors who are to meet in each State to vote for him, may be easily influenced. To prevent the certain evils of attempting to elect a new President, it will be necessary to continue the old one. The only way to alter this, would be to render him ineligible after a certain number of years, and then no foreign nation would interfere to keep *in* a man who was utterly ineligible. Nothing is so essential to the preservation of a Republican Government, as a periodical rotation. Nothing so strongly impels a man to regard the interest of his constituents, as the certainty of returning to the general mass of the people, from whence he was taken; where he must participate their burdens. It is a great defect in the Senate, that they are not ineligible at the end of six years. The biennial exclusion of one third of them, will have no effect, as they can be re-elected. Some stated time ought to be fixed, when the President ought to be reduced to a private station. I should be contented that he might be elected for eight years: But I would wish him to be capable of holding the office only eight years, out of twelve or sixteen years. But as it now stands, he may continue in office for life; or in other words, it will be an elective Monarchy.

Governor *Edmund Randolph,*—Mr. Chairman.—The Honorable Gentleman last up, says that I do not mention the parts to which I object. I have hitherto mentioned my objections with freedom and candour. But, Sir, I considered that our critical situation rendered adoption necessary, were it even more defective than it is. I observed, that if opinions ought to lead the Committee on one side, they ought on the other. Every Gentleman who has turned his thoughts to the subject of politics, and has considered of the most eligible mode of Republican Government, agrees that the greatest difficulty arises from the Executive, as to the time of his election, mode of his election, quantum of power, &c. I will acknowledge that at one stage of this business, I had embraced the idea of the Honorable Gentleman, that the re-eligibility of the President was improper. But I will acknowledge, that on a further consideration of the subject, and attention to the lights which were thrown upon it by others, I altered my opinion of the limitation of his eligibility. When we consider the advantages arising to us from it, we cannot object to it. That which has produced my opinion against the limitation of his eligibility, is this—that it renders him more independent in his place, and more solicitous of promoting the interest of his constituents: For, unless you put it in his power to be re-elected, instead of being attentive to their interests, he will lean to the augmentation of his private emoluments. This subject will admit of high coloring and plausible arguments; but on considering it attentively and coolly, I believe it will be found less exceptionable than any other mode. The mode of election here, excludes that faction which is productive of those hostilities and confusion in Poland. It renders it unnecessary and impossible for foreign force or aid to interpose. The Electors must be elected by the people at large.* To procure his re-election, his influence must be co-extensive with the Continent. And there can be no combination between the Electors, as they elect him on the same day in every State. When this is the case, how can foreign influence or intrigues enter? There is no reason to conclude, from the experience of these States, that he will be continually re-elected. There has been several instances, where officers have been displaced where they were re-eligible. This has been the case with the Executive of Massachusetts, and I believe of New-Hampshire. It happens from the mutation of sentiments though the officers be good.

There is another provision against the danger mentioned by the Honorable Member, of the President receiving emoluments from foreign powers. If discovered he may be impeached. If he be not impeachable he may be displaced at the end of the four years. By the ninth section, of the first article, "No person holding an office of profit or trust, shall accept of any present or emolument whatever, from any foreign power, without the consent of the Representatives of the people;" and by the first section, of the second article, his compensation is neither to be increased or diminished, during the time for which he shall have been elected; and he shall not, during that period, receive any emolument from the United States or any of them. I consider therefore, that he is restrained from receiving any present or emoluments whatever. It is impossible to guard better against corruption. The Honorable Member seems to think, that he may hold his office without being re-elected. He cannot hold over four years, unless he be re-elected, any more than if he were prohibited. As to forwarding and transmitting the certificates of the Electors, I think the regulation as good as could be provided.

Mr. *George Mason*,—Mr. Chairman.—The Vice-President appears to me to be not only an unnecessary but a dangerous officer. He is, contrary to the usual course of Parliamentary proceedings, to be President of the

---

*Article II, section 1 of the Constitution provides that the state legislatures could determine how Presidential Electors would be elected.

Senate. The State from which he comes may have two votes, when the others will have but one. Besides, the Legislative and Executive are hereby mixed and incorporated together. I cannot at this distance of time foresee the consequences; but I think, that in the course of human affairs, he will be made a tool of in order to bring about his own interest, and aid in overturning the liberties of his country. There is another part which I disapprove of, but which perhaps I do not understand. "In case of removal of the President from office, or of his death, resignation, or inability to discharge the powers and duties of the said office, the same shall devolve on the Vice-President, and the Congress may by law provide for the case of removal, death, resignation, or inablility both of the President and Vice-President, declaring what officer shall then act as President, and such officer shall act accordingly, until the disability be removed, or a President shall be elected."—The power of Congress is right and proper so far as it enables them to provide what officer shall act, in case both the President and Vice-President be dead or disabled. But Gentlemen ought to take notice that the election of this officer is only for four years. There is no provision for a speedy election of another President, when the former is dead or removed. The influence of the Vice-President may prevent the election of the President. But perhaps I may be mistaken.

Mr. *James Madison*,—Mr. Chairman.—I think there are some peculiar advantages incident to this office, which recommend it to us. There is in the first place a great probability this officer will be taken from one of the largest States, and if so, the circumstance of his having an eventual vote will be so far favorable. The consideration which recommends it to me, is, that he will be the choice of the people at large.—There are to be ninety one Electors,* each of whom has two votes: If he have one-fourth of the whole number of votes, he is elected Vice-President. There is much more propriety in giving this office to a person chosen by the people at large, than to one of the Senate who is only the choice of the Legislature of one State. His eventual vote is an advantage too obvious to comment upon. I differ from the Honorable Member [George Mason] in the case which enables the Congress to make a temporary appointment. When the President and Vice-President die, the election of another President will immediately take place, and suppose it would not, all that Congress could do, would be to make an appointment between the expiration of the four years and the last election, and to continue only till such expiration. This can rarely happen. This power continues the Government in motion, and is well guarded.

---

*Each state was entitled to the same number of Presidential Electors as the sum of their U.S. Representatives and Senators. The first House of Representatives was to contain 65 members; the Senate 26.

18 JUNE 1788

Mr. *James Monroe*, after a brief exordium in which he insisted, that on the judicious organization of the executive power, the security of our interest and happiness greatly depended; that in the construction of this part of the Government, we should be cautious in avoiding the defects of other Governments, and that our circumspection should be commensurate to the extent of the powers delegated; proceeded as follows: The President ought to act under the strongest impulses of rewards and punishments, which are the strongest incentives to human actions. There are two ways of securing this point. He ought to depend on the people of America for his appointment and continuance in office: He ought also to be responsible in an equal degree to all the States; and to be tried by dispassionate Judges: His responsibility ought further to be direct and immediate. Let us consider in the first place then, how far he is dependent on the people of America. He is to be elected by Electors, in a manner perfectly dissatisfactory to my mind. I believe that he will owe his election, in fact, to the State Governments, and not to the people at large. It is to be observed, that Congress have it in their power to appoint the time of choosing the Electors, and of electing the President. Is it not presumeable they will appoint the times of choosing the Electors, and electing the President, at a considerable distance from each other, so as to give an opportunity to the Electors to form a combination? If they know that such a man as they wish, for instance the actual President, cannot possibly be elected by a majority of the whole number of Electors appointed, yet if they can prevent the election by such majority, of any one they disapprove of, and if they can procure such a number of votes as will be sufficient to make their favourite one of the five highest on the list, they may ultimately carry the election into the General Congress; where the votes in choosing him shall be taken by States, each State having one vote. Let us see how far this is compatible with the security of republicanism. Although this State is to have ten and Massachusetts eight Representatives, and Delaware and Rhode-Island are to have but one each, yet the votes are to be by States only. The consequence will be, that a majority of the States, and these consisting of the smallest, may elect him. This will give an advantage to the small States. He will depend therefore on the States for his re-election and continuance in office, and not on the people. Does it not bear the complection of the late Confederation? He will conduct himself in accommodation to them, since by them he is chosen, and may be again. If he accommodates himself to the interest of particular States, will they not be obliged by State policy to support him afterwards?—Let me inquire into his responsibility if he does not depend on the people.

To whom is he responsible? To the Senate, his own council. If he makes a treaty bartering the interests of his country, by whom is he to be tried?— By the very persons who advised him to perpetrate the act. Is this any security? I am persuaded that the Gentleman who will be first elected, may continue in the office for life.

The situation of the United States, as it applies to the European States, demands attention. We may hold the balance among those States. Their Western territories are contiguous to us. What we may do without any offensive operations, may have considerable influence. Will they not then endeavor to influence his general councils? May we not suppose that they will endeavour to attach him to their interest, and support him, in order to make him serve their purposes? If this be the case, does not the mode of election present a favorable opportunity to continue in office the person that shall be President? I am persuaded they may, by their power and intrigues, influence his re-election. There being nothing to prevent his corruption, but his virtue, which is but precarious, we have not sufficient security. If there be a propriety in giving him a right of making leagues, he ought not to be connected with the Senate.—If the Senate have a right to make leagues, there ought to be a majority of the States.

The Vice-President is an unnecessary officer. I can see no reason for such an officer. The Senate might of their own body elect a President, who would have no dangerous influence. He is to succeed the President in case of removal, disability, &c. and is to have the casting vote in the Senate. This gives an undue advantage to the State he comes from, and will render foreign powers desirous of securing his favor, to obtain which they will exert themselves in his behalf. I am persuaded that the advantage of his information will not counterbalance the disadvantages attending his office.

The President might be elected by the people, dependent upon them, and responsible for mal-administration. As this is not the case, I must disapprove of this clause in its present form.

Mr. *William Grayson,*—Mr. Chairman.—One great objection with me is this. If we advert to the Democratical, Aristocratical, or Executive branch, we will find their powers are perpetually varying and fluctuating throughout the whole. Perhaps the Democratic branch would be well constructed were it not for this defect. The Executive is still worse in this respect than the Democratic branch. He is to be elected by a number of Electors in the country; but the principle is changed, when no person has a majority of the whole number of Electors appointed, or when more than one have such a majority, and have an equal number of votes, for then the Lower House is to vote by States. It is thus changing throughout the whole. It seems rather founded on accident, than any principle of

Government I ever heard of. We know that there scarcely ever was an election of such an officer, without the interposition of foreign powers. Two causes prevail to make them intermeddle in such cases: One is to preserve the balance of power; the other to preserve their trade. These causes have produced interferences of foreign powers in the election of the King of Poland. All the great powers of Europe interfered in an election which took place not very long ago, and would not let the people choose for themselves.* We know how much the powers of Europe have interfered with *Sweden*.—Since the death of Charles the XIIth, that country has been a Republican Government. Some powers were willing it should be so: Some were willing her imbecility should continue: Others wished the contrary: And at length the Court of France brought about a revolution, which converted it into an absolute Government.† Can America be free from these interferences? France after losing Holland will wish to make America entirely her own. Great-Britain will wish to increase her influence by a still closer connection. It is the interest of Spain, from the contiguity of her possessions in the Western hemisphere to the United States, to be in an intimate connection with them, and influence their deliberations if possible. I think we have every thing to apprehend from such interferences. It is highly probable the President will be continued in office for life. To gain his favor they will support him. Consider the means of importance he will have by creating officers. If he has a good understanding with the Senate, they will join to prevent a discovery of his misdeeds.

Whence comes this extreme confidence, that we disregard the example of ancient and modern nations? We find that Aristocracies never invested their officers with such immense powers. *Rome* had not only an Aristocratical, but also a Democratical branch; yet the Consuls were in office only two years. This quadrennial power cannot be justified by ancient history. There is hardly an instance where a Republic trusted its Executive so long with much power.—Nor is it warranted by modern Republics. The delegation of power is in most of them only for one year.

When you have a strong Democratical and a strong Aristocratical branch, you may have a strong Executive.—But when those are weak, the

---

*When King Augustus III of Poland died in 1763, two candidates for the crown emerged: Count Stanislas Poniatowski, a member of the pro-Russian faction of the Polish nobility, and the Elector of Saxony, supported by Austria and France. Russian troops occupied Poland and the Russian envoy used bribes and intimidation to obtain the election of Poniatowski.

†Sweden's constitutional laws of 1720–23 gave the parliament of Sweden control of the government until August 1772. At that time, with the assistance of France, King Gustavus III seized control of the government in a bloodless coup and restored the Crown's ancient rights and privileges (Michael Roberts, *The Age of Liberty: Sweden, 1719–1772* [Cambridge, England, 1986], 198–205).

balance will not be preserved if you give the Executive extensive powers
for so long a time. As this Government is organized, it would be dangerous
to trust the President with such powers. How will you punish him if he
abuse his power? Will you call him before the Senate? They are his
counsellors and partners in crimes. Where are your checks? We ought
to be extremely cautious in this country. If ever the Government be
changed, it will probably be into a Despotism.—The first object in England
was to destroy the Monarchy: But the Aristocratic branch restored him,
and of course the Government was organized on its ancient principles.
But were a revolution to happen here, there would be no means of restoring the Government to its former organization.—This is a caution to
us not to trust extensive powers. I have an extreme objection to the mode
of his election. I presume the seven Eastern States will always elect him.
As he is vested with the power of making treaties, and as there is a material
distinction between the carrying and productive States, the former will
be disposed to have him themselves. He will accommodate himself to their
interests in forming treaties, and they will continue him perpetually in
office.—Thus, mutual interest will lead them reciprocally to support one
another. It will be a Government of a faction, and this observation will
apply to every part of it. For, having a majority, they may do what they
please. I have made an estimate which shews, with what facility they will
be able to re-elect him. The number of Electors is equal to the number
of Representatives and Senators, viz: ninety-one. They are to vote for
two persons. They give therefore one hundred and eighty-two votes. Let
there be forty-five votes for four different candidates, and two for the
President. He is one of the five highest, if he have but two votes which
he may easily purchase. In this case, by the third clause, of the first section,
of the second article, the election is to be by the Representatives, according
to States.

Let New-Hampshire be for him; a majority of its

	3 Representatives is	2
Rhode-Island,		1
Connecticut,	5	3
New-Jersey,	4	3
Delaware,		1
Georgia,	3	2
North-Carolina,	5	3
A majority of seven States, is		15

Thus the majority of seven States is but 15, while the minority amounts
to 50.

The total number of voices, 91 Electors, and 65 Representatives, is
156.

Voices in favor of the President, are two State Electors, and 15 Representatives, which are in all $^{17}/_{139}$ So that the President may be re-elected by the voices of 17 against 139. It may be said, that this is an extravagant case, and will never happen. In my opinion, it will often happen. A person who is a favorite with Congress if he gets but two votes of Electors, may, by the subsequent choice of 15 Representatives, be elected President. Surely the possibility of such a case, ought to be excluded. I shall postpone mentioning in what manner he ought to be elected, till we come to offer amendments.

Mr. *George Mason* contended, that this mode of election was a mere deception—a mere *ignus fatuus* on the people of America, and thrown out to make them believe they were to choose him; whereas it would not be once out of fifty that he would be chosen by them in the first instance; because a majority of the whole number of votes was required. If the localities of the States were considered, and the probable diversity of opinions of the people attended to, he thought it would be found, that so many persons would be voted for, that there seldom or never could be a majority in favor of one, except one great name, who he believed would be unanimously elected. He then continued thus:—A majority of *the whole number* of Electors is necessary to elect the President. It is not the greatest number of votes that is required, but a majority of the whole number of Electors. If there be more than one having such majority, and an equal number, one of them is to be chosen by ballot of the House of Representatives. But if no one have a majority of the actual number of Electors appointed, how is he to be chosen? From the five highest on the list, by ballot of the Lower House, and the votes to be taken by States!—I conceive he ought to be chosen from the two highest on the list. This would be simple and easy. Then indeed the people would have some agency in the election. But when it is extended to the five highest, a person having a very small number of votes may be elected. This will almost constantly happen. The States may choose the man in whom they have most confidence. This is, in my opinion, a very considerable defect. The people will in reality have no hand in his election.

It has been wittily observed, that the Constitution has married the President and Senate—has made them man and wife. I believe the consequence that generally results from marriage, will happen here. They will be continually supporting and aiding each other: They will always consider their interests as united. We know the advantage the few have over the many. They can with facility act in concert and on an uniform system: They may join scheme and plot against the people without any chance of detection. The Senate and President will form a combination that cannot be prevented by the Representatives. The Executive and Legislative powers thus connected, will destroy all balances: This would have been prevented by a Constitutional Council to aid the President in the discharge of his office; vesting the Senate at the same time with power of impeaching them. Then we should have real responsibility. In its present form, the guilty try themselves. The President is tried by his counsellors. He is not removed from office during his trial. When he is arraigned for treason he has the command of the army and navy, and may surround the Senate with 30,000 troops. It brings to my recollection the remarkable trial of *Milo* at *Rome.** We may expect to see similar instances here. But I suppose, that the cure for all evils—the virtue and integrity of our Representatives, will be thought a sufficient security. On this great and important subject, I am one of those (and ever shall be) who object to it.

Mr. *James Madison,*—Mr. Chairman.—I will take the liberty of making a few observations which may place this in such a light as may obviate objections. It is observable, that none of the Honorable Members objecting to this, have pointed out the right mode of election. It was found difficult in the Convention, and will be found so by any Gentleman who will take the liberty of delineating a mode of electing the President, that would exclude those inconveniences which they apprehend. I would not contend against some of the principles laid down by some Gentlemen if the interests of some States only were to be consulted. But there is a great diversity of interests. The choice of the people ought to be attended to. I have found no better way of selecting the man in whom they place the highest confidence, than that delineated in the plan of the Convention— nor has the Gentleman told us. Perhaps it will be found impracticable to elect him by the immediate suffrages of the people. Difficulties would arise from the extent and population of the States. Instead of this, the people choose the Electors.—This can be done with ease and convenience, and will render the choice more judicious. As to the eventual voting by States, it has my approbation. The lesser States, and some large States, will be generally pleased by that mode. The Deputies from the small States argued, (and there is some force in their reasoning) that when the people voted, the large States evidently had the advantage over the rest, and without varying the mode, the interests of the little States might be neglected or sacrificed. Here is a compromise.—For in the eventual election, the small States will have the advantage. In so extensive a country, it is probable

---

*Titus Annius Milo was a supporter of Pompey the Great and an enemy of Publius Clodius, Julius Caesar's agent. In the year 52 BC, a confrontation between Milo and Clodius ended in Clodius' murder. Milo was tried for the murder, and during the trial, Milo's enemies used a variety of means to intimidate his supporters. Cicero, one of Milo's friends, had prepared an oration in Milo's defense but was afraid to speak at the trial. Milo went into exile at Massilia (Marseilles).

that many persons will be voted for, and the lowest of the five highest on the list may not be so inconsiderable as he supposes. With respect to the possibility, that a small number of votes may decide his election, I do not know how, nor do I think that a bare calculation of possibility ought to govern us. One Honorable Gentleman [William Grayson] has said, that the Eastern States may, in the eventual election, choose him. But in the extravagant calculation he has made, he has been obliged to associate North-Carolina and Georgia, with the five smallest Northern States. There can be no union of interests or sentiments between States so differently situated.

The Honorable Member last up [George Mason] has committed a mistake in saying, there must be a majority of the *whole* number of Electors appointed. A majority of votes, equal to a majority of the Electors appointed, will be sufficient. Forty-six is a majority of ninety-one, and will suffice to elect the President.

Mr. *Mason* arose, and insisted that the person having the greatest number of votes would not be elected, unless such majority consisted of the whole number of Electors appointed: That it would rarely happen that any one would have such a majority, and as he was then to be chosen from the five highest on the list, his election was entirely taken from the people.

Mr. *Madison*, expressed astonishment at the construction of the Honorable Member, and insisted, that nothing was necessary but a number of votes equal to a majority of the Electors, which was forty-six. For the clause expressly said, that "The person having the greatest number of votes shall be President, if such number be a majority of the whole number of Electors appointed." Each had two votes, because one vote was intended for the Vice President. I am surprised, continued Mr. *Madison*, that the Honorable Member has not pointed out a more proper mode, since he objects to this.

But the Honorable Gentleman tells us, that the President and Senate will be in alliance against the Representatives, and that from the advantage of the few over the many, they may seduce, or over-rule the Representatives. But if this be the case, how can he contend for the augmentation of the number of the latter? For the more you increase their number, the more danger in the disproportion. The diversity of circumstances, situation and extent of the different States, will render a previous combination, with respect to the election of the President, impossible.

Federalist

AN AMERICAN CITIZEN I (TENCH COXE)
Philadelphia *Independent Gazetteer*, 26 September 1787 (excerpt)*

In the first place let us look at the nature and powers of the head of that country, and those of the ostensible head of ours.

The British King is the great Bishop or Supreme Head of an established church, with an immense patronage annexed. In this capacity he commands a number of votes in the House of Lords, by creating Bishops, who, besides their great incomes, have votes in that assembly, and are judges in the last resort. They have also many honorable and lucrative places to bestow, and thus from their wealth, learning, dignities, powers and patronage give a great lustre and an enormous influence to the crown.

In America our President will not only be *without* these influencing advantages, *but they will be in the possession of the people at large, to strengthen their hands in the event of a contest with him.* All religious funds, honors and powers, are in the gift of numberless, unconnected, disunited, and contending corporations, wherein the principle of perfect equality universally prevails. In short, danger from ecclesiastical tyranny, that long standing and still remaining curse of the people—that sacrilegious engine of royal power in some countries, can be feared by no man in the United States. In Britain their king is for life—In America our president will always be *one of the people* at the end of four years. In that country the king is hereditary and may be an idiot, a knave, or a tyrant by nature, or ignorant from neglect of his education, yet cannot be removed, for *"he can do no wrong."* In America, as the president is to be one of the people at the end of his short term, so will he and his fellow citizens remember, *that he was originally one of the people; and that he is created by their breath*— Further, he cannot be an idiot, probably not a knave or a tyrant, for those whom nature makes so, discover it before the age of thirty-five, until which period he cannot be elected. It appears we have not admitted that he can do no wrong, but have rather pre-supposed he may and will sometimes do wrong, by providing for *his impeachment, his trial, and his peaceable and complete removal.*

In England the king has a power to create members of the upper house, who are judges in the highest court, as well as legislators. Our

---

*This was the first of four "American Citizen" essays. By the end of the year, it was reprinted in twenty-four newspapers from New Hampshire to South Carolina, in the Philadelphia *American Museum*, as a broadside (with the other three "American Citizen" essays), and in two Richmond, Va., Federalist anthologies.

president not only cannot make members of the upper house, but their creation, like his own, is by *the people* through their representatives, and a member of assembly may and will be as certainly dismissed at the end of his year for electing a weak or wicked senator, as for any other blunder or misconduct.

The King of England has legislative power, while our president can only use it when the other servants of the people are divided. But in all great cases affecting the national interests or safety, his modified and restrained power must give way to the sense of two-thirds of the legislature. In fact it amounts to no more, than a serious duty imposed upon him to request both houses to reconsider any matter on which he entertains doubts or feels apprehensions; and here the people have a strong hold upon him *from his sole and personal responsibility.*

The president of the upper house (or the chancellor) in England is appointed by the king, while our vice-president, who is chosen *by the people* through the electors and the senate, *is not at all dependant on the president*, but may exercise equal powers on some occasions. In all royal governments an helpless infant or an unexperienced youth, may wear the crown. *Our president must be matured by the experience of years*, and being born among us, his character at thirty-five must be fully understood. Wisdom, virtue, and active qualities of mind and body can alone make him the first servant of a free and enlightened people.

Our president will fall very far short indeed of any prince in his annual income, which will not be hereditary, but *the absolute allowance of the people passing through the hands of their other servants from year to year as it becomes necessary.* There will be no burdens on the nation to provide for his heir or other branches of his family. 'Tis probable, from the state of property in America and other circumstances, that many citizens will *exceed* him in shew and expence, those dazzling trappings of kingly rank and power. He will have no authority to make a treaty without *two-thirds of the senate*, nor can he appoint ambassadors or other great officers *without their approbation*, which will remove the idea of *patronage and influence*, and of personal obligation and dependance. The appointment of even the inferior officers may be taken out of his hands by an act of Congress at any time; he can create no nobility or titles of honor, nor take away offices during good behaviour. *His person is not so much protected as that of a member of the house of representatives; for he may be proceeded against like any other man in the ordinary course of law.* He appoints *no officer of the separate states.* He will have no influence *from placemen in the legislature*, nor can he prorogue or dissolve it. He will have no power *over the treasures of the state*; and lastly, as he is *created* through the electors by the people at large, *he must ever look up to the support of his creators.* From such a servant with powers so limited and transitory, there can be no danger, especially when we consider the solid foundations on which our national liberties are immovably fixed by the other provisions of this excellent constitution. Whatever of dignity or authority he possesses, *is a delegated part of their Majesty and their political omnipotence, transiently vested in him by the people themselves for their own happiness.*

PUBLIUS: THE FEDERALIST 67 (ALEXANDER HAMILTON)
New York Packet, 11 March 1788 (excerpt)*

To the People of the State of New-York.

The Constitution of the executive department of the proposed government claims next our attention.

There is hardly any part of the system, which could have been attended with great[er] difficulty in the arrangement of it than this; and there is perhaps none, which has been inveighed against with less candor, or criticised with less judgment.

Here the writers against the Constitution seem to have taken pains to signalize their talent of misrepresentation, calculating upon the aversion of the people to monarchy, they have endeavoured to inlist all their jealousies and apprehensions in opposition to the intended President of the United States; not merely as the embryo but as the full grown progeny of that detested parent. To establish the pretended affinity they have not scrupled to draw resources even from the regions of fiction. The authorities of a magistrate, in few instances greater, and in some instances less, than those of a Governor of New-York, have been magnified into more than royal prerogatives. He has been decorated with attributes superior in dignity and splendor to those of a King of Great-Britain. He has been shown to us with the diadem sparkling on his brow, and the imperial purple flowing in his train. He has been seated on a throne surrounded with minions and mistresses; giving audience to the envoys of foreign potentates, in all the supercilious pomp of majesty. The images of Asiatic despotism and voluptuousness have scarcely been wanting to crown the exaggerated scene. We have been almost taught to tremble at the terrific visages of murdering janizaries; and to blush at the unveiled mysteries of a future seraglio.

Attempts so extravagant as these to disfigure, or it might rather be said, to metamorphose the object, render it necessary to take an accurate view of its real nature and form; in order as well to ascertain its true

*Reprinted: New York *Independent Journal*, 12 March.

aspect and genuine appearance, as to unmask the disingenuity and expose the fallacy of the counterfeit resemblances which have been so insidiously as well as industriously propagated.

PUBLIUS: THE FEDERALIST 69 (ALEXANDER HAMILTON) New York Packet, 14 March 1788*

To the People of the State of New-York.

I proceed now to trace the real characters of the proposed executive as they are marked out in the plan of the Convention. This will serve to place in a strong light the unfairness of the representations which have been made in regard to it.

The first thing which strikes our attention is that the executive authority, with few exceptions, is to be vested in a single magistrate. This will scarcely however be considered as a point upon which any comparison can be grounded; for if in this particular there be a resemblance to the King of Great-Britain, there is not less a resemblance to the Grand Signior, to the Khan of Tartary, to the man of the seven mountains, or to the Governor of New-York.

That magistrate is to be elected for *four* years; and is to be re-eligible as often as the People of the United States shall think him worthy of their confidence. In these circumstances, there is a total dissimilitude between *him* and a King of Great-Britain; who is an *hereditary* monarch, possessing the crown as a patrimony descendible to his heirs forever; but there is a close analogy between *him* and a Governor of New-York, who is elected for *three* years, and is re-eligible without limitation or intermission. If we consider how much less time would be requisite for establishing a dangerous influence in a single State, than for establishing a like influence throughout the United States, we must conclude that a duration of *four* years for the Chief Magistrate of the Union, is a degree of permanency far less to be dreaded in that office, than a duration of *three* years for a correspondent office in a single State.

The President of the United States would be liable to be impeached, tried, and upon conviction of treason, bribery, or other high crimes or misdemeanors, removed from office; and would afterwards be liable to prosecution and punishment in the ordinary course of law. The person of the King of Great-Britain is sacred and inviolable: There is no constitutional tribunal to which he is amenable; no punishment to which he can be subjected without involving the crisis of a national revolution. In

*Reprinted: New York *Independent Journal*, 15 March.

this delicate and important circumstance of personal responsibility, the President of confederated America would stand upon no better ground than a Governor of New-York, and upon worse ground than the Governors of Maryland and Delaware.

The President of the United States is to have power to return a bill, which shall have passed the two branches of the Legislature, for re-consideration; but the bill so returned is to become a law, if upon that reconsideration it be approved by two thirds of both houses. The King of Great Britain, on his part, has an absolute negative upon the acts of the two houses of Parliament. The disuse of that power for a considerable time past, does not affect the reality of its existence; and is to be ascribed wholly to the crown's having found the means of substituting influence to authority, or the art of gaining a majority in one or the other of the two houses, to the necessity of exerting a prerogative which could seldom be exerted without hazarding some degree of national agitation. The qualified negative of the President differs widely from this absolute negative of the British sovereign; and tallies exactly with the revisionary authority of the Council of revision of this State, of which the Governor is a constituent part. In this respect, the power of the President would exceed that of the Governor of New-York; because the former would possess singly what the latter shares with the Chancellor and Judges: But it would be precisely the same with that of the Governor of Massachusetts, whose constitution, as to this article, seems to have been the original from which the Convention have copied.

The President is to be the "Commander in Chief of the army and navy of the United States, and of the militia of the several States, when called into the actual service of the United States. He is to have power to grant reprieves and pardons for offences against the United States, *except in cases of impeachment*; to recommend to the consideration of Congress such measures as he shall judge necessary and expedient; to convene on extraordinary occasions both houses of the Legislature, or either of them, and in case of disagreement between them *with respect to the time of adjournment*, to adjourn them to such time as he shall think proper; to take care that the laws be faithfully executed; and to commission all officers of the United States." In most of these particulars the power of the President will resemble equally that of the King of Great-Britain and the Governor of New-York. The most material points of difference are these—First; the President will have only the occasional command of such part of the militia of the nation, as by legislative provision may be called into the actual service of the Union—The King of Great-Britain and the Governor of New-York have at all times the entire command of all the militia within their several jurisdictions. In this article therefore the power of the President would be inferior to that of either the Monarch or the Governor.—Secondly; the President is to be Commander in Chief of the army and navy of the United States. In this respect his authority would be nominally the same with that of the King of Great-Britain, but in substance much inferior to it. It would amount to nothing more than the supreme command and direction of the military and naval forces, as first General and Admiral of the confederacy; while that of the British King extends to the *declaring* of war and to the *raising* and *regulating* of fleets and armies; all which by the Constitution under consideration would appertain to the Legislature.[a] The Governor of New-York on the other hand, is by the Constitution of the State vested only with the command of its militia and navy. But the Constitutions of several of the States, expressly declare their Governors to be the Commanders in Chief as well of the army as navy; and it may well be a question whether those of New-Hampshire and Massachusetts, in particular, do not in this instance confer larger powers upon their respective Governors, than could be claimed by a President of the United States.—Thirdly; the power of the President in respect to pardons would extend to all cases, *except those of impeachment.* The Governor of New-York may pardon in all cases, even in those of impeachment, except for treason and murder. Is not the power of the Governor in this article, on a calculation of political consequences, greater than that of the President? All conspiracies and plots against the government, which have not been matured into actual treason, may be screened from punishment of every kind, by the interposition of the prerogative of pardoning. If a Governor of New-York therefore should be at the head of any such conspiracy, until the design had been ripened into actual hostility, he could ensure his accomplices and adherents an entire impunity. A President of the Union on the other hand, though he may even pardon treason, when prosecuted in the ordinary course of law, could shelter no offender in any degree from the effects of impeachment & conviction. Would not the prospect of a total indemnity for all the pre-

[a]*A writer in a Pennsylvania paper, under the signature of* Tamony *has asserted that the King of Great-Britain owes his prerogatives as Commander in Chief to an annual mutiny bill.—The truth is on the contrary that his prerogative in this respect is immemorial, and was only disputed "contrary to all reason and precedent," as Blackstone, vol. I, p. 262, expresses it, by the long parliament of Charles the first, but by the statute the 13, of Charles second, ch. 6, it was declared to be in the King alone, for that the sole supreme government and command of the militia within his Majesty's realms and dominions, and of all forces by sea and land, and of all forts and places of strength,* ever was and is *the undoubted right of his Majesty and his royal predecessors Kings and Queens of England, and that both or either House of Parliament cannot nor ought to pretend to the same.*

liminary steps be a greater temptation to undertake and persevere in an enterprise against the public liberty than the mere prospect of an exemption from death and confiscation, if the final execution of the design, upon an actual appeal to arms, should miscarry? Would this last expectation have any influence at all, when the probability was computed that the person who was to afford that exemption might himself be involved in the consequences of the measure; and might be incapacitated by his agency in it, from affording the desired impunity. The better to judge of this matter, it will be necessary to recollect that by the proposed Constitution the offence of treason is limited "to levying war upon the United States, and adhering to their enemies, giving them aid and comfort," and that by the laws of New-York it is confined within similar bounds.—Fourthly; the President can only adjourn the national Legislature in the single case of disagreement about the time of adjournment. The British monarch may prorogue or even dissolve the Parliament. The Governor of New-York may also prorogue the Legislature of this State for a limited time; a power which in certain situations may be employed to very important purposes.

The President is to have power with the advice and consent of the Senate to make treaties; provided two thirds of the Senators present concur. The King of Great-Britain is the sole and absolute representative of the nation in all foreign transactions. He can of his own accord make treaties of peace, commerce, alliance, and of every other description. It has been insinuated, that his authority in this respect is not conclusive, and that his conventions with foreign powers are subject to revision, and stand in need of the ratification of Parliament. But I believe this doctrine was never heard of 'till it was broached upon the present occasion. Every jurist[b] of that kingdom, and every other man acquainted with its constitution knows, as an established fact, that the prerogative of making treaties exists in the crown in its utmost plenitude; and that the compacts entered into by the royal authority have the most complete legal validity and perfection, independent of any other sanction. The Parliament, it is true, is sometimes seen employing itself in altering the existing laws to conform them to the speculations in a new treaty; and this may have possibly given birth to the imagination that its co-operation was necessary to the obligatory efficacy of the treaty. But this parliamentary interposition proceeds from a different cause; from the necessity of adjusting a most artificial and intricate system of revenue and commercial laws to the changes made in them by the operation of the treaty; and of adapting new provisions and precautions to the new state of things, to keep the machine from running into disorder. In this respect therefore, there is no comparison

[b] *Vide Blackstone's Commentaries, page 257.*

between the intended power of the President, and the actual power of the British sovereign. The one can perform alone, what the other can only do with the concurrence of a branch of the Legislature. It must be admitted that in this instance the power of the fœderal executive would exceed that of any State executive. But this arises naturally from the exclusive possession by the Union of that part of the sovereign power, which relates to treaties. If the confederacy were to be dissolved, it would become a question, whether the executives of the several States were not solely invested with that delicate and important prerogative.

The President is also to be authorised to receive Ambassadors and other public Ministers. This, though it has been a rich theme of declamation, is more a matter of dignity than of authority. It is a circumstance, which will be without consequence in the administration of the government, and it was far more convenient that it should be arranged in this manner, than that there should be a necessity of convening the Legislature, or one of its branches, upon every arrival of a foreign minister; though it were merely to take the place of a departed predecessor.

The President is to nominate and *with the advice and consent of the Senate* to appoint Ambassadors and other public Ministers, Judges of the Supreme Court, and in general all officers of the United States established by law and whose appointments are not otherwise provided for by the Constitution. The King of Great-Britain is emphatically and truly stiled the fountain of honor. He not only appoints to all offices, but can create offices. He can confer titles of nobility at pleasure; and has the disposal of an immense number of church preferments. There is evidently a great inferiority, in the power of the President in this particular, to that of the British King; nor is it equal to that of the Governor of New-York, if we are to interpret the meaning of the constitution of the State by the practice which has obtained under it. The power of appointment is with us lodged in a Council composed of the Governor and four members of the Senate chosen by the Assembly. The Governor *claims* and has frequently *exercised* the right of nomination, and is *entitled* to a casting vote in the appointment. If he really has the right of nominating, his authority is in this respect equal to that of the President, and exceeds it in the article of the casting vote. In the national government, if the Senate should be divided, no appointment could be made: In the government of New-York, if the Council should be divided the Governor can turn the scale and confirm his own nomination.[c] If we compare the publicity which must necessarily

---

[c]*Candor however demands an acknowledgement, that I do not think the claim of the Governor to a right of nomination well founded. Yet it is always justifiable to reason from the practice of a government till its propriety has been constitutionally*

attend the mode of appointment by the President and an entire branch of the national Legislature, with the privacy in the mode of appointment by the Governor of New-York, closeted in a secret apartment with at most four, and frequently with only two persons, and if we at the same time consider how much more easy it must be to influence the small number of which a Council of Appointment consist than the considerable number of which the national Senate would consist, we cannot hesitate to pronounce, that the power of the Chief Magistrate of this State in the disposition of offices must in practice be greatly superior to that of the Chief Magistrate of the Union.

Hence it appears, that except as to the concurrent authority of the President in the article of treaties, it would be difficult to determine whether that Magistrate would in the aggregate, possess more or less power than the Governor of New-York. And it appears yet more unequivocally that there is no pretence for the parallel which has been attempted between him and the King of Great-Britain. But to render the contrast, in this respect, still more striking, it may be of use to throw the principal circumstances of dissimilitude into a closer groupe.

The President of the United States would be an officer elected by the people for *four* years. The King of Great-Britain is a perpetual and *hereditary* prince. The one would be amenable to personal punishment and disgrace: The person of the other is sacred and inviolable. The one would have a *qualified* negative upon the acts of the legislative body: The other has an *absolute* negative. The one would have a right to command the military and naval forces of the nation: The other in addition to this right, possesses that of *declaring* war, and of *raising* and *regulating* fleets and armies by his own authority. The one would have a concurrent power with a branch of the Legislature in the formation of treaties: The other is the *sole possessor* of the power of making treaties. The one would have a like concurrent authority in appointing to offices: The other is the sole author of all appointments. The one can infer no privileges whatever: The other can make denizens of aliens, noblemen of commoners, can erect corporations with all the rights incident to corporate bodies. The one can prescribe no rules concerning the commerce or currency of the nation: The other is in several respects the arbiter of commerce, and in this capacity can establish markets and fairs, can regulate weights and measures, can lay embargoes for a limited time, can coin money, can

---

questioned. And independent of this claim, when we take into view the other consideration[s] and pursue them through all their consequences, we shall be inclined to draw much the same conclusion.

authorise or prohibit the circulation of foreign coin. The one has no particle of spiritual jurisdiction: The other is the supreme head and Governor of the national church!—What answer shall we give to those who would persuade us that things so unlike resemble each other?—The same that ought to be given to those who tell us, that a government, the whole power of which would be in the hands of the elective and periodical servants of the people, is an aristocracy, a monarchy, and a despotism.

PUBLIUS: THE FEDERALIST 73 (ALEXANDER HAMILTON)
New York Packet, 21 March 1788*

To the People of the State of New-York.
The third ingredient towards constituting the vigor of the executive authority is an adequate provision for its support. It is evident that without proper attention to this article, the separation of the executive from the legislative department would be merely nominal and nugatory. The Legislature, with a discretionary power over the salary and emoluments of the Chief Magistrate, could render him as obsequious to their will, as they might think proper to make him. They might in most cases either reduce him by famine, or tempt him by largesses, to surrender at discretion his judgment to their inclinations. These expressions taken in all the latitude of the terms would no doubt convey more than is intended.—There are men who could neither be distressed nor won into a sacrifice of their duty; but this stern virtue is the growth of few soils: And in the main it will be found, that a power over a man's support is a power over his will. If it were necessary to confirm so plain a truth by facts, examples would not be wanting, even in this country, of the intimidation or seduction of the executive by the terrors, or allurements, of the pecuniary arrangements of the legislative body.

It is not easy therefore to commend too highly the judicious attention which has been paid to this subject in the proposed Constitution. It is there provided that "The President of the United States shall, at stated times, receive for his services a compensation, *which shall neither be increased nor diminished, during the period for which he shall have been elected,* and he shall not *receive within that period any other emolument* from the United States or any of them." It is impossible to imagine any provision which would have been more eligible than this—The Legislature on the appointment of a President is once for all to declare what shall be the compensation for his services during the time for which he shall have

*Reprinted: New York *Independent Journal*, 22 March.

been elected. This done, they will have no power to alter it either by increase or diminution, till a new period of service by a new election commences—They can neither weaken his fortitude by operating upon his necessities; nor corrupt his integrity, by appealing to his avarice. Neither the Union nor any of its members will be at liberty to give, nor will he be at liberty to receive any other emolument, than that which may have been determined by the first act. He can of course have no pecuniary inducement to renounce or desert the independence intended for him by the Constitution.

The last of the requisites to energy which have been enumerated are competent powers. Let us proceed to consider those which are proposed to be vested in the President of the United States.

The first thing that offers itself to our observation, is the qualified negative of the President upon the acts or resolutions of the two Houses of the Legislature; or in other words his power of returning all bills with objections; to have the effect of preventing their becoming laws, unless they should afterwards be ratified by two thirds of each of the component members of the legislative body.

The propensity of the legislative department to intrude upon the rights and to absorb the powers of the other departments, has been already suggested and repeated; the insufficiency of a mere parchment delineation of the boundaries of each, has also been remarked upon; and the necessity of furnishing each with constitutional arms for its own defence, has been inferred and proved. From these clear and indubitable principles results the propriety of a negative, either absolute or qualified, in the executive, upon the acts of the legislative branches. Without the one or the other the former would be absolutely unable to defend himself against the depredations of the latter. He might gradually be stripped of his authorities by successive resolutions, or annihilated by a single vote. And in the one mode or the other, the legislative and executive powers might speedily come to be blended in the same hands. If even no propensity had ever discovered itself in the legislative body, to invade the rights of the executive, the rules of just reasoning and theoretic propriety would of themselves teach us, that the one ought not to be left at the mercy of the other, but ought to possess a constitutional and effectual power of self defence.

But the power in question has a further use. It not only serves as a shield to the executive, but it furnishes an additional security against the enaction of improper laws. It establishes a salutary check upon the legislative body calculated to guard the community against the effects of faction, precipitancy, or of any impulse unfriendly to the public good, which may happen to influence a majority of that body.

The propriety of a negative, has upon some occasions been combated by an observation, that it was not to be presumed a single man would possess more virtue or wisdom, than a number of men; and that unless this presumption should be entertained, it would be improper to give the executive magistrate any species of controul over the legislative body.

But this observation when examined will appear rather specious than solid. The propriety of the thing does not turn upon the supposition of superior wisdom or virtue in the executive: But upon the supposition that the legislative will not be infallible: That the love of power may sometimes betray it into a disposition to encroach upon the rights of the other members of the government; that a spirit of faction may sometimes pervert its deliberations; that impressions of the moment may sometimes hurry it into measures which itself on maturer reflection would condemn. The primary inducement to conferring the power in question upon the executive, is to enable him to defend himself; the secondary one is to encrease the chances in favor of the community, against the passing of bad laws, through haste, inadvertence, or design. The oftner a measure is brought under examination, the greater the diversity in the situations of those who are to examine it, the less must be the danger of those errors which flow from want of due deliberation, or of those missteps which proceed from the contagion of some common passion or interest. It is far less probable, that culpable views of any kind should infect all the parts of the government, at the same moment and in relation to the same object, than that they should by turns govern and mislead every one of them.

It may perhaps be said, that the power of preventing bad laws includes that of preventing good ones; and may be used to the one purpose as well as to the other. But this objection will have little weight with those who can properly estimate the mischiefs of that inconstancy and mutability in the laws, which forms the greatest blemish in the character and genius of our governments. They will consider every institution calculated to restrain the excess of law-making, and to keep things in the same state, in which they may happen to be at any given period, as much more likely to do good than harm; because it is favorable to greater stability in the system of legislation. The injury which may possibly be done by defeating a few good laws will be amply compensated by the advantage of preventing a number of bad ones.

Nor is this all. The superior weight and influence of the legislative body in a free government, and the hazard to the executive in a trial of strength with that body, afford a satisfactory security, that the negative would generally be employed with great caution, and that there would oftener be room for a charge of timidity than of rashness, in the exercise of it. A King of Great-Britain, with all his train of sovereign attributes, and with all the influence he draws from a thousand sources, would at this day hesitate to put a negative upon the joint resolutions of the two houses of Parliament. He would not fail to exert the utmost resources of that influence to strangle a measure disagreeable to him, in its progress to the throne, to avoid being reduced to the dilemma of permitting it to take effect, or of risking the displeasure of the nation, by an opposition to the sense of the legislative body. Nor is it probable that he would ultimately venture to exert his prerogatives, but in a case of manifest propriety, or extreme necessity. All well informed men in that kingdom will accede to the justness of this remark. A very considerable period has elapsed since the negative of the crown has been exercised.

If a magistrate, so powerful and so well fortified as a British monarch, would have scruples about the exercise of the power under consideration, how much greater caution may be reasonably expected in a President of the United States, cloathed for the short period of four years with the executive authority of a government wholly and purely republican?

It is evident that there would be greater danger of his not using his power when necessary, than of his using it too often, or too much. An argument indeed against its expediency has been drawn from this very source. It has been represented on this account as a power odious in appearance, useless in practice. But it will not follow, that because it might be rarely exercised, it would never be exercised. In the case for which it is chiefly designed, that of an immediate attack upon the constitutional rights of the executive, or in a case in which the public good was evidently and palpably sacrificed, a man of tolerable firmness would avail himself of his constitutional means of defence, and would listen to the admonitions of duty and responsibility. In the former supposition, his fortitude would be stimulated by his immediate interest in the power of his office; in the latter by the probability of the sanction of his constituents; who though they would naturally incline to the legislative body in a doubtful case, would hardly suffer their partiality to delude them in a very plain case. I speak now with an eye to a magistrate possessing only a common share of firmness. There are men, who under any circumstances will have the courage to do their duty at every hazard.

But the Convention have pursued a mean in this business; which will both facilitate the exercise of the power vested in this respect in the executive magistrate, and make its efficacy to depend on the sense of a considerable part of the legislative body. Instead of an absolute negative, it is proposed to give the executive the qualified negative already described. This is a power, which would be much more readily exercised than the other. A man who might be afraid to defeat a law by his single VETO, might not scruple to return it for re-consideration; subject to being finally rejected only in the event of more than one third of each house concurring in the sufficiency of his objections. He would be encouraged by the reflection, that if his opposition should prevail, it would embark in it a very respectable proportion of the legislative body, whose influence would be united with his in supporting the propriety of his conduct, in the public opinion. A direct and categorical negative has something in the appearance of it more harsh, and more apt to irritate, than the mere suggestion of argumentative objections to be approved or disapproved, by those to whom they are addressed—In proportion as it would be less apt to offend, it would be more apt to be exercised; and for this very reason it may in practice be found more effectual. It is to be hoped that it will not often happen, that improper views will govern so large a proportion as two-thirds of both branches of the Legislature at the same time; and this too in spite of the counterpoising weight of the executive. It is at any rate far less probable, that this should be the case, than that such views should taint the resolutions and conduct of a bare majority. A power of this nature, in the executive, will often have a silent and unpercieved though forcible operation. When men engaged in unjustifiable pursuits are aware, that obstructions may come from a quarter which they cannot controul, they will often be restrained, by the bare apprehension of opposition, from doing what they would with eagerness rush into, if no such external impediments were to be feared.

This qualified negative, as has been elsewhere remarked, is in this State vested in a council, consisting of the Governor, with the Chancellor and Judges of the Supreme Court, or any two of them. It has been freely employed upon a variety of occasions, and frequently with success. And its utility has become so apparent, that persons who in compiling the Constitution were violent opposers of it, have from experience become its declared admirers.[a]

I have in another place remarked, that the Convention in the formation of this part of their plan, had departed from the model of the Constitution of this State, in favor of that of Massachusetts—two strong reasons may be imagined for this preference. One is that the Judges, who are to be the interpreters of the law, might receive an improper bias from having given a previous opinion in their revisionary capacities. The other is that by being often associated with the executive they might be induced to embark too far in the political views of that magistrate, and thus a dangerous combination might by degrees be cemented between the executive and judiciary departments. It is impossible to keep the Judges too

[a] *Mr. Abraham Yates, a warm opponent of the plan of the Convention, is of this number.*

distinct from every other avocation than that of expounding the laws. It is peculiarly dangerous to place them in a situation to be either corrupted or influenced by the executive.

PUBLIUS: THE FEDERALIST 74 (ALEXANDER HAMILTON) *New York Packet*, 25 March 1788*

To the People of the State of New-York.
The President of the United States is to be "Commander in Chief of the army and navy of the United States, and of the militia of the several States *when called into the actual service* of the United States." The propriety of this provision is so evident in itself; and it is at the same time so consonant to the precedents of the State constitutions in general, that little need be said to explain or enforce it. Even those of them, which have in other respects coupled the Chief Magistrate with a Council, have for the most part concentred the military authority in him alone. Of all the cares or concerns of government, the direction of war most peculiarly demands those qualities which distinguish the exercise of power by a single hand. The direction of war implies the direction of the common strength; and the power of directing and employing the common strength, forms an usual and essential part in the definition of the executive authority.

"The President may require the opinion in writing of the principal officer in each of the executive departments upon any subject relating to the duties of their respective offices." This I consider as a mere redundancy in the plan; as the right for which it provides would result of itself from the office.

He is also to be authorised "to grant reprieves and pardons for offences against the United States *except in cases of impeachment.*" Humanity and good policy conspire to dictate, that the benign prerogative of pardoning should be as little as possible fettered or embarrassed. The criminal code of every country partakes so much of necessary severity, that without an easy access to exceptions in favor of unfortunate guilt, justice would wear a countenance too sanguinary and cruel. As the sense of responsibility is always strongest in proportion as it is undivided, it may be inferred that a single man would be most ready to attend to the force of those motives, which might plead for a mitigation of the rigor of the law, and least apt to yield to considerations, which were calculated to shelter a fit object of its vengeance. The reflection, that the fate of a fellow creature depended on his *sole fiat*, would naturally inspire scru-

*Reprinted: New York *Independent Journal*, 26 March.

pulousness and caution: The dread of being accused of weakness or connivance would beget equal circumspection, though of a different kind. On
the other hand, as men generally derive confidence from their numbers,
they might often encourage each other in an act of obduracy, and might
be less sensible to the apprehension of suspicion or censure for an injudicious or affected clemency. On these accounts, one man appears to
be a more eligible dispenser of the mercy of the government than a body
of men.

The expediency of vesting the power of pardoning in the President
has, if I mistake not, been only contested in relation to the crime of treason.
This, it has been urged, ought to have depended upon the assent of one
or both of the branches of the legislative body. I shall not deny that there
are strong reasons to be assigned for requiring in this particular the concurrence of that body or of a part of it. As treason is a crime levelled at
the immediate being of the society, when the laws have once ascertained
the guilt of the offender, there seems a fitness in refering the expediency
of an act of mercy towards him to the judgment of the Legislature. And
this ought the rather to be the case, as the supposition of the connivance
of the Chief Magistrate ought not to be entirely excluded. But there are
also strong objections to such a plan. It is not to be doubted that a single
man of prudence and good sense, is better fitted, in delicate conjunctures,
to balance the motives, which may plead for and against the remission of
the punishment, than any numerous body whatever. It deserves particular
attention, that treason will often be connected with seditions, which embrace a large proportion of the community; as lately happened in Massachusetts. In every such case, we might expect to see the representation
of the people tainted with the same spirit, which had given birth to the
offence. And when parties were pretty equally matched, the secret sympathy of the friends and favorers of the condemned person, availing itself
of the good nature and weakness of others, might frequently bestow impunity where the terror of an example was necessary. On the other hand,
when the sedition had proceeded from causes which had inflamed the
resentments of the major party, they might often be found obstinate and
inexorable, when policy demanded a conduct of forbearance and clemency.
But the principal argument for reposing the power of pardoning in this
case in the Chief Magistrate is this—In seasons of insurrection or rebellion,
there are often critical moments, when a well timed offer of pardon to
the insurgents or rebels may restore the tranquility of the commonwealth;
and which, if suffered to pass unimproved, it may never be possible afterwards to recall. The dilatory process of convening the Legislature, or
one of its branches, for the purpose of obtaining its sanction to the measure, would frequently be the occasion of letting slip the golden oppor-

tunity. The loss of a week, a day, an hour, may sometimes be fatal. If it should be observed that a discretionary power with a view to such contingencies might be occasionally confered upon the President; it may be answered in the first place, that it is questionable whether, in a limited constitution, that power could be delegated by law; and in the second place, that it would generally be impolitic before-hand to take any step which might hold out the prospect of impunity. A proceeding of this kind, out of the usual course, would be likely to be construed into an argument of timidity or of weakness, and would have a tendency to embolden guilt.

5

The Judiciary

ANTIFEDERALISTS VIEWED *the federal judiciary as another source of danger to individual liberty and to the independent existence of the states. They were concerned that the judicial power of the United States would compromise the right to trial by jury in civil cases: though the Constitution guaranteed jury trials in criminal cases, it said nothing about civil cases. Even in criminal cases, the Constitution did not guarantee juries of the "vicinage," but only that trials would take place in the state in which a crime was committed. This might entail a distance of hundreds of miles. And in matters that might come before the Supreme Court, travel of thousands of miles would be involved.*

The Constitution gave the federal courts appellate jurisdiction not only in matters of law, which was traditional, but also in determining matters of fact that would normally have been decided by a jury in the lower court. This profoundly disturbed Antifederalists as another threat to the jury system.

Antifederalists worried that the jurisdiction of the federal courts was too broad, and as federal power grew, which they believed was inevitable, more cases would be taken to federal courts rather than state courts, thus reducing the importance of the state courts. They expected the federal courts to encourage their own aggrandizement of power. As interpreters of the ambiguities in the Constitution, federal courts would accrue more power to themselves as they allowed federal power to expand at state expense.

Federalists responded that of the three branches, the judicial branch was the "least dangerous," because it had the power only of judgment. They denied that jury trials were always necessary or were endangered, either by the silence of the Constitution or by the appellate jurisdiction of the federal courts in matters of fact. They defended the jurisdiction of the federal courts as the only means to provide justice in foreign and interstate cases, and to impose uniform obedience to the Constitution and to federal law. Federalists viewed the courts as the intermediary between the people and the Congress. The courts, through judicial review, would uphold the Constitution against the attempts by Congress to enlarge its power. As such, it was a protector of the people, not a danger.

Antifederalist

BRUTUS XI
New York Journal, 31 January 1788

The nature and extent of the judicial power of the United States, proposed to be granted by this constitution, claims our particular attention.

Much has been said and written upon the subject of this new system on both sides, but I have not met with any writer, who has discussed the judicial powers with any degree of accuracy. And yet it is obvious, that we can form but very imperfect ideas of the manner in which this government will work, or the effect it will have in changing the internal police and mode of distributing justice at present subsisting in the respective states, without a thorough investigation of the powers of the judiciary and of the manner in which they will operate. This government is a complete system, not only for making, but for executing laws. And the courts of law, which will be constituted by it, are not only to decide upon the constitution and the laws made in pursuance of it, but by officers subordinate to them to execute all their decisions. The real effect of this system of government, will therefore be brought home to the feelings of the people, through the medium of the judicial power. It is, moreover, of great importance, to examine with care the nature and extent of the judicial power, because those who are to be vested with it, are to be placed in a situation altogether unprecedented in a free country. They are to be rendered totally independent, both of the people and the legislature, both with respect to their offices and salaries. No errors they may commit can be corrected by any power above them, if any such power there be, nor can they be removed from office for making ever so many erroneous adjudications.

The only causes for which they can be displaced, is, conviction of treason, bribery, and high crimes and misdemeanors.

This part of the plan is so modelled, as to authorise the courts, not only to carry into execution the powers expressly given, but where these are wanting or ambiguously expressed, to supply what is wanting by their own decisions.

That we may be enabled to form a just opinion on this subject, I shall, in considering it,

1st. Examine the nature and extent of the judicial powers—and

2d. Enquire, whether the courts who are to exercise them, are so constituted as to afford reasonable ground of confidence, that they will exercise them for the general good.

With a regard to the nature and extent of the judicial powers, I have to regret my want of capacity to give that full and minute explanation of them that the subject merits. To be able to do this, a man should be possessed of a degree of law knowledge far beyond what I pretend to. A number of hard words and technical phrases are used in this part of the system, about the meaning of which gentlemen learned in the law differ.

Its advocates know how to avail themselves of these phrases. In a number of instances, where objections are made to the powers given to the judicial, they give such an explanation to the technical terms as to avoid them.

Though I am not competent to give a perfect explanation of the powers granted to this department of the government, I shall yet attempt to trace some of the leading features of it, from which I presume it will appear, that they will operate to a total subversion of the state judiciaries, if not, to the legislative authority of the states.

In article 3d, sect. 2d, it is said, "The judicial power shall extend to all cases in law and equity arising under this constitution, the laws of the United States, and treaties made, or which shall be made, under their authority, &c."

The first article to which this power extends, is, all cases in law and equity arising under this constitution.

What latitude of construction this clause should receive, it is not easy to say. At first view, one would suppose, that it meant no more than this, that the courts under the general government should exercise, not only the powers of courts of law, but also that of courts of equity, in the manner in which those powers are usually exercised in the different states. But this cannot be the meaning, because the next clause authorises the courts to take cognizance of all cases in law and equity arising under the laws of the United States; this last article, I conceive, conveys as much power to the general judicial as any of the state courts possess.

The cases arising under the constitution must be different from those arising under the laws, or else the two clauses mean exactly the same thing.

The cases arising under the constitution must include such, as bring into question its meaning, and will require an explanation of the nature and extent of the powers of the different departments under it.

This article, therefore, vests the judicial with a power to resolve all questions that may arise on any case on the construction of the constitution, either in law or in equity.

1st. They are authorised to determine all questions that may arise upon the meaning of the constitution in law. This article vests the courts with authority to give the constitution a legal construction, or to explain it according to the rules laid down for construing a law.—These rules give a certain degree of latitude of explanation. According to this mode of construction, the courts are to give such meaning to the constitution as comports best with the common, and generally received acceptation of the words in which it is expressed, regarding their ordinary and popular use, rather than their grammatical propriety. Where words are dubious, they will be explained by the context. The end of the clause will be attended to, and the words will be understood, as having a view to it; and the words will not be so understood as to bear no meaning or a very absurd one.

2d. The judicial are not only to decide questions arising upon the meaning of the constitution in law, but also in equity.

By this they are empowered, to explain the constitution according to the reasoning spirit of it, without being confined to the words or letter.

"From this method of interpreting laws (says Blackstone) by the reason of them, arises what we call equity;" which is thus defined by Grotius, "the correction of that, wherein the law, by reason of its universality, is deficient; for since in laws all cases cannot be foreseen, or expressed, it is necessary, that when the decrees of the law cannot be applied to particular cases, there should some where be a power vested of defining those circumstances, which had they been foreseen the legislator would have expressed; and these are the cases, which according to Grotius, lex non exacte definit, sed arbitrio boni viri permittet."

The same learned author observes, "That equity, thus depending essentially upon each individual case, there can be no established rules and fixed principles of equity laid down, without destroying its very essence, and reducing it to a positive law."

From these remarks, the authority and business of the courts of law, under this clause, may be understood.

They will give the sense of every article of the constitution, that may from time to time come before them. And in their decisions they will not confine themselves to any fixed or established rules, but will determine, according to what appears to them, the reason and spirit of the constitution. The opinions of the supreme court, whatever they may be, will have the force of law; because there is no power provided in the constitution, that can correct their errors, or controul their adjudications. From this court there is no appeal. And I conceive the legislature themselves, cannot set aside a judgment of this court, because they are authorised by the constitution to decide in the last resort. The legislature must be controuled by the constitution, and not the constitution by them. They have therefore no more right to set aside any judgment pronounced upon the construction of the constitution, than they have to take from the president, the chief command of the army and navy, and commit it to some other person. The reason is plain; the judicial and executive derive their authority from the same source, that the legislature do theirs; and therefore in all cases, where the constitution does not make the one responsible to, or controulable by the other, they are altogether independent of each other.

The judicial power will operate to effect, in the most certain, but yet silent and imperceptible manner, what is evidently the tendency of the constitution:—I mean, an entire subversion of the legislative, executive and judicial powers of the individual states. Every adjudication of the supreme court, on any question that may arise upon the nature and extent of the general government, will affect the limits of the state jurisdiction. In proportion as the former enlarge the exercise of their powers, will that of the latter be restricted.

That the judicial power of the United States, will lean strongly in favour of the general government, and will give such an explanation to the constitution, as will favour an extension of its jurisdiction, is very evident from a variety of considerations.

1st. The constitution itself strongly countenances such a mode of construction. Most of the articles in this system, which convey powers of any considerable importance, are conceived in general and indefinite terms, which are either equivocal, ambiguous, or which require long definitions to unfold the extent of their meaning. The two most important powers committed to any government, those of raising money, and of raising and keeping up troops, have already been considered, and shewn to be unlimitted by any thing but the discretion of the legislature. The clause which vests the power to pass all laws which are proper and necessary, to carry the powers given into execution,* it has been shewn, leaves the legislature at liberty, to do every thing, which in their judgment is best. It is said, I know, that this clause confers no power on the legislature, which they would not have had without it—though I believe this is not the fact, yet, admitting it to be, it implies that the constitution is not to receive an explanation strictly, according to its letter; but more

*Article I, section 8, last clause.

power is implied than is expressed. And this clause, if it is to be considered, as explanatory of the extent of the powers given, rather than giving a new power, is to be understood as declaring, that in construing any of the articles conveying power, the spirit, intent and design of the clause, should be attended to, as well as the words in their common acceptation.

This constitution gives sufficient colour for adopting an equitable construction, if we consider the great end and design it professedly has in view—there appears from its preamble to be, "to form a more perfect union, establish justice, insure domestic tranquillity, provide for the common defence, promote the general welfare, and secure the blessings of liberty to ourselves and posterity." The design of this system is here expressed, and it is proper to give such a meaning to the various parts, as will best promote the accomplishment of the end; this idea suggests itself naturally upon reading the preamble, and will countenance the court in giving the several articles such a sense, as will the most effectually promote the ends the constitution had in view—how this manner of explaining the constitution will operate in practice, shall be the subject of future enquiry.

2d. Not only will the constitution justify the courts in inclining to this mode of explaining it, but they will be interested in using this latitude of interpretation. Every body of men invested with office are tenacious of power; they feel interested, and hence it has become a kind of maxim, to hand down their offices, with all its rights and privileges, unimpared to their successors; the same principle will influence them to extend their power, and increase their rights; this of itself will operate strongly upon the courts to give such a meaning to the constitution in all cases where it can possibly be done, as will enlarge the sphere of their own authority. Every extension of the power of the general legislature, as well as of the judicial powers, will increase the powers of the courts; and the dignity and importance of the judges, will be in proportion to the extent and magnitude of the powers they exercise. I add, it is highly probable the emolument of the judges will be increased, with the increase of the business they will have to transact and its importance. From these considerations the judges will be interested to extend the powers of the courts, and to construe the constitution as much as possible, in such a way as to favour it; and that they will do it, appears probable.

3d. Because they will have precedent to plead, to justify them in it. It is well known, that the courts in England, have by their own authority, extended their jurisdiction far beyond the limits set them in their original institution, and by the laws of the land.

The court of exchequer is a remarkable instance of this. It was originally intended principally to recover the king's debts, and to order the revenues of the crown. It had a common law jurisdiction, which was established merely for the benefit of the king's accomptants. We learn from Blackstone, that the proceedings in this court are grounded on a writ called quo minus, in which the plaintiff suggests, that he is the king's farmer or debtor, and that the defendant hath done him the damage complained of, by which he is less able to pay the king. These suits, by the statute of Rutland [1282], are expressly directed to be confined to such matters as specially concern the king, or his ministers in the exchequer. And by the articuli super cartas [1300], it is enacted, that no common pleas be thenceforth held in the exchequer contrary to the form of the great charter: but now any person may sue in the exchequer. The surmise of being debtor to the king being matter of form, and mere words of course; and the court is open to all the nation.

When the courts will have a president [precedent] before them of a court which extended its jurisdiction in opposition to an act of the legislature, is it not to be expected that they will extend theirs, especially when there is nothing in the constitution expressly against it? and they are authorised to construe its meaning, and are not under any controul?

This power in the judicial, will enable them to mould the government, into almost any shape they please.—The manner in which this may be effected we will hereafter examine.

FEDERAL FARMER
c. 8 November 1787 (excerpt)

There are some powers proposed to be lodged in the general government in the judicial department, I think very unnecessarily, I mean powers respecting questions arising upon the internal laws of the respective states. It is proper the federal judiciary should have powers co-extensive with the federal legislature—that is, the power of deciding finally on the laws of the union. By Art. 3. Sect. 2. the powers of the federal judiciary are extended (among other things) to all cases between a state and citizens of another state—between citizens of different states—between a state or the citizens thereof, and foreign states, citizens or subjects. Actions in all these cases, except against a state government, are now brought and finally determined in the law courts of the states respectively; and as there are no words to exclude these courts of their jurisdiction in these cases, they will have concurrent jurisdiction with the inferior federal courts in them; and, therefore, if the new constitution be adopted without any amendment in this respect, all those numerous actions, now brought in the state courts between our citizens and foreigners, between citizens of different states, by state governments against foreigners, and by state governments against citizens of other states, may also be brought in the federal courts; and an appeal will lay in them from the state courts, or federal inferior courts, to the supreme judicial court of the union. In almost all these cases, either party may have the trial by jury in the state courts; excepting paper money and tender laws, which are wisely guarded against in the proposed constitution; justice may be obtained in these courts on reasonable terms; they must be more competent to proper decisions on the laws of their respective states, than the federal courts can possibly be. I do not, in any point of view, see the need of opening a new jurisdiction to these causes—of opening a new scene of expensive law suits—of suffering foreigners, and citizens of different states, to drag each other many hundred miles into the federal courts. It is true, those courts may be so organized by a wise and prudent legislature, as to make the obtaining of justice in them tolerably easy; they may in general be organized on the common law principles of the country: But this benefit is by no means secured by the constitution. The trial by jury is secured only in those few criminal cases, to which the federal laws will extend—as crimes committed on the seas against the laws of nations, treason and counterfeiting the federal securities and coin: But even in these cases, the jury trial of the vicinage is not secured, particularly in the large states, a citizen may be tried for a crime committed in the state, and yet tried in some states 500 miles from the place where it was committed; but the jury trial is not secured at all in civil causes. Though the convention have not established this trial, it is to be hoped that congress, in putting the new system into execution, will do it by a legislative act, in all cases in which it can be done with propriety. Whether the jury trial is not excluded [in] the supreme judicial court, is an important question. By Art. 3. Sect. 2. all cases affecting ambassadors, other public ministers, and consuls, and in those cases in which a state shall be party, the supreme court shall have jurisdiction. In all the other cases before mentioned, the supreme court shall have appellate jurisdiction, both as to LAW and FACT, with such exception, and under such regulations, as the congress shall make. By court is understood a court consisting of judges; and the idea of a jury is excluded. This court, or the judges, are to have jurisdiction on appeals, in all the cases enumerated, as to law and fact; the judges are to decide the law and try the fact, and the trial of the fact being assigned to the judges by the constitution, a jury for trying the fact is excluded; however, under the exceptions and powers to make regulations, Congress may, perhaps, introduce the jury, to try the fact in most necessary cases.

There can be but one supreme court in which the final jurisdiction will centre in all federal causes—except in cases where appeals by law shall not be allowed: The judicial powers of the federal courts extends in law and equity to certain cases: and, therefore, the powers to determine on the law, in equity, and as to the fact, all will concentre in the supreme court:—These powers, which by this constitution are blended in the same hands, the same judges, are in Great-Britain deposited in different hands— to wit, the decision of the law in the law judges, the decision in equity in the chancellor, and the trial of the fact in the jury. It is a very dangerous thing to vest in the same judge power to decide on the law, and also general powers in equity; for if the law restrain him, he is only to step into his shoes of equity, and give what judgment his reason or opinion may dictate; we have no precedents in this country, as yet, to regulate the divisions as in equity in Great-Britain; equity, therefore, in the supreme court for many years, will be mere discretion. I confess in the constitution of the supreme court, as left by the constitution, I do not see a spark of freedom or a shadow of our own or the British common law.

This court is to have appellate jurisdiction in all the other cases before mentioned: Many sensible men suppose that cases before-mentioned respect, as well the criminal cases as the civil ones, mentioned antecedently in the constitution, if so an appeal is allowed in criminal cases—contrary to the usual sense of law. How far it may be proper to admit a foreigner or the citizen of another state to bring actions against state governments, which have failed in performing so many promises made during the war, is doubtful: How far it may be proper so to humble a state, as to bring it to answer to an individual in a court of law, is worthy of consideration; the states are now subject to no such actions; and this new jurisdiction will subject the states, and many defendants to actions, and processes, which were not in the contemplation of the parties, when the contract was made; all engagements existing between citizens of different states, citizens and foreigners, states and foreigners; and states and citizens of other states were made the parties contemplating the remedies then existing on the laws of the states—and the new remedy proposed to be given in the federal courts, can be founded on no principle whatever.

CENTINEL II (SAMUEL BRYAN)
Philadelphia *Freeman's Journal*, 24 October 1787 (excerpt)*

Such a body as the intended Congress, unless particularly inhibited and restrained, must grasp at omnipotence, and before long swallow up the Legislative, the Executive, and the Judicial powers of the several States.

*This was the second of eighteen essays signed "Centinel" that appeared in the Philadelphia *Independent Gazetteer* and *Freeman's Journal* between 5 October and 9 April 1788. Contemporaries incorrectly attributed the essays to George Bryan, one of the leaders of the state

In addition to the respectable authorities quoted in my first number, to shew that the right of *taxation* includes all the powers of government, I beg leave to adduce the Farmer's Letters, see particularly letter 9th, in which Mr. Dickinson* has clearly proved, that if the British Parliament assumed the power of taxing the colonies, *internally*, as well as *externally*, and it should be submitted to, the several colony legislatures would soon become contemptible, and before long fall into disuse.—Nothing, says he, would be left for them to do, higher than to frame bye-laws for empounding of cattle or the yoking of hogs.

By the proposed plan, there are divers cases of judicial authority to be given to the courts of the United States, besides the two mentioned by Mr. *Wilson*.†—In maritime causes about property, jury trial has not been usual; but in suits in *equity*, with all due deference to Mr. *Wilson*'s professional abilities, (which he calls to his aid) jury trial, as to facts, is in full exercise. Will this jurisperitus say that if the question in equity should be, did *John Doe* make a will, that the chancellor of England would decide upon it? He well knows that in this case, there being no mode of jury trial before the chancellor, the question would be referred to the court of king's bench for discussion according to the common law, and when the judge in equity should receive the *verdict*, the fact so established, could never by re-examined or controverted. Maritime causes and those appertaining to a court of equity, are, however, but *two* of the many and extensive subjects of federal cognizance mentioned in the plan. This jurisdiction will embrace all suits arising under the laws of impost, excise and other revenue of the United States. In England if goods be seized, if a ship be prosecuted for non-compliance with, or breach of the laws of the customs, or those for regulating trade, in the court of exchequer, the claimant is secured of the transcendent privilege of Englishmen, *trial by a jury of his peers*. Why not in the United States of America? This jurisdiction also goes to all cases under the laws of the United States, that is to say, under all statutes and ordinances of Congress. How far this may extend, it is easy to foresee; for upon the decay of the state powers of legislation, in consequence of the loss of the *purse strings*, it will be found necessary for the federal legislature to make laws upon every subject of legislation. Hence the state courts of justice, like the barony and hundred courts of England, will be eclipsed and gradually fall into disuse.

Constitutionalist Party and a justice of the state supreme court. Samuel Bryan was his son, and was a clerk of the Assembly, 1784-86. "Centinel" II was reprinted six times by 13 December: Mass. (1), R.I. (1), N.Y. (2), Md. (1), Va. (1). It was also printed as a broadside in Philadelphia and New York, and in pamphlet anthologies in New York and Richmond.

*John Dickinson's "Letters from a Farmer in Pennsylvania" were printed in the *Pennsylvania Chronicle* in 1767–68.

†A reference to James Wilson's 6 October speech.

The jurisdiction of the federal court goes, likewise, to the laws to be created by treaties, made by the President and Senate, (a species of legislation) with other nations; "to all cases affecting foreign ministers and consuls; to controversies wherein the United States shall be a party; to controversies between citizens of different states,"* as when an inhabitant of *New-York* has a demand on an inhabitant of *New-Jersey.*—This last is a very invidious jurisdiction, implying an improper distrust of the impartiality and justice of the tribunals of the states. It will include all legal debates between foreigners in Britain, or elsewhere, and the people of this country.—A reason hath been assigned for it, viz. "That large tracts of land, in neighbouring states, are claimed under royal or other grants, disputed by the states where the lands lie, so that justice cannot be expected from the state tribunals."—Suppose it were proper indeed to provide for such case, why include all cases, and for all time to come? Demands as to land for 21 years would have satisfied this. A London merchant shall come to America, and sue for his supposed debt, and the citizen of this country shall be deprived of jury trial, and subjected to an appeal (tho' nothing but the *fact* is disputed) to a court 500 or 1000 miles from home; when if this American has a claim upon an inhabitant of England, his adversary is secured of the privilege of jury trial.—This jurisdiction goes also to controversies between any state and its citizens; which, though *probably* not intended, may hereafter be set up as a ground to divest the states, severally, of the trial of criminals; inasmuch as every charge of felony or misdemeanour, is a controversy between the state and a citizen of the same: that is to say, the state is plaintiff and the party accused is defendant in the prosecution. In all doubts about jurisprudence, as was observed before, the paramount courts of Congress will decide, and the judges of the state, being *sub graviore lege*, under the paramount law, must acquiesce.

Mr. *Wilson* says, that it would have been impracticable to have made a general rule for jury trial in the civil cases assigned to the federal judiciary, because of the want of uniformity in the mode of jury trial, as practised by the several states. This objection proves too much, and therefore amounts to nothing. If it precludes the mode of common law in civil cases, it certainly does in criminal. Yet in these we are told "the oppression of government is effectually barred by declaring that in all criminal cases *trial by jury* shall be preserved." Astonishing, that provision could not be made for a jury in civil controversies, of 12 men, whose verdict should be unanimous, *to be taken from the vicinage*; a precaution which is omitted as to trial of crimes, which may be any where in the state within which

*Article III, section 2.

they have been committed. So that an inhabitant of *Kentucky* may be tried for treason at *Richmond*.

The abolition of jury trial in civil cases, is the more considerable, as at length the courts of Congress will supersede the state courts, when such mode of trial will fall into disuse among the people of the United States.

The northern nations of the European continent, have all lost this invaluable privilege: *Sweden*, the last of them, by the artifices of the *aristocratic* senate, which depressed the king and reduced the house of commons to insignificance. But the nation a few years ago, preferring the absolute authority of a monarch to the *vexatious* domination of the *wellborn* few, an end was suddenly put to their power.

"The policy of this right of juries, (says judge Blackstone) to decide upon *fact*, is founded on this: That if the power of judging were entirely trusted with the magistrates, or any select body of men, named by the executive authority, their decisions, in spite of their own natural integrity, would have a biass towards those of their own rank and dignity; for it is not to be expected, that the *few* should be attentive to the rights of the *many*. This therefore preserves in the hands of the people, that share which they ought to have in the administration of justice, and prevents the encroachments of the more powerful and wealthy citizens."

The attempt of governor [Cadwallader] *Colden*, of New-York, before the revolution to re-examine the *facts* and re-consider the *damages*, in the case of *Forsey* against *Cunningham*, produced about the year 1764, a flame of patriotic and successful opposition, that will not be easily forgotten.

To manage the various and extensive judicial authority, proposed to be vested in Congress, there will be one or more inferior courts immediately requisite in each state; and laws and regulations must be forthwith provided to direct the judges—here is a wide door for inconvenience to enter. Contracts made under the acts of the states respectively, will come before courts acting under new laws and new modes of proceeding, not thought of when they were entered into.—An inhabitant of Pennsylvania residing at Pittsburgh, finds the goods of his debtor, who resides in Virginia, within the reach of his attachment; but no writ can be had to authorise the marshal, sheriff, or other officer of Congress, to seize the property, about to be removed, nearer than 200 miles: suppose that at Carlisle, for instance, such a writ may be had, mean while the object escapes. Or if an inferior court, whose judges have ample salaries, be established in every county, would not the expence be enormous? Every reader can extend in his imagination, the instances of difficulty which would proceed from this needless interference with the judicial rights of the separate states, and which as much as any other circumstance in the new plan, implies that the dissolution of their forms of government is designed.

AN OLD WHIG III
Philadelphia *Independent Gazetteer*, 20 October 1787 (excerpt)*

As to the trial by jury, the question may be decided in a few words. Any future Congress sitting under the authority of the proposed new constitution, may, if they chuse, enact that there shall be no more trial by jury, in any of the United States; except in the trial of crimes; and this "SUPREME LAW" will at once annul the trial by jury, in all other cases. The author of the speech† supposes that no danger "can possibly ensue, since the proceedings of the supreme court are to be regulated by the Congress, which is a faithful representation of the people; and the oppression of government is effectually barred; by declaring that in all criminal cases the trial by jury shall be preserved." Let us examine the last clause of this sentence first.—I know that an affected indifference to the trial by jury has been expressed, by some persons high in the confidence of the present ruling party in some of the states;—and yet for my own part I cannot change the opinion I had early formed of the excellence of this mode of trial even in civil causes. On the other hand I have no doubt that whenever a settled plan shall be formed for the extirpation of liberty, the banishment of jury trials will be one of the means adopted for the purpose.—But how is it that "the oppression of government is effectually barred by declaring that in all criminal cases the trial by jury shall be preserved?"—Are there not a thousand civil cases in which the government is a party?—In all actions for penalties, forfeitures and public debts, as well as many others, the government is a party and the whole weight of government is thrown into the scale of the prosecution yet these are all of them civil causes.— These penalties, forfeitures and demands of public debts may be multiplied at the will and pleasure of government.—These modes of harrassing the subject have perhaps been more effectual than direct criminal prosecutions.—In the reign of Henry the Seventh of England, Empson and Dudley acquired an infamous immortality by these prosecutions for penalties and forfeitures:—Yet all these prosecutions were in the form of civil actions; they are undoubtedly objects highly alluring to a government.—They fill the public coffers and enable government to reward its minions at a cheap rate.—They are a profitable kind of revenge and gratify the officers about

---

*Reprinted: *New York Journal*, 1 December.
†A reference to James Wilson's 6 October speech.

a court, who study their own interests more than corporal punishment.—
Perhaps they have at all times been more eagerly pursued than mere criminal prosecutions.—Shall trial by jury be taken away in all these cases and
shall we still be told that "we are effectually secured against the oppressions
of government?" At this rate Judges may sit in the United States, as they
did in some instances before the war, without a jury to condemn people's
property and extract money from their pockets, to be put into the pockets
of the judges themselves who condemn them; and we shall be told that
we are safe from the oppression of government.—No, Mr. Printer, we
ought not to part with the trial by jury; we ought to guard this and many
other privileges by a bill of rights, which cannot be invaded. The reason
that is pretended in the speech why such a declaration; as a bill of rights
requires, cannot be made for the protection of the trial by jury;—"that we
cannot with any propriety say 'that the trial by jury shall be as heretofore' "
in the case of a federal system of jurisprudence, is almost too contemptible
to merit notice.—Is this the only form of words that language could afford
on such an important occasion? Or if it were to what did these words
refer when adopted in the constitutions of the states?—Plainly sir, to the
trial by juries as established by the common law of England in the state
of its purity;—That common law for which we contended so eagerly at
the time of the revolution, and which now after the interval of a very few
years, by the proposed new constitution we seem ready to abandon forever;
at least in that article which is the most invaluable part of it; the trial by
jury.

DISSENT OF THE MINORITY OF THE PENNSYLVANIA CONVENTION
(SAMUEL BRYAN)
Pennsylvania Packet, 18 December 1787 (excerpt)*

We have before noticed the judicial power as it would effect a consolidation of the states into one government; we will now examine it, as
it would affect the liberties and welfare of the people, supposing such a
government were practicable and proper.

The judicial power, under the proposed constitution, is founded on
the well-known principles of the *civil law*, by which the judge determines

*The Pennsylvania Convention ratified the Constitution on 12 December 1787 by a vote
of 46–23. On 18 December this dissent was published in the *Pennsylvania Packet* and as a broadside.
It was signed by twenty-one of the twenty-three dissenters. The Dissent was reprinted in thirteen
newspapers by 14 March 1788: R.I. (2), N.Y. (3), Pa. (6), Va. (1), S.C. (1), and in the Philadelphia
American Museum, a nationally circulated magazine. It was also published in an anthology and
as pamphlets in Boston and Richmond.

both on law and fact, and appeals are allowed from the inferior tribunals to the superior, upon the whole question; so that *facts* as well as *law*, would be re-examined, and even new facts brought forward in the court of appeals; and to use the words of a very eminent Civilian—"The cause is many times another thing before the court of appeals, than what it was at the time of the first sentence."

That this mode of proceeding is the one which must be adopted under this constitution, is evident from the following circumstances:—1st. That the trial by jury, which is the grand characteristic of the common law, is secured by the constitution, only in criminal cases.—2d. That the appeal from both *law* and *fact* is expressly established, which is utterly inconsistent with the principles of the common law, and trials by jury. The only mode in which an appeal from law and fact can be established, is, by adopting the principles and practice of the civil law; unless the United States should be drawn into the absurdity of calling and swearing juries, merely for the purpose of contradicting their verdicts, which would render juries contemptible and worse than useless.—3d. That the courts to be established would decide on all cases *of law and equity*, which is a well known characteristic of the civil law, and these courts would have conusance [cognizance] not only of the laws of the United States and of treaties, and of cases affecting ambassadors, but of all cases of *admiralty and maritime jurisdiction*, which last are matters belonging exclusively to the civil law, in every nation in Christendom.

Not to enlarge upon the loss of the invaluable right of trial by an unbiassed jury, so dear to every friend of liberty, the monstrous expence and inconveniences of the mode of proceeding to be adopted, are such as will prove intolerable to the people of this country. The lengthy proceedings of the civil law courts in the chancery of England, and in the courts of Scotland and France, are such that few men of moderate fortune can endure the expence of; the poor man must therefore submit to the wealthy. Length of purse will too often prevail against right and justice. For instance, we are told by the learned judge *Blackstone*, that a question only on the property of an *ox*, of the value of *three* guineas, originating under the civil law proceedings in Scotland, after many interlocutory orders and sentences below, was carried at length from the court of sessions, the highest court in that part of Great Britain, by way of *appeal* to the house of lords, where the question of law and fact was finally determined. He adds, that no pique or spirit could in the court of king's bench or common pleas at Westminster, have given continuance to such a cause for a tenth part of the time, nor have cost a twentieth part of the expence. Yet the costs in the courts of king's bench and common pleas in England, are infinitely greater than those which the people of this country have ever experienced. We abhor the idea of losing the transcendant privilege of trial by jury, with the loss of which, it is remarked by the same learned author, that in Sweden, the liberties of the commons were extinguished by an aristocratic senate: and that *trial by jury* and the liberty of the people went out together. At the same time we regret the intolerable delay, the enormous expences and infinite vexation to which the people of this country will be exposed from the voluminous proceedings of the courts of civil law, and especially from the appellate jurisdiction, by means of which a man may be drawn from the utmost boundaries of this extensive country to the seat of the supreme court of the nation to contend, perhaps with a wealthy and powerful adversary. The consequence of this establishment will be an absolute confirmation of the power of aristocratical influence in the courts of justice; for the common people will not be able to contend or struggle against it.

Trial by jury in criminal cases may also be excluded by declaring that the libeller for instance shall be liable to an action of debt for a specified sum; thus evading the common law prosecution by indictment and trial by jury. And the common course of proceeding against a ship for breach of revenue laws by information (which will be classed among civil causes) will at the civil law be within the resort of a court, where no jury intervenes. Besides, the benefit of jury trial, in cases of a criminal nature, which cannot be evaded, will be rendered of little value, by calling the accused to answer far from home; there being no provision that the trial be by a jury of the neighbourhood or country. Thus an inhabitant of Pittsburgh, on a charge of crime committed on the banks of the Ohio, may be obliged to defend himself at the side of the Delaware, and so *vice versa*. To conclude this head: we observe that the judges of the courts of Congress would not be independent, as they are not debarred from holding other offices, during the pleasure of the president and senate, and as they may derive their support in part from fees, alterable by the legislature.

Federalist

PUBLIUS: THE FEDERALIST 78 (ALEXANDER HAMILTON)
28 May 1788*

We proceed now to an examination of the judiciary department of the proposed government.

In unfolding the defects of the existing confederation, the utility and necessity of a federal judicature have been clearly pointed out. It is the less necessary to recapitulate the considerations there urged; as the propriety of the institution in the abstract is not disputed: The only questions which have been raised being relative to the manner of constituting it, and to its extent. To these points therefore our observations shall be confined.

The manner of constituting it seems to embrace these several objects—1st. The mode of appointing the judges—2d. The tenure by which they are to hold their place—3d. The partition of the judiciary authority between different courts, and their relations to each other.

First. As to the mode of appointing the judges: This is the same with that of appointing the officers of the union in general, and has been so fully discussed in the two last numbers, that nothing can be said here which would not be useless repetition.

Second. As to the tenure by which the judges are to hold their places: This chiefly concerns their duration in office; the provisions for their support; and the precautions for their responsibility.

According to the plan of the convention, all the judges who may be appointed by the United States are to hold their offices *during good behaviour*, which is conformable to the most approved of the state constitutions; and among the rest, to that of this state. Its propriety having been drawn into question by the adversaries of that plan, is no light symptom of the rage for objection which disorders their imaginations and judgments. The standard of good behaviour for the continuance in office of the judicial magistracy is certainly one of the most valuable of the modern improvements in the practice of government. In a monarchy it is an excellent barrier to the despotism of the prince: In a republic it is a no less excellent barrier to the encroachments and oppressions of the representative body. And it is the best expedient which can be devised in any government, to secure a steady, upright and impartial administration of the laws.

*Reprinted: New York *Independent Journal*, 14 June; *New York Packet*, 17, 20 June.

Whoever attentively considers the different departments of power must perceive, that in a government in which they are separated from each other, the judiciary, from the nature of its functions, will always be the least dangerous to the political rights of the constitution; because it will be least in a capacity to annoy or injure them. The executive not only dispenses the honors, but holds the sword of the community. The legislative not only commands the purse, but prescribes the rules by which the duties and rights of every citizen are to be regulated. The judiciary on the contrary has no influence over either the sword or the purse, no direction either of the strength or of the wealth of the society, and can take no active resolution whatever. It may truly be said to have neither FORCE nor WILL, but merely judgment; and must ultimately depend upon the aid of the executive arm even for the efficacy of its judgments.

This simple view of the matter suggests several important consequences. It proves incontestibly that the judiciary is beyond comparison the weakest of the three departments of power;[a] that it can never attack with success either of the other two; and that all possible care is requisite to enable it to defend itself against their attacks. It equally proves, that though individual oppression may now and then proceed from the courts of justice, the general liberty of the people can never be endangered from that quarter: I mean, so long as the judiciary remains truly distinct from both the legislative and executive. For I agree that "there is no liberty, if the power of judging be not separated from the legislative and executive powers."[b] And it proves, in the last place, that as liberty can have nothing to fear from the judiciary alone, but would have every thing to fear from its union with either of the other departments; that as all the effects of such an union must ensue from a dependence of the former on the latter, notwithstanding a nominal and apparent separation; that as from the natural feebleness of the judiciary, it is in continual jeopardy of being overpowered, awed or influenced by its coordinate branches; and that as nothing can contribute so much to its firmness and independence, as permanency in office, this quality may therefore be justly regarded as an indispensable ingredient in its constitution; and in a great measure as the citadel of the public justice and the public security.

The complete independence of the courts of justice is peculiarly essential in a limited constitution. By a limited constitution I understand one which contains certain specified exceptions to the legislative authority;

[a]The celebrated Montesquieu speaking of them says, "of the three powers above mentioned, the JUDICIARY is next to nothing." Spirit of Laws, vol. I, page 186.

[b]Idem. page 181.

such for instance as that it shall pass no bills of attainder, no *ex post facto* laws, and the like. Limitations of this kind can be preserved in practice no other way than through the medium of the courts of justice; whose duty it must be to declare all acts contrary to the manifest tenor of the constitution void. Without this, all the reservations of particular rights or privileges would amount to nothing.

Some perplexity respecting the right of the courts to pronounce legislative acts void, because contrary to the constitution, has arisen from an imagination that the doctrine would imply a superiority of the judiciary to the legislative power. It is urged that the authority which can declare the acts of another void, must necessarily be superior to the one whose acts may be declared void. As this doctrine is of great importance in all the American constitutions, a brief discussion of the grounds on which it rests cannot be unacceptable.

There is no position which depends on clearer principles, than that every act of a delegated authority, contrary to the tenor of the commission under which it is exercised, is void. No legislative act therefore contrary to the constitution can be valid. To deny this would be to affirm that the deputy is greater than his principal; that the servant is above his master; that the representatives of the people are superior to the people themselves; that men acting by virtue of powers may do not only what their powers do not authorise, but what they forbid.

If it be said that the legislative body are themselves the constitutional judges of their own powers, and that the construction they put upon them is conclusive upon the other departments, it may be answered, that this cannot be the natural presumption, where it is not to be collected from any particular provisions in the constitution. It is not otherwise to be supposed that the constitution could intend to enable the representatives of the people to substitute their *will* to that of their constituents. It is far more rational to suppose that the courts were designed to be an inter-mediate body between the people and the legislature, in order, among other things, to keep the latter within the limits assigned to their authority. The interpretation of the laws is the proper and peculiar province of the courts. A constitution is in fact, and must be, regarded by the judges as a fundamental law. It therefore belongs to them to ascertain its meaning as well as the meaning of any particular act proceeding from the legislative body. If there should happen to be an irreconcileable variance between the two, that which has the superior obligation and validity ought of course to be prefered; or in other words, the constitution ought to be prefered to the statute, the intention of the people to the intention of their agents.

Nor does this conclusion by any means suppose a superiority of the judicial to the legislative power. It only supposes that the power of the people is superior to both; and that where the will of the legislature declared in its statutes, stands in opposition to that of the people declared in the constitution, the judges ought to be governed by the latter, rather than the former. They ought to regulate their decisions by the fundamental laws, rather than by those which are not fundamental.

This exercise of judicial discretion in determining between two contradictory laws, is exemplified in a familiar instance. It not uncommonly happens, that there are two statutes existing at one time, clashing in whole or in part with each other, and neither of them containing any repealing clause or expression. In such a case, it is the province of the courts to liquidate and fix their meaning and operation: So far as they can by any fair construction be reconciled to each other; reason and law conspire to dictate that this should be done: Where this is impracticable, it becomes a matter of necessity to give effect to one, in exclusion of the other. The rule which has obtained in the courts for determining their relative validity is that the last in order of time shall be preferred to the first. But this is mere rule of construction, not derived from any positive law, but from the nature and reason of the thing. It is a rule not enjoined upon the courts by legislative provision, but adopted by themselves, as consonant to truth and propriety, for the direction of their conduct as interpreters of the law. They thought it reasonable, that between the interfering acts of an *equal* authority, that which was the last indication of its will, should have the preference.

But in regard to the interfering acts of a superior and subordinate authority, of an original and derivative power, the nature and reason of the thing indicate the converse of that rule as proper to be followed. They teach us that the prior act of a superior ought to be prefered to the subsequent act of an inferior and subordinate authority; and that, accordingly, whenever a particular statute contravenes the constitution, it will be the duty of the judicial tribunals to adhere to the latter, and disregard the former.

It can be of no weight to say, that the courts on the pretence of a repugnancy, may substitute their own pleasure to the constitutional intentions of the legislature. This might as well happen in the case of two contradictory statutes; or it might as well happen in every adjudication upon any single statute. The courts must declare the sense of the law; and if they should be disposed to exercise WILL instead of JUDGMENT, the consequence would equally be the substitution of their pleasure to that of the legislative body. The observation, if it proved any thing, would prove that there ought to be no judges distinct from that body.

If then the courts of justice are to be considered as the bulwarks of a limited constitution against legislative encroachments, this consideration will afford a strong argument for the permanent tenure of judicial offices, since nothing will contribute so much as this to that independent spirit in the judges, which must be essential to the faithful performance of so arduous a duty.

This independence of the judges is equally requisite to guard the constitution and the rights of individuals from the effects of those ill humours which the arts of designing men, or the influence of particular conjunctures sometimes disseminate among the people themselves, and which, though they speedily give place to better information and more deliberate reflection, have a tendency in the mean time to occasion dangerous innovations in the government, and serious oppressions of the minor party in the community. Though I trust the friends of the proposed constitution will never concur with its enemies[c] in questioning that fundamental principle of republican government, which admits the right of the people to alter or abolish the established constitution whenever they find it inconsistent with their happiness; yet it is not to be inferred from this principle, that the representatives of the people, whenever a momentary inclination happens to lay hold of a majority of their constituents incompatible with the provisions in the existing constitution, would on that account be justifiable in a violation of those provisions; or that the courts would be under a greater obligation to connive at infractions in this shape, than when they had proceeded wholly from the cabals of the representative body. Until the people have by some solemn and authoritative act annulled or changed the established form, it is binding upon themselves collectively, as well as individually; and no presumption, or even knowledge of their sentiments, can warrant their representatives in a departure from it, prior to such an act. But it is easy to see that it would require an uncommon portion of fortitude in the judges to do their duty as faithful guardians of the constitution, where legislative invasions of it had been instigated by the major voice of the community.

But it is not with a view to infractions of the constitution only that the independence of the judges may be an essential safeguard against the effects of occasional ill humours in the society. These sometimes extend no farther than to the injury of the private rights of particular classes of citizens, by unjust and partial laws. Here also the firmness of the judicial magistracy is of vast importance in mitigating the severity, and confining the operation of such laws. It not only serves to moderate the immediate mischiefs of those which may have been passed, but it operates as a check upon the legislative body in passing them; who, perceiving that obstacles

[c]Vide Protest of the minority of the convention of Pennsylvania, Martin's speech, &c.

to the success of an iniquitous intention are to be expected from the scruples of the courts, are in a manner compelled by the very motives of the injustice they meditate, to qualify their attempts. This is a circumstance calculated to have more influence upon the character of our governments, than but few may be aware of. The benefits of the integrity and moderation of the judiciary have already been felt in more states than one; and though they may have displeased those whose sinister expectations they may have disappointed, they must have commanded the esteem and applause of all the virtuous and disinterested. Considerate men of every description ought to prize whatever will tend to beget or fortify that temper in the courts; as no man can be sure that he may not be to-morrow the victim of a spirit of injustice, by which he may be a gainer to-day. And every man must now feel that the inevitable tendency of such a spirit is to sap the foundations of public and private confidence, and to introduce in its stead, universal distrust and distress.

That inflexible and uniform adherence to the rights of the constitution and of individuals, which we perceive to be indispensable in the courts of justice, can certainly not be expected from judges who hold their offices by a temporary commission. Periodical appointments, however regulated, or by whomsoever made, would in some way or other be fatal to their necessary independence. If the power of making them was committed either to the executive or legislative, there would be danger of an improper complaisance to the branch which possessed it; if to both, there would be an unwillingness to hazard the displeasure of either; if to the people, or to persons chosen by them for the special purpose, there would be too great a disposition to consult popularity, to justify a reliance that nothing would be consulted but the constitution and the laws.

There is yet a further and a weighty reason for the permanency of the judicial offices; which is deducible from the nature of the qualifications they require. It has been frequently remarked with great propriety, that a voluminous code of laws is one of the inconveniencies necessarily connected with the advantages of a free government. To avoid an arbitrary discretion in the courts, it is indispensable that they should be bound down by strict rules and precedents, which serve to define and point out their duty in every particular case that comes before them; and it will readily be conceived from the variety of controversies which grow out of the folly and wickedness of mankind, that the records of those precedents must unavoidably swell to a very considerable bulk, and must demand long and laborious study to acquire a competent knowledge of them. Hence it is that there can be but few men in the society, who will have sufficient skill in the laws to qualify them for the stations of judges. And making the proper deductions for the ordinary depravity of human nature, the number must be still smaller of those who unite the requisite integrity with the requisite knowledge. These considerations apprise us, that the government can have no great option between fit characters; and that a temporary duration in office, which would naturally discourage such characters from quiting a lucrative line of practice to accept a seat on the bench, would have a tendency to throw the administration of justice into hands less able, and less well qualified to conduct it with utility and dignity. In the present circumstances of this country, and in those in which it is likely to be for a long time to come, the disadvantages on this score would be greater than they may at first sight appear; but it must be confessed that they are far inferior to those which present themselves under the other aspects of the subject.

Upon the whole there can be no room to doubt that the convention acted wisely in copying from the models of those constitutions which have established *good behaviour* as the tenure of their judicial offices in point of duration; and that so far from being blameable on this account, their plan would have been inexcuseably defective if it had wanted this important feature of good government. The experience of Great Britain affords an illustrious comment on the excellence of the institution.

PUBLIUS: THE FEDERALIST 80 (ALEXANDER HAMILTON)
28 May 1788*

To judge with accuracy of the proper extent of the federal judicature, it will be necessary to consider in the first place what are its proper objects.

It seems scarcely to admit of controversy that the judiciary authority of the union ought to extend to these several descriptions of causes. 1st. To all those which arise out of the laws of the United States, passed in pursuance of their just and constitutional powers of legislation; 2d. to all those which concern the execution of the provisions expressly contained in the articles of union; 3d. to all those in which the United States are a party; 4th. to all those which involve the PEACE of the CONFEDERACY, whether they relate to the intercourse between the United States and foreign nations, or to that between the States themselves; 5th. to all those which originate on the high seas, and are of admiralty or maritime jurisdiction; and lastly, to all those in which the state tribunals cannot be supposed to be impartial and unbiassed.

The first point depends upon this obvious consideration that there ought always to be a constitutional method of giving efficacy to consti-

*Reprinted: New York *Independent Journal*, 21 June; *New York Packet*, 27 June, 1 July.

tutional provisions. What for instance would avail restrictions on the authority of the state legislatures, without some constitutional mode of enforcing the observance of them? The states, by the plan of the convention are prohibited from doing a variety of things; some of which are incompatible with the interests of the union, and others with the principles of good government. The imposition of duties on imported articles, and the emission of paper money, are specimens of each kind. No man of sense will believe that such prohibitions would be scrupulously regarded, without some effectual power in the government to restrain or correct the infractions of them. This power must either be a direct negative on the state laws, or an authority in the federal courts, to over-rule such as might be in manifest contravention of the articles of union. There is no third course that I can imagine. The latter appears to have been thought by the convention preferable to the former, and I presume will be most agreeable to the states.

As to the second point, it is impossible by any argument or comment to make it clearer than it is in itself. If there are such things as political axioms, the propriety of the judicial power of a government being co-extensive with its legislative, may be ranked among the number. The mere necessity of uniformity in the interpretation of the national laws, decides the question. Thirteen independent courts of final jurisdiction over the same causes, arising upon the same laws, is a hydra in government, from which nothing but contradiction and confusion can proceed.

Still less need be said in regard to the third point. Controversies between the nation and its members or citizens, can only be properly referred to the national tribunals. Any other plan would be contrary to reason, to precedent, and to decorum.

The fourth point rests on this plain proposition, that the peace of the WHOLE ought not to be left at the disposal of a PART. The union will undoubtedly be answerable to foreign powers for the conduct of its members. And the responsibility for an injury ought ever to be accompanied with the faculty of preventing it. As the denial or perversion of justice by the sentences of courts, as well as in any other manner, is with reason classed among the just causes of war, it will follow that the federal judiciary ought to have cognizance of all causes in which the citizens of other countries are concerned. This is not less essential to the preservation of the public faith, than to the security of the public tranquility. A distinction may perhaps be imagined between cases arising upon treaties and the laws of nations, and those which may stand merely on the footing of the municipal law. The former kind may be supposed proper for the federal jurisdiction, the latter for that of the states. But it is at least problematical whether an unjust sentence against a foreigner, where the subject of controversy was wholly relative to the *lex loci*, would not, if unredressed, be an aggression upon his sovereign, as well as one which violated the stipulations in a treaty or the general laws of nations. And a still greater objection to the distinction would result from the immense difficulty, if not impossibility, of a practical discrimination between the cases of one complection and those of the other. So great a proportion of the cases in which foreigners are parties involve national questions, that it is by far most safe and most expedient to refer all those in which they are concerned to the national tribunals.

The power of determining causes between two states, between one state and the citizens of another, and between the citizens of different states, is perhaps not less essential to the peace of the union than that which has been just examined. History gives us a horrid picture of the dissentions and private wars which distracted and desolated Germany prior to the institution of the IMPERIAL CHAMBER by Maximilian, towards the close of the fifteenth century; and informs us at the same time of the vast influence of that institution in appeasing the disorders and establishing the tranquillity of the empire. This was a court invested with authority to decide finally all differences between the members of the Germanic body.

A method of terminating territorial disputes between the states, under the authority of the federal head, was not unattended to, even in the imperfect system by which they have been hitherto held together. But there are many other sources, besides interfering claims of boundary, from which bickerings and animosities may spring up among the members of the union. To some of these we have been witnesses in the course of our past experience. It will readily be conjectured that I allude to the fraudulent laws which have been passed in too many of the states. And though the proposed constitution establishes particular guards against the repetition of those instances which have heretofore made their appearance, yet it is warrantable to apprehend that the spirit which produced them will assume new shapes that could not be foreseen, nor specifically provided against. Whatever practices may have a tendency to disturb the harmony between the states, are proper objects of federal superintendence and control.

It may be esteemed the basis of the union, that "the citizens of each state shall be entitled to all the privileges and immunities of citizens of the several states."* And if it be a just principle that every government *ought to possess the means of executing its own provisions by its own authority,* it will follow, that in order to the inviolable maintenance of that equality of privileges and immunities to which the citizens of the union will be

*Article IV, section 2.

entitled, the national judiciary ought to preside in all cases in which one state or its citizens are opposed to another state or its citizens. To secure the full effect of so fundamental a provision against all evasion and subterfuge, it is necessary that its construction should be committed to that tribunal, which, having no local attachments, will be likely to be impartial between the different states and their citizens, and which, owing its official existence to the union, will never be likely to feel any bias inauspicious to the principles on which it is founded.

The fifth point will demand little animadversion. The most bigotted idolizers of state authority have not thus far shewn a disposition to deny the national judiciary the cognizance of maritime causes. These so generally depend on the laws of nations, and so commonly affect the rights of foreigners, that they fall within the considerations which are relative to the public peace. The most important part of them are by the present confederation submitted to federal jurisdiction.

The reasonableness of the agency of the national courts in cases in which the state tribunals cannot be supposed to be impartial, speaks for itself. No man ought certainly to be a judge in his own cause, or in any cause in respect to which he had the least interest or bias. This principle has no inconsiderable weight in designating the federal courts as the proper tribunals for the determination of controversies between different states and their citizens. And it ought to have the same operation in regard to some cases between the citizens of the same state. Claims to land under grants of different states, founded upon adverse pretensions of boundary, are of this description. The courts of neither of the granting states could be expected to be unbiassed. The laws may have even prejudged the question, and tied the courts down to decisions in favour of the grants of the state to which they belonged. And even where this had not been done, it would be natural that the judges, as men, should feel a strong predilection to the claims of their own government.

Having thus laid down and discussed the principles which ought to regulate the constitution of the federal judiciary, we will proceed to test, by these principles, the particular powers of which, according to the plan of the convention, it is to be composed. It is to comprehend, "all cases in law and equity arising under the constitution, the laws of the United States, and treaties made, or which shall be made under their authority; to all cases affecting ambassadors, other public ministers and consuls; to all cases of admiralty and maritime jurisdiction; to controversies to which the United States shall be a party; to controversies between two or more states, between a state and citizens of another state, between citizens of different states, between citizens of the same state claiming lands under grants of different states, and between a state or the citizens thereof, and foreign states, citizens and subjects."* This constitutes the entire mass of the judicial authority of the union. Let us now review it in detail. It is then to extend,

First. To all cases in law and equity *arising under the constitution* and *the laws of the United States.* This corresponds to the two first classes of causes which have been enumerated as proper for the jurisdiction of the United States. It has been asked what is meant by "cases arising under the constitution," in contradistinction from those "arising under the laws of the United States." The difference has been already explained. All the restrictions upon the authority of the state legislatures, furnish examples of it. They are not, for instance, to emit paper money; but the interdiction results from the constitution, and will have no connection with any law of the United States. Should paper money, notwithstanding, be emitted, the controversies concerning it would be cases arising upon the constitution, and not upon the laws of the United States, in the ordinary signification of the terms. This may serve as a sample of the whole.

It has also been asked, what need of the word "equity"? What equitable causes can grow out of the constitution and laws of the United States? There is hardly a subject of litigation between individuals, which may not involve those ingredients of *fraud, accident, trust* or *hardship,* which would render the matter an object of equitable, rather than of legal jurisdiction, as the distinction is known and established in several of the states. It is the peculiar province, for instance, of a court of equity to relieve against what are called hard bargains: These are contracts, in which, though there may have been no direct fraud or deceit, sufficient to invalidate them in a court of law; yet there may have been some undue and unconscionable advantage taken of the necessities or misfortunes of one of the parties, which a court of equity would not tolerate. In such cases, where foreigners were concerned on either side, it would be impossible for the federal judicatories to do justice without an equitable, as well as a legal jurisdiction. Agreements to convey lands claimed under the grants of different states, may afford another example of the necessity of an equitable jurisdiction in the federal courts. This reasoning may not be so palpable in those states where the formal and technical distinction between LAW and EQUITY is not maintained as in this state, where it is exemplified by every day's practice.

The judiciary authority of the union is to extend—

Second. To treaties made, or which shall be made under the authority of the United States, and to all cases affecting ambassadors, other public ministers and consuls. These belong to the fourth class of the enumerated

*Article III, section 2.

cases, as they have an evident connection with the preservation of the national peace.

Third. To cases of admiralty and maritime jurisdiction. These form altogether the fifth of the enumerated classes of causes proper for the cognizance of the national courts.

Fourth. To controversies to which the United States shall be a party. These constitute the third of those classes.

Fifth. To controversies between two or more states, between a state and citizens of another state, between citizens of different states. These belong to the fourth of those classes, and partake in some measure of the nature of the last.

Sixth. To cases between the citizens of the same state, *claiming lands under grants of different states.* These fall within the last class, and *are the only instance in which the proposed constitution directly contemplates the cognizance of disputes between the citizens of the same state.*

Seventh. To cases between a state and the citizens thereof, and foreign states, citizens, or subjects. These have been already explained to belong to the fourth of the enumerated classes, and have been shewn to be in a peculiar manner the proper subjects of the national judicature.

From this review of the particular powers of the federal judiciary, as marked out in the constitution, it appears, that they are all conformable to the principles which ought to have governed the structure of that department, and which were necessary to the perfection of the system. If some partial inconveniencies should appear to be connected with the incorporation of any of them into the plan, it ought to be recollected that the national legislature will have ample authority to make such *exceptions* and to prescribe such regulations as will be calculated to obviate or remove these inconveniencies. The possibility of particular mischiefs can never be viewed by a well-informed mind as a solid objection to a general principle, which is calculated to avoid general mischiefs, and to obtain general advantages.

PUBLIUS: THE FEDERALIST 81 (ALEXANDER HAMILTON)
28 May 1788 (excerpt)*

Let us resume the train of our observations; we have seen that the original jurisdiction of the supreme court would be confined to two classes of causes, and those of a nature rarely to occur. In all other causes of federal cognizance, the original jurisdiction would appertain to the inferior

*Reprinted: New York *Independent Journal*, 25, 28 June; *New York Packet*, 4, 8 July.

tribunals, and the supreme court would have nothing more than an appellate jurisdiction, "with such *exceptions*, and under such *regulations* as the congress shall make."

The propriety of this appellate jurisdiction has been scarcely called in question in regard to matters of law; but the clamours have been loud against it as applied to matters of fact. Some well intentioned men in this state, deriving their notions from the language and forms which obtain in our courts, have been induced to consider it as an implied supersedure of the trial by jury, in favour of the civil law mode of trial, which prevails in our courts of admiralty, probates and chancery. A technical sense has been affixed to the term "appellate", which in our law parlance is commonly used in reference to appeals in the course of the civil law. But if I am not misinformed, the same meaning would not be given to it in any part of New-England. There an appeal from one jury to another is familiar both in language and practice, and is even a matter of course, until there have been two verdicts on one side. The word "appellate" therefore will not be understood in the same sense in New-England as in New-York, which shews the impropriety of a technical interpretation derived from the jurisprudence of any particular state. The expression taken in the abstract, denotes nothing more than the power of one tribunal to review the proceedings of another, either as to the law or fact, or both. The mode of doing it may depend on ancient custom or legislative provision, (in a new government it must depend on the latter) and may be with or without the aid of a jury, as may be judged adviseable. If therefore the re-examination of a fact, once determined by a jury, should in any case be admitted under the proposed constitution, it may be so regulated as to be done by a second jury, either by remanding the cause to the court below for a second trial of the fact, or by directing an issue immediately out of the supreme court.

But it does not follow that the re-examination of a fact once ascertained by a jury, will be permitted in the supreme court. Why may it not be said, with the strictest propriety, when a writ of error is brought from an inferior to a superior court of law in this state, that the latter has jurisdiction of the fact, as well as the law? It is true it cannot institute a new enquiry concerning the fact, but it takes cognizance of it as it appears upon the record, and pronounces the law arising upon it.[a] This is jurisdiction of both fact and law, nor is it even possible to separate them. Though the common law courts of this state ascertain disputed facts by a jury, yet they unquestionably have jurisdiction of both fact and law; and

[a]This word is a compound of JUS and DICTIO, juris, dictio, or a speaking or pronouncing of the law.

accordingly, when the former is agreed in the pleadings, they have no recourse to a jury, but proceed at once to judgment. I contend therefore on this ground, that the expressions, "appellate jurisdiction, both as to law and fact," do not necessarily imply a re-examination in the supreme court of facts decided by juries in the inferior courts.

The following train of ideas may well be imagined to have influenced the convention in relation to this particular provision. The appellate jurisdiction of the supreme court (may it have been argued) will extend to causes determinable in different modes, some in the course of the COMMON LAW, and others in the course of the CIVIL LAW. In the former, the revision of the law only, will be, generally speaking, the proper province of the supreme court; in the latter, the re-examination of the fact is agreeable to usage, and in some cases, of which prize causes are an example, might be essential to the preservation of the public peace. It is therefore necessary, that the appellate jurisdiction should, in certain cases, extend in the broadest sense to matters of fact. It will not answer to make an express exception of cases, which shall have been originally tried by a jury, because in the courts of some of the states, *all causes* are tried in this mode;[b] and such an exception would preclude the revision of matters of fact, as well where it might be proper, as where it might be improper. To avoid all inconveniencies, it will be safest to declare generally, that the supreme court shall possess appellate jurisdiction, both as to law and *fact*, and that this jurisdiction shall be subject to such *exceptions* and regulations as the national legislature may prescribe. This will enable the government to modify it in such a manner as will best answer the ends of public justice and security.

This view of the matter, at any rate puts it out of all doubt that the supposed *abolition* of the trial by jury, by the operation of this provision, is fallacious and untrue. The legislature of the United States would certainly have full power to provide that in appeals to the supreme court there should be no re-examination of facts where they had been tried in the original causes by juries. This would certainly be an authorised exception; but if for the reason already intimated it should be thought too extensive, it might be qualified with a limitation to such causes only as are determinable at common law in that mode of trial.

The amount of the observations hitherto made on the authority of the judicial department is this—that it has been carefully restricted to those causes which are manifestly proper for the cognizance of the national

[b]I hold that the states will have concurrent jurisdiction with the subordinate federal judicatories, in many cases of federal cognizance, as will be explained in my next paper.

judicature, that in the partition of this authority a very small portion of original jurisdiction has been reserved to the supreme court, and the rest consigned to the subordinate tribunals—that the supreme court will possess an appellate jurisdiction both as to law and fact in all the cases refered to them, but subject to any *exceptions* and *regulations* which may be thought adviseable; that this appellate jurisdiction does in no case *abolish* the trial by jury, and that an ordinary degree of prudence and integrity in the national councils will insure us solid advantages from the establishment of the proposed judiciary, without exposing us to any of the inconveniencies which have been predicted from that source.

6

The Bill of Rights

ANTIFEDERALISTS ARGUED *that in a state of nature people were entirely free. In society some rights were yielded for the common good. But there were rights that were so basic and important that to give them up would be contrary to the common good. These rights, which should always be retained by the people, had to be precisely stated in the form of a bill of rights. A bill of rights would be a landmark, clearly defining limits for those in power, and would be a firebell for the people, enabling them at once to know when their rights were threatened.*

The protection of a bill of rights was especially important in the new Constitution, which was an original compact with the people. State bills of rights offered no protection from oppressive acts of the federal government because the Constitution, treaties and laws made in pursuance of the Constitution were declared the supreme law of the land. The Constitution, Antifederalists maintained, was so ambiguous and the powers that could be construed by implication were so broad that a bill of rights, a guidepost, was necessary.

Federalists rejected the proposition that a bill of rights was needed. They made a clear distinction between the state constitutions and the U.S. Constitution. Using the language of social compact, Federalists asserted that when the people formed their state constitutions, they delegated to the states all rights and power which were not explicitly reserved to the people. The state governments had authority to regulate even personal and private matters. But in the U.S. Constitution, the people or the states retained all rights and powers that were not positively granted to the federal government. In short, everything not given was reserved. The U.S. government had strictly delegated powers, limited to the general interests of the nation.

Therefore, Federalists argued, a bill of rights was not only unnecessary, but might even be dangerous. Unnecessary, because the new federal government could in no way endanger the freedom of the press or religion, for instance, since it was given no constitutional power to regulate either. Dangerous, because a listing of rights could be interpreted as inclusive. Rights omitted might be considered as not retained. And the listing of rights, such as freedom of the press, might imply that a power to regulate the press existed absent the provision.

Finally, Federalists believed that bills of rights were paper protections, useless just when they were most needed: in times of crisis they would be overridden. The people's rights are best secured not by bills of rights but by a representative form of government in which officeholders are responsible to the people, derive their power from the people, and would themselves suffer from the loss of basic rights.

Antifederalist

RICHARD HENRY LEE TO GOVERNOR EDMUND RANDOLPH
New York, 16 October 1787 (excerpts)*

DEAR SIR, I was duly honored with your favor of September 17th, from Philadelphia, which should have been acknowledged long before now, if the nature of the business that it related to had not required time.

The establishment of the new plan of government, in its present form, is a question that involves such immense consequences to the present times and to posterity, that it calls for the deepest attention of the best and wisest friends of their country and of mankind. If it be found good after mature deliberation, adopt it, if wrong, amend it at all events, for to say (as many do) that a bad government must be established for fear of anarchy, is really saying that we must kill ourselves for fear of dying. Experience and the actual state of things, shew that there is no difficulty

*Published in the Petersburg *Virginia Gazette*, 6 December (not extant). The text is taken from the *Pennsylvania Packet*, 20 December, the earliest known reprint. Between 20 December and 16 February 1788, the letter and amendments were reprinted in twelve newspapers from New Hampshire to Virginia. They also appeared in a pamphlet anthology in mid-December and in the Philadelphia *American Museum*, a nationally circulated magazine. Lee was one of the major political figures of the Revolutionary Era. It was he, as a Virginia delegate to Congress, who moved for independence from Great Britain on 7 June 1776. He assisted in devising the Articles of Confederation. In 1784-85, Lee served as president of Congress. He was appointed a delegate to the Constitutional Convention, but declined to serve because he was then still serving in Congress.

in procuring a general convention; the late one being collected without any obstruction: Nor does external war, or internal discord prevent the most cool, collected, full, and fair discussion of this all-important subject. If with infinite ease, a convention was obtained to prepare a system, why may not another with equal ease be procured to make proper and necessary amendments? Good government is not the work of a short time, or of sudden thought. From *Moses* to *Montesquieu* the greatest geniuses have been employed on this difficult subject, and yet experience has shewn capital defects in the system produced for the government of mankind. But since it is neither prudent or easy to make frequent changes in government, and as bad governments have been generally found the most fixed; so it becomes of the last consequence to frame the first establishment upon ground the most unexceptionable, and such as the best theories with experience justify; not trusting as our new constitution does, and as many approve of doing, to time and future events to correct errors, that both reason and experience in similar cases, point out in the new system. It has hitherto been supposed a fundamental maxim that in governments rightly balanced, the different branches of legislature should be unconnected, and that the legislative and executive powers should be separate:— In the new constitution, the president and senate have all the executive and two thirds of the legislative power. In some weighty instances (as making all kinds of treaties which are to be the laws of the land) they have the whole legislative and executive powers. They jointly, appoint all officers civil and military, and they (the senate) try all impeachments either of their own members, or of the officers appointed by themselves.

Is there not a most formidable combination of power thus created in a few, and can the most critic eye, if a candid one, discover responsibility in this potent corps? Or will any sensible man say, that great power without responsibility can be given to rulers with safety to liberty? It is most clear that the parade of impeachment is nothing to them or any of them—as little restraint is to be found, I presume from the fear of offending constituents.—The president is for four years duration (and Virginia for example) has one vote of thirteen in the choice of him, and this thirteenth vote not of the people, but electors, two removes from the people. The senate is a body of six years duration, and as in the choice of president, the largest state has but a thirteenth vote, so is it in the choice of senators.— This latter statement is adduced to shew that responsibility is as little to be apprehended from amenability to constituents, as from the terror of impeachment. You are, therefore, Sir, well warranted in saying, either a monarchy or aristocracy will be generated, perhaps the most grievous system of government may arise. It cannot be denied with truth, that this new constitution is, in its first principles, highly and dangerously oligarchic; and it is a point agreed that a government of the few, is, of all governments, the worst. The only check to be found in favor of the democratic principle in this system is, the house of representatives; which I believe may justly be called a mere shread or rag of representation: It being obvious to the least examination, that smallness of number and great comparative disparity of power, renders that house of little effect to promote good, or restrain bad government. But what is the power given to this ill constructed body? To judge of what may be for the general welfare, and such judgments when made, the acts of Congress become the supreme laws of the land. This seems a power co-extensive with every possible object of human legislation.—Yet there is no restraint in form of a bill of rights, to secure (what Doctor Blackstone calls) that residuum of human rights, which is not intended to be given up to society, and which indeed is not necessary to be given for any good social purpose.—The rights of conscience, the freedom of the press, and the trial by jury are at mercy. It is there stated, that in criminal cases, the trial shall be by jury. But how? In the state. What then becomes of the jury of the vicinage or at least from the county in the first instance, for the states being from 50 to 700 miles in extent? This mode of trial even in criminal cases may be greatly impaired, and in civil causes the inference is strong, that it may be altogether omitted as the constitution positively assumes it in criminal, and is silent about it in civil causes.—Nay, it is more strongly discountenanced in civil cases by giving the supreme court in appeals, jurisdiction both as to law and fact. Judge Blackstone in his learned commentaries, art. jury trial, says, it is the most transcendant privilege which any subject can enjoy or wish for, that he cannot be affected either in his property, his liberty, his person, but by the unanimous consent of 12 of his neighbours and equals. A constitution that I may venture to affirm has under providence, secured the just liberties of this nation for a long succession of ages.—The impartial administration of justice, which secures both our persons and our properties, is the great end of civil society. But if that be entirely *entrusted* to the magistracy, a select body of men, and those generally selected by the prince, or such as enjoy the highest offices of the state, these decisions in spite of their own natural integrity, will have frequently an involuntary bias towards those of their own rank and dignity. It is not to be expected from human nature, that the few should always be attentive to the good of the many. The learned judge further says, that every tribunal selected for the decision of *facts*, is a step towards establishing aristocracy; the most oppressive of all governments. The answer to these objections is, that the new legislature may provide remedies!— But as they may, so they may not, and if they did, a succeeding assembly may repeal the provisions.—The evil is found resting upon constitutional bottom, and the remedy upon the mutable ground of legislation, revocable at any annual meeting. It is the more unfortunate that this great security of human rights, the trial by jury, should be weakened in this system, as power is unnecessarily given in the second section of the third article, to call people from their own country in all cases of controversy about property between citizens of different states and foreigners, with citizens of the United States, to be tried in a distant court where the Congress may sit. For although inferior congressional courts may for the above purposes be instituted in the different states, yet this is a matter altogether in the pleasure of the new legislature, so that if they please not to institute them, or if they do not regulate the right of appeal reasonably, the people will be exposed to endless oppression, and the necessity of submitting in multitudes of cases, to pay unjust demands, rather than follow suitors, through great expence, to far distant tribunals, and to be determined upon there, as it may be, without a jury. . . . With the constitution came from the convention, so many members of that body to Congress, and of those too, who were among the most fiery zealots for their system, that the votes of three states being of them, two states divided by them, and many others mixed with them, it is easy to see that Congress could have little opinion upon the subject.* Some denied our right to make amendments, whilst others more moderate agreed to the right, but denied the expediency of amending; but it was plain that a majority was ready to send it on in terms of approbation—my judgment and conscience forbid the last, and therefore I moved the amendments that I have the honor to send you inclosed herewith, and demanded the yeas and nays that they might appear on the journal. This seemed to alarm and to prevent such appearance on the journal, it was agreed to transmit the constitution without a syllable of approbation of disapprobation; so that the term unanimously only applied to the transmission, as you will observe by attending to the terms of the resolve for transmitting. Upon the whole, Sir, my opinion is, that as this constitution abounds with useful regulations, at the same time that it is liable to strong and fundamental objections, the plan for us to pursue, will be to propose the necessary amendments, and express our willingness to adopt it with the amendments, and to suggest the calling of a new convention for the purpose of considering them. To this I see no well founded objection, but great safety and much good to be the probable result. I am perfectly satisfied that you make such use of this letter as you

---

*Lee had believed for some time that it was a conflict of interest for Convention delegates to sit in Congress and pass judgment on their work in the Convention. In fact, he had refused appointment to the Convention for this reason (to John Adams, 3 September 1787). On 27 October Lee wrote Samuel Adams that his concern on this matter had been "fully verified" by the events in Congress respecting the transmission of the Constitution to the states.

shall think to be for the public good; and now after begging your pardon for so great a trespass on your patience, and presenting my best respects to your lady, I will conclude with assuring you, that I am with the sincerest esteem and regard, dear Sir, your most affectionate and obedient servant, RICHARD HENRY LEE.

POSTSCRIPT.

It having been found from universal experience, that the most express declarations and reservations are necessary to protect the just rights and liberty of mankind from the silent, powerful and ever active conspiracy of those who govern; and it appearing to be the sense of the good people of America, by the various bills or declarations of rights whereon the government of the greater number of states are founded. That such precautions are necessary to restrain and regulate the exercise of the great powers given to rulers. In conformity with these principles, and from respect for the public sentiment on this subject, it is submitted,—That the new constitution proposed for the government of the United States be bottomed upon a declaration or bill of rights, clearly and precisely stating the principles upon which this social compact is founded, to wit: That the rights of conscience in matters of religion ought not to be violated—That the freedom of the press shall be secured—That the trial by jury in criminal and civil cases, and the modes prescribed by the common law for the safety of life in criminal prosecutions, shall be held sacred—That standing armies in times of peace are dangerous to liberty, and ought not to be permitted, unless assented to by two-thirds of the members composing each house of the legislature under the new constitution—That the elections should be free and frequent; That the right administration of justice should be secured by the independency of the judges; That excessive bail, excessive fines, or cruel and unusual punishments, should not be demanded or inflicted; That the right of the people to assemble peaceably, for the purpose of petitioning the legislature, shall not be prevented; that the citizens shall not be exposed to unreasonable searches, seizure of their persons, houses, papers or property. . . . That such parts of the new constitution be amended as provide imperfectly for the trial of criminals by a jury of the vicinage, and to supply the omission of a jury trial in civil causes or disputes about property between individuals, whereby the common law is directed, and as generally it is secured by the several state constitutions. That such parts of the new constitution be amended, as permit the vexatious and oppressive callings of citizens from their own country, and all controversies between citizens of different states and between citizens and foreigners, to be tried in a far distant court, and as it may be without a jury, whereby in a multitude of cases, the circumstances of distance and expence may compel numbers to submit to the most unjust and ill-founded demand—That in order to secure the rights of the people more effectually from violation, the power and respectability of the house of representatives be increased, by increasing the number of delegates to that house, where the popular interest must chiefly depend for protection— That the constitution be so amended as to increase the number of votes necessary to determine questions in cases where a bare majority may be seduced by strong motives of interest to injure and oppress the minority of the community, as in commercial regulations, where advantage may be taken of circumstances to ordain rigid and premature laws, that will in effect amount to monopolies, to the great impoverishment of those states whose peculiar situation expose them to such injuries.

AN OLD WHIG IV
Philadelphia *Independent Gazetteer*, 27 October 1787 (excerpt)*

In this country perhaps we are possessed of more than our share of political virtue. If we will exercise a little patience, and bestow our best endeavours on the business, I do not think it impossible, that we may yet form a federal constitution, much superior to any form of government, which has ever existed in the world;—but, whenever this important work shall be accomplished, I venture to pronounce, that it will not be done without a *careful attention to the framing of a bill of rights.*

Much has been said and written, on the subject of a bill of rights;— possibly without sufficient attention to the necessity of conveying distinct and precise ideas of the true meaning of a bill of rights. Your readers, I hope, will excuse me, if I conclude this letter with an attempt to throw some light on this subject.

Men when they enter into society, yield up a part of their natural liberty, for the sake of being protected by government. If they yield up all their natural rights they are absolute slaves to their governors. If they yield up less than is necessary, the government is so feeble, that it cannot protect them.—To yield up so much, as is necessary for the purposes of government; and to retain all beyond what is necessary, is the great point, which ought, if possible, to be attained in the formation of a constitution. At the same time that by these means, the liberty of the subject is secured, the government is really strengthened; because wherever the subject is

*Reprinted as a broadside in Philadelphia and in the Philadelphia *Freeman's Journal*, 31 October; *New York Morning Post*, 3 November; Baltimore *Maryland Gazette*, 6 November (excerpt); *Massachusetts Gazette*, 27 November; and *New York Journal*, 8 December.

convinced that nothing more is required from him, than what is necessary for the good of the community, he yields a chearful obedience, which is more useful than the constrained service of slaves.—To define what portion of his natural liberty, the subject shall at all times be entitled to retain, is one great end of a bill of rights. To these may be added in a bill of rights some particular engagements of protection, on the part of government, without such a bill of rights, firmly securing the privileges of the subject, the government is always in danger of degenerating into tyranny; for it is certainly true, that "in establishing the powers of government, the rulers are invested with every right and authority, which is not in explicit terms reserved."—Hence it is, that we find the rulers so often lording over the people at their will and pleasure. Hence it is that we find the patriots, in all ages of the world, so very solicitous to obtain explicit engagements from their rulers, stipulating, expressly, for the preservation of particular rights and privileges.

In different nations, we find different grants or reservations of privileges appealed to in the struggles between the rulers and the people, many of which in the different nations of Europe, have long since been swallowed up and lost by time, or destroyed by the arbitrary hand of power. In England we find the people, with the Barons at their head, exacting a solemn resignation of their rights from king John, in their celebrated *magna charta* [1215], which was many times renewed in Parliament, during the reigns of his successors. The *petition of rights* [1628] was afterwards consented to by Charles the first, and contained a declaration of the liberties of the people. The *habeus corpus act,* after the restoration of Charles the Second [1679], *the bill of rights* [1689], which was obtained from the Prince and Princess of Orange on their accession to the throne and the act of settlement [1701], at the accession of the Hanover family, are other instances to shew the care and watchfulness of that nation, to improve every opportunity, of the reign of a weak prince, or the revolution in their government, to obtain the most explicit declarations in favor of their liberties. In like manner the people of this country, at the revolution, having all power in their own hands, in forming the constitutions of the several states, took care to secure themselves by bills of rights, so as to prevent, as far as possible, the encroachments of their future rulers upon the rights of the people. Some of these rights are said to be *unalienable,* such as the rights of conscience: yet even these have been often invaded, where they have not been carefully secured by express and solemn bills and declarations in their favor.

Before we establish a government, whose acts will be THE SUPREME LAW OF THE LAND, and whose power will extend to almost every case without exception, we ought carefully to guard ourselves by a BILL OF

RIGHTS, against the invasion of those liberties which it is essential for us to retain, which it is of no real use to government to strip us of; but which in the course of human events have been too often insulted with all the wantonness of an idle barbarity.

BRUTUS II
New York Journal, 1 November 1787*

To the CITIZENS of the STATE of NEW-YORK.

I flatter myself that my last address established this position, that to reduce the Thirteen States into one government, would prove the destruction of your liberties.

But lest this truth should be doubted by some, I will now proceed to consider its merits.

Though it should be admitted, that the argument against reducing all the states into one consolidated government, are not sufficient fully to establish this point; yet they will, at least, justify this conclusion, that in forming a constitution for such a country, great care should be taken to limit and define its powers, adjust its parts, and guard against an abuse of authority. How far attention has been paid to these objects, shall be the subject of future enquiry. When a building is to be erected which is intended to stand for ages, the foundation should be firmly laid. The constitution proposed to your acceptance, is designed not for yourselves alone, but for generations yet unborn. The principles, therefore, upon which the social compact is founded, ought to have been clearly and precisely stated, and the most express and full declaration of rights to have been made—But on this subject there is almost an entire silence.

If we may collect the sentiments of the people of America, from their own most solemn declarations, they hold this truth as self evident, that all men are by nature free. No one man, therefore, or any class of men, have a right, by the law of nature, or of God, to assume or exercise authority over their fellows. The origin of society then is to be sought, not in any natural right which one man has to exercise authority over another, but in the united consent of those who associate. The mutual wants of men, at first dictated the propriety of forming societies; and when they were established, protection and defence pointed out the necessity of instituting government. In a state of nature every individual pursues his own interest; in this pursuit it frequently happened, that the possessions or enjoyments of one were sacrificed to the views and designs

*Reprinted in the Boston *Independent Chronicle*, 30 November.

of another; thus the weak were a prey to the strong, the simple and unwary were subject to impositions from those who were more crafty and designing. In this state of things, every individual was insecure; common interest therefore directed, that government should be established, in which the force of the whole community should be collected, and under such directions, as to protect and defend every one who composed it. The common good, therefore, is the end of civil government, and common consent, the foundation on which it is established. To effect his end, it was necessary that a certain portion of natural liberty should be surrendered, in order, that what remained should be preserved: how great a proportion of natural freedom is necessary to be yielded by individuals, when they submit to government, I shall not now enquire. So much, however, must be given up, as will be sufficient to enable those, to whom the administration of the government is committed, to establish laws for the promoting the happiness of the community, and to carry those laws into effect. But it is not necessary, for this purpose, that individuals should relinquish all their natural rights. Some are of such a nature that they cannot be surrendered. Of this kind are the rights of conscience, the right of enjoying and defending life, &c. Others are not necessary to be resigned, in order to attain the end for which government is instituted, these therefore ought not to be given up. To surrender them, would counteract the very end of government, to wit, the common good. From these observations it appears, that in forming a government on its true principles, the foundation should be laid in the manner I before stated, by expressly reserving to the people such of their essential natural rights, as are not necessary to be parted with. The same reasons which at first induced mankind to associate and institute government, will operate to influence them to observe this precaution. If they had been disposed to conform themselves to the rule of immutable righteousness, government would not have been requisite. It was because one part exercised fraud, oppression, and violence on the other, that men came together, and agreed that certain rules should be formed, to regulate the conduct of all, and the power of the whole community lodged in the hands of rulers to enforce an obedience to them. But rulers have the same propensities as other men; they are as likely to use the power with which they are vested for private purposes, and to the injury and oppression of those over whom they are placed, as individuals in a state of nature are to injure and oppress one another. It is therefore as proper that bounds should be set to their authority, as that government should have at first been instituted to restrain private injuries.

This principle, which seems so evidently founded in the reason and nature of things, is confirmed by universal experience. Those who have governed, have been found in all ages ever active to enlarge their powers and abridge the public liberty. This has induced the people in all countries, where any sense of freedom remained, to fix barriers against the encroachments of their rulers. The country from which we have derived our origin, is an eminent example of this. Their magna charta and bill of rights have long been the boast, as well as the security, of that nation. I need say no more, I presume, to an American, than, that this principle is a fundamental one, in all the constitutions of our own states; there is not one of them but what is either founded on a declaration or bill of rights, or has certain express reservation of rights interwoven in the body of them. From this it appears, that at a time when the pulse of liberty beat high and when an appeal was made to the people to form constitutions for the government of themselves, it was their universal sense, that such declarations should make a part of their frames of government. It is therefore the more astonishing, that this grand security, to the rights of the people, is not to be found in this constitution.

It has been said, in answer to this objection, that such declaration of rights, however requisite they might be in the constitutions of the states, are not necessary in the general constitution, because, "in the former case, every thing which is not reserved is given, but in the latter the reverse of the proposition prevails, and every thing which is not given is reserved."* It requires but little attention to discover, that this mode of reasoning is rather specious than solid. The powers, rights, and authority, granted to the general government by this constitution, are as complete, with respect to every object to which they extend, as that of any state government—It reaches to every thing which concerns human happiness—Life, liberty, and property, are under its controul. There is the same reason, therefore, that the exercise of power, in this case, should be restrained within proper limits, as in that of the state governments. To set this matter in a clear light, permit me to instance some of the articles of the bills of rights of the individual states, and apply them to the case in question.

For the security of life, in criminal prosecutions, the bills of rights of most of the states have declared, that no man shall be held to answer for a crime until he is made fully acquainted with the charge brought against him; he shall not be compelled to accuse, or furnish evidence against himself—The witnesses against him shall be brought face to face, and he shall be fully heard by himself or counsel. That it is essential to the security of life and liberty, that trial of facts be in the vicinity where they happen. Are not provisions of this kind as necessary in the general government, as in that of a particular state? The powers vested in the

---

*See James Wilson's 6 October speech, below.

new Congress extend in many cases to life; they are authorised to provide for the punishment of a variety of capital crimes, and no restraint is laid upon them in its exercise, save only, that "the trial of all crimes, except in cases of impeachment, shall be by jury; and such trial shall be in the state where the said crimes shall have been committed."* No man is secure of a trial in the county where he is charged to have committed a crime; he may be brought from Niagara to New-York, or carried from Kentucky to Richmond† for trial for an offence, supposed to be committed. What security is there, that a man shall be furnished with a full and plain description of the charges against him? That he shall be allowed to produce all proof he can in his favor? That he shall see the witnesses against him face to face, or that he shall be fully heard in his own defence by himself or counsel?

For the security of liberty it has been declared, "that excessive bail should not be required, nor excessive fines imposed, nor cruel or unusual punishments inflicted—That all warrants, without oath or affirmation, to search suspected places, or seize any person, his papers or property, are grievous and oppressive."

These provisions are as necessary under the general government as under that of the individual states; for the power of the former is as complete to the purpose of requiring bail, imposing fines, inflicting punishments, granting search warrants, and seizing persons, papers, or property, in certain cases, as the other.

For the purpose of securing the property of the citizens, it is declared by all the states, "that in all controversies at law, respecting property, the ancient mode of trial by jury is one of the best securities of the rights of the people, and ought to remain sacred and inviolable."

Does not the same necessity exist of reserving this right, under this national compact, as in that of this state? Yet nothing is said respecting it. In the bills of rights of the states it is declared, that a well regulated militia is the proper and natural defence of a free government—That as standing armies in time of peace are dangerous, they are not to be kept up, and that the military should be kept under strict subordination to, and controuled by the civil power.

The same security is as necessary in this constitution, and much more so; for the general government will have the sole power to raise and to pay armies, and are under no controul in the exercise of it; yet nothing of this is to be found in this new system.

I might proceed to instance a number of other rights, which were as necessary to be reserved, such as, that elections should be free, that

*Article III, section 2, clause 3.
†Kentucky was still part of Virginia.

the liberty of the press should be held sacred; but the instances adduced, are sufficient to prove, that this argument is without foundation.—Besides, it is evident, that the reason here assigned was not the true one, why the framers of this constitution omitted a bill of rights; if it had been, they would not have made certain reservations, while they totally omitted others of more importance. We find they have, in the 9th section of the 1st article, declared, that the writ of habeas corpus shall not be suspended, unless in cases of rebellion—that no bill of attainder, or expost facto law, shall be passed—that no title of nobility shall be granted by the United States, &c. If every thing which is not given is reserved, what propriety is there in these exceptions? Does this constitution any where grant the power of suspending the habeas corpus, to make expost facto laws, pass bills of attainder, or grant titles of nobility? It certainly does not in express terms. The only answer that can be given is, that these are implied in the general powers granted. With equal truth it may be said, that all the powers, which the bills of right, guard against the abuse of, are contained or implied in the general ones granted by this constitution.

So far it is from being true, that a bill of rights is less necessary in the general constitution than in those of the states, the contrary is evidently the fact.—This system, if it is possible for the people of America to accede to it, will be an original compact; and being the last, will, in the nature of things, vacate every former agreement inconsistent with it. For it being a plan of government received and ratified by the whole people, all other forms, which are in existence at the time of its adoption, must yield to it. This is expressed in positive and unequivocal terms, in the 6th article, "That this constitution and the laws of the United States, which shall be made in pursuance thereof, and all treaties made, or which shall be made, under the authority of the United States, shall be the supreme law of the land; and the judges in every state shall be bound thereby, any thing in the *constitution*, or laws of any state, *to the contrary* notwithstanding.

"The senators and representatives before-mentioned, and the members of the several state legislatures, and all executive and judicial officers, both of the United States, and of the several states, shall be bound, by oath or affirmation, to support this constitution."

It is therefore not only necessarily implied thereby, but positively expressed, that the different state constitutions are repealed and entirely done away, so far as they are inconsistent with this, with the laws which shall be made in pursuance thereof, or with treaties made, or which shall be made, under the authority of the United States; of what avail will the constitutions of the respective states be to preserve the rights of its citizens? should they be plead, the answer would be, the constitution of the United States, and the laws made in pursuance thereof, is the supreme law, and all legislatures and judicial officers, whether of the general or state governments, are bound by oath to support it. No priviledge, reserved by the bills of rights, or secured by the state government, can limit the power granted by this, or restrain any laws made in pursuance of it. It stands therefore on its own bottom, and must receive a construction by itself without any reference to any other—And hence it was of the highest importance, that the most precise and express declarations and reservations of rights should have been made.

This will appear the more necessary, when it is considered, that not only the constitution and laws made in pursuance thereof, but all treaties made, or which shall be made, under the authority of the United States, are the supreme law of the land, and supersede the constitutions of all the states. The power to make treaties, is vested in the president, by and with the advice and consent of two thirds of the senate. I do not find any limitation, or restriction, to the exercise of this power. The most important article in any constitution may therefore be repealed, even without a legislative act. Ought not a government, vested with such extensive and indefinite authority, to have been restricted by a declaration of rights? It certainly ought.

So clear a point is this, that I cannot help suspecting, that persons who attempt to persuade people, that such reservations were less necessary under this constitution than under those of the states, are wilfully endeavouring to deceive, and to lead you into an absolute state of vassalage.

John Smilie
Speech in Pennsylvania Ratifying Convention, 28 November 1787*

The arguments which have been urged, Mr. President, have not in my opinion, satisfactorily shewn that a bill of rights would have been an improper, nay, that it is not a necessary appendage to the proposed system. As it has been denied [by James Wilson] that Virginia possesses a bill of rights, I shall on that subject only observe, that Mr. [George] Mason, a gentleman certainly of great information and integrity, has assured me that such a thing does exist, and I am persuaded, I shall be able at a future period to lay it before the convention. But, Sir, the state of Delaware has a bill of rights, and I believe one of the honourable members (Mr. M'Kean) who now contests the necessity and propriety of that instrument, took a

*Pennsylvania Herald, 12 December 1787. John Smilie came from Ireland to Pennsylvania in 1760. He served in the state Assembly, 1784–86, and was a member of the Supreme Executive Council, 1786–89. He voted against the Constitution in the state Convention. Smilie later served in the U.S. House of Representatives as a Republican, 1793–95, 1799–1813.

very conspicuous part in the formation of the Delaware government. It seems however that the members of the federal convention were themselves convinced, in some degree, of the expediency and propriety of a bill of rights, for we find them expressly declaring that the writ of Habeas Corpus and the trial by jury in criminal cases shall not be suspended or infringed. How does this indeed agree with the maxim that whatever is not given is reserved? Does it not rather appear from the reservation of these two articles that every thing else, which is not specified, is included in the powers delegated to the government? This, sir, must prove the necessity of a full and explicit declaration of rights; and when we further consider the extensive, the undefined powers vested in the administrators of this system, when we consider the system itself as a great political compact between the governors and the governed, a plain, strong, and accurate, criterion by which the people might at once determine when, and in what instance, their rights were violated, is a preliminary, without which this plan ought not to be adopted. So loosely, so inaccurately are the powers which are enumerated in this constitution defined, that it will be impossible, without a test of that kind, to ascertain the limits of authority, and to declare when government has degenerated into oppression. In that event the contest will arise between the people and the rulers: "You have exceeded the powers of your office, you have oppressed us," will be the language of the suffering citizens. The answer of the government will be short—"We have not exceeded our power: you have no test by which you can prove it." Hence, Sir, it will be impracticable to stop the progress of tyranny, for there will be no check but the people, and their exertions must be futile and uncertain; since it will be difficult indeed, to communicate to them, the violation that has been committed, and their proceedings will be neither systematical nor unanimous. It is said, however, that the difficulty of framing a bill of rights was insurmountable: but, Mr. President, I cannot agree in this opinion. Our experience, and the numerous precedents before us, would have furnished a very sufficient guide. At present there is no security, even for the rights of conscience, and under the sweeping force of the sixth article every principle of a bill of rights, every stipulation for the most sacred and invaluable privileges of man, are left at the mercy of government.

ROBERT WHITEHILL
Speech in Pennsylvania Ratifying Convention, 28 November 1787*

... If indeed the constitution itself so well defined the powers of the government that no mistake could arise, and we were well assured that our governors, would always act right, then we might be satisfied without an explicit reservation of those rights with which the people ought not, and mean not to part. But, Sir, we know that it is the nature of power to seek its own augmentation, and thus the loss of liberty is the necessary consequence of a loose or extravagant delegation of authority. National freedom has been, and will be the sacrifice of ambition and power, and it is our duty to employ the present opportunity in stipulating such restrictions as are best calculated to protect us from oppression and slavery. Let us then, Mr. President, if other countries cannot supply an adequate example, let us proceed upon our own principles, and with the great end of government in view, the happiness of the people, it will be strange if we err. Government we have been told, sir, is yet in its infancy, we ought not therefore to submit to the shackles of foreign schools and opinions. In entering into the social compact, men ought not to leave their rulers at large, but erect a permanent land mark by which they may learn the extent of their authority, and the people be able to discover the first encroachments on their liberties.

Federalist

JAMES WILSON
Speech at a Public Meeting in Philadelphia, 6 October 1787
(excerpt)†

Mr. Chairman and Fellow Citizens, Having received the honor of an appointment to represent you in the late convention, it is perhaps, my duty to comply with the request of many gentlemen whose characters and

---

*Pennsylvania Herald, 12 December 1787. Robert Whitehill was born in Pennsylvania, the son of an immigrant from Northern Ireland. He helped to write the state constitution in 1776. He served in the state Assembly, 1776–78, 1783–87, and in the Supreme Executive Council, 1779–81. He voted against the Constitution in the state Convention. He again served in the legislature in the 1790s and was a Republican member of the U.S. House of Representatives, 1805–13.

†Pennsylvania Herald, 9 October (Extra). This speech was reprinted thirty-four times from Vermont to Georgia by 29 December. It was also reprinted in a four-page broadside anthology in Philadelphia, in the nationally circulated Philadelphia American Museum, and in a pamphlet anthology in Richmond, Va.

judgments I sincerely respect, and who have urged, that this would be a proper occasion to lay before you any information which will serve to explain and elucidate the principles and arrangements of the constitution, that has been submitted to the consideration of the United States. I confess that I am unprepared for so extensive and so important a disquisition; but the insidious attempts which are clandestinely and industriously made to pervert and destroy the new plan, induce me the more readily to engage in its defence; and the impressions of four months constant attention to the subject, have not been so easily effaced as to leave me without an answer to the objections which have been raised.

It will be proper however, before I enter into the refutation of the charges that are alledged, to mark the leading descrimination between the state constitutions, and the constitution of the United States. When the people established the powers of legislation under their separate governments, they invested their representatives with every right and authority which they did not in explicit terms reserve; and therefore upon every question, respecting the jurisdiction of the house of assembly, if the frame of government is silent, the jurisdiction is efficient and complete. But in delegating fœderal powers, another criterion was necessarily introduced, and the congressional authority is to be collected, not from tacit implication, but from the positive grant expressed in the instrument of union. Hence it is evident, that in the former case every thing which is not reserved is given, but in the latter the reverse of the proposition prevails, and every thing which is not given, is reserved. This distinction being recognized, will furnish an answer to those who think the omission of a bill of rights, a defect in the proposed constitution: for it would have been superfluous and absurd to have stipulated with a fœderal body of our own creation, that we should enjoy those privileges, of which we are not divested either by the intention or the act, that has brought that body into existence. For instance, the liberty of the press, which has been a copious source of declamation and opposition, what controul can proceed from the fœderal government to shackle or destroy that sacred palladium of national freedom? If indeed, a power similar to that which has been granted for the regulation of commerce, had been granted to regulate literary publications, it would have been as necessary to stipulate that the liberty of the press should be preserved inviolate, as that the impost should be general in its operation. With respect likewise to the particular district of ten miles, which is to be made the seat of fœderal government, it will undoubtedly be proper to observe this salutary precaution, as there the legislative power will be exclusively lodged in the president, senate, and house of representatives of the United States. But this could not be an object with the convention, for it must naturally depend upon a future compact, to which the citizens immediately interested will, and ought to be parties; and there is no reason to suspect that so popular a privilege will in that case be neglected. In truth then, the proposed system possesses no influence whatever upon the press, and it would have been merely nugatory to have introduced a formal declaration upon the subject—nay, that very declaration might have been construed to imply that some degree of power was given, since we undertook to define its extent.

A COUNTRYMAN II (ROGER SHERMAN)
New Haven Gazette, 22 November 1787*

To the PEOPLE of CONNECTICUT.

It is fortunate that you have been but little distressed with that torrent of impertinence and folly, with which the newspaper politicians have overwhelmed many parts of our country.

It is enough that you should have heard, that one party has seriously urged, that we should adopt the *New Constitution* because it has been approved by *Washington* and *Franklin*: and the other, with all the solemnity of apostolic address to *Men, Brethren, Fathers, Friends and Countrymen*, have urged that we should reject, as dangerous, every clause thereof, because that *Washington* is more used to command as a soldier, than to reason as a politician—*Franklin* is *old*—others are *young*—and *Wilson* is *haughty*. You are too well informed to decide by the opinion of others, and too independent to need a caution against undue influence.

Of a very different nature, tho' only one degree better than the other reasoning, is all that sublimity of *nonsense* and *alarm*, that has been thundered against it in every shape of *metaphoric terror*, on the subject of a *bill of rights*, the *liberty of the press, rights of conscience, rights of taxation and election, trials in the vicinity, freedom of speech, trial by jury*, and a *standing army*. These last are undoubtedly important points, much too important to depend on mere paper protection. For, guard such privileges by the strongest expressions, still if you leave the legislative and executive power in the hands of those who are or may be disposed to deprive you of them—you are but slaves. Make an absolute monarch—give him the

*This was the second of five essays that appeared in the *New Haven Gazette* between 15 November and 20 December. The last four were signed "A Countryman." This essay was reprinted in the *New York Journal*, 3 December; *New Jersey Journal*, 5 December; *Pennsylvania Gazette*, 26 December; and the *Massachusetts Gazette*, 11 January 1788. Roger Sherman was a New Haven lawyer. He was a delegate to Congress, 1774–81, 1783–84, and signed the Declaration of Independence and Articles of Confederation. He was a delegate to the Constitutional Convention and signed the Constitution. He served in the U.S. House of Representatives, 1789–91, and in the U.S. Senate, 1791–93.

supreme authority, and guard as much as you will by bills of right, your liberty of the press, and trial by jury;—he will find means either to take them from you, or to render them useless.

The only real security that you can have for all your important rights must be in the nature of your government. If you suffer any man to govern you who is not strongly interested in supporting your privileges, you will certainly lose them. If you are about to trust your liberties with people whom it is necessary to bind by stipulation, that they shall not keep a standing army, your stipulation is not worth even the trouble of writing. No bill of rights ever yet bound the supreme power longer than the *honey moon* of a new married couple, unless the *rulers were interested* in preserving the rights; and in that case they have always been ready enough to declare the rights, and to preserve them when they were declared.— The famous English *Magna Charta* is but an act of parliament, which every subsequent parliament has had just as much constitutional power to repeal and annul, as the parliament which made it had to pass it at first. But the security of the nation has always been, that their government was so formed, that at least *one branch* of their legislature must be strongly interested to preserve the rights of the nation.

You have a bill of rights in Connecticut (i.e.) your legislature many years since enacted that the subjects of this state should enjoy certain privileges. Every assembly since that time, could, by the same authority, enact that the subjects should enjoy none of those privileges; and the only reason that it has not long since been so enacted, is that your legislature were as strongly interested in preserving those rights as any of the subjects; and this is your only security that it shall not be so enacted at the next session of assembly: and it is security enough.

Your General Assembly under your present constitution are supreme. They may keep troops on foot in the most profound peace, if they think proper. They have heretofore abridged the trial by jury in some causes, and they can again in all. They can restrain the press, and may lay the most burdensome taxes if they please, and who can forbid? But still the people are perfectly safe that not one of these events shall take place so long as the members of the General assembly are as much interested, and interested in the same manner as the other subjects.

On examining the new proposed constitution, there can not be a question, but that there is authority enough lodged in the proposed federal Congress, if abused, to do the greatest injury. And it is perfectly idle to object to it, that there is no bill of rights, or to propose to add to it a provision that a trial by jury shall in no case be omitted, or to patch it up by adding a stipulation in favor of the press, or to guard it by removing the paltry objection to the right of Congress to regulate the time and manner of elections.

If you can not prove by the best of all evidence, viz. by the *interest of the rulers*, that this authority will not be abused, or at least that those powers are not more likely to be abused by the Congress, than by those who now have the same powers, you must by no means adopt the constitution:—No, not with all the bills of rights and all the stipulations in favour of the people that can be made.

But if the members of Congress are to be interested just as you and I are, and just as the members of our present legislatures are interested, we shall be just as safe, with even supreme power, (if that were granted) in Congress, as in the General Assembly. If the members of Congress can take no improper step which will not affect them as much as it does us, we need not apprehend that they will usurp authorities not given them to injure that society of which they are a part.

The sole question, (so far as any apprehension of tyranny and oppression is concerned) ought to be, how are Congress formed? how far are the members interested to preserve your rights? how far have you a controul over them?—Decide this, and then all the questions about their power may be dismissed for the amusement of those politicians whose business it is to catch flies, or may occasionally furnish subjects for *George Bryan's* POMPOSITY, or the declamations of *Cato—An Old Whig—Son of Liberty—Brutus—Brutus junior—An Officer of the Continental Army,*—the more contemptible *Timoleon*—and the residue of that rabble of writers.*

JAMES WILSON
Speech in Pennsylvania Ratifying Convention, 28 November 1787†

I am called upon to give a reason, why the convention omitted to add a bill of rights to the work before you. I confess, Sir, I did think that in point of propriety, the honourable gentleman [John Smilie] ought first to have furnished some reasons, to shew such an addition to be necessary; it is natural to prove the affirmative of a proposition; and if he had established the propriety of this addition, he might then have asked, why it was not made.

I cannot say, Mr. President, what were the reasons, of every member of that convention, for not adding a bill of rights; I believe the truth is,

---

*George Bryan of Pennsylvania was incorrectly believed to be the author of the "Centinel" essays, which were, like the other essays mentioned here, Antifederalist.

†Thomas Lloyd, comp. and ed., *Debates of the Convention, of the State of Pennsylvania on the Constitution, proposed for the Government of the United States* (Philadelphia, 1788), 41–44.

that such an idea never entered the mind of many of them. I don't recollect to have heard the subject mentioned, till within about three days of the time of our rising, and even then there was no direct motion offered for any thing of this kind.—I may be mistaken in this; but as far as my memory serves me, I believe it was the case. A proposition to adopt a measure, that would have supposed that we were throwing into the general government, every power not expressly reserved by the people, would have been spurned at, in that house, with the greatest indignation; even in a single government, if the powers of the people rest on the same establishment, as is expressed in this constitution, a bill of rights is by no means a necessary measure. In a government possessed of enumerated powers, such a measure would be not only unnecessary, but preposterous and dangerous: whence comes this notion, that in the United States there is no security without a bill of rights? Have the citizens of South-Carolina no security for their liberties? they have no bill of rights. Are the citizens on the eastern side of the Delaware less free, or less secured in their liberties, than those on the western side? The state of New-Jersey has no bill of rights.—The state of New-York has no bill of rights.—The states of Connecticut and Rhode-Island have no bills of rights.—I know not whether I have exactly enumerated the states who have thought it unnecessary to add a bill of rights to their constitutions; but this enumeration, Sir, will serve to shew by experience, as well as principle, that even in single governments, a bill of rights is not an essential or necessary measure.—But in a government, consisting of enumerated powers, such as is proposed for the United States, a bill of rights would not only be unnecessary, but, in my humble judgment, highly imprudent. In all societies, there are many powers and rights, which cannot be particularly enumerated. A bill of rights annexed to a constitution, is an enumeration of the powers reserved. If we attempt an enumeration, every thing that is not enumerated, is presumed to be given. The consequence is, that an imperfect enumeration would throw all implied power into the scale of the government; and the rights of the people would be rendered incomplete. On the other hand; an imperfect enumeration of the powers of government, reserves all implied power to the people; and, by that means the constitution becomes incomplete; but of the two it is much safer to run the risk on the side of the constitution; for an omission in the enumeration of the powers of government, is neither so dangerous, nor important, as an omission in the enumeration of the rights of the people.

Mr. President, as we are drawn into this subject, I beg leave to pursue its history a little further. The doctrine and practice of declarations of rights have been borrowed from the conduct of the people of England, on some remarkable occasion; but the principles and maxims, on which their government is constituted, are widely different from those of ours. I have already stated the language of magna charta. After repeated confirmations of that instrument, and after violations of it, repeated equally often, the next step taken in this business, was, when the petition of rights was presented to Charles the first.

It concludes in this manner, "all of which they most humbly *pray* to be allowed, as their rights and liberties, according to the laws and statutes of this realm." One of the most material statutes of the realm was magna charta; so that we find they continue upon the old ground, as to the foundation on which they rest their liberties. It was not till the æra of the revolution [of 1688], that the two houses assume an higher tone, and "*demand* and insist upon all the premises as their undoubted rights and liberties."[a] But when the whole transaction is considered, we shall find that those rights, and liberties, are claimed only on the foundation of an original contract, supposed to have been made at some former period, between the king and the people.[b]

But, in this constitution, the citizens of the United States appear dispensing a part of their original power, in what manner and what proportion they think fit. They never part with the whole; and they retain the right of re-calling what they part with. When, therefore, they possess, as I have already mentioned, the fee-simple of authority, why should they have recourse to the minute and subordinate remedies, which can be necessary only to those, who pass the fee, and reserve only a rent-charge?

To every suggestion concerning a bill of rights, the citizens of the United States may always say, WE reserve the right to do what we please.

[a]2 Par. Deb. 261. [John Torbuck, *A Collection of the Parliamentary Debates in England...*, 21 vols., London, 1741–1742), II, 261.]
[b]1 Blackstone, 233. [Blackstone, III, 233.]

PUBLIUS: THE FEDERALIST 84 (ALEXANDER HAMILTON) 28 May 1788 (excerpt)*

In the course of the foregoing review of the constitution I have taken notice of, and endeavoured to answer, most of the objections which have appeared against it. There however remain a few which either did not fall naturally under any particular head, or were forgotten in their proper places. These shall now be discussed; but as the subject has been

*Reprinted: New York *Independent Journal*, 26 July, 9 August; and *New York Packet*, 8, 12 August.

drawn into great length, I shall so far consult brevity as to comprise all my observations on these miscellaneous points in a single paper.

The most considerable of these remaining objections is, that the plan of the convention contains no bill of rights. Among other answers given to this, it has been upon different occasions remarked, that the constitutions of several of the states are in a similar predicament. I add, that New-York is of this number. And yet the opposers of the new system in this state, who profess an unlimited admiration for its constitution, are among the most intemperate partizans of a bill of rights. To justify their zeal in this matter, they alledge two things; one is, that though the constitution of New-York has no bill of rights prefixed to it, yet it contains in the body of it various provisions in favour of particular privileges and rights, which in substance amount to the same thing; the other is, that the constitution adopts in their full extent the common and statute law of Great-Britain, by which many other rights not expressed in it are equally secured.

To the first I answer, that the constitution proposed by the convention contains, as well as the constitution of this state, a number of such provisions.

Independent of those, which relate to the structure of the government, we find the following:—Article I. section 3. clause 7. "Judgment in cases of impeachment shall not extend further than to removal from office, and disqualification to hold and enjoy any office of honour, trust or profit under the United States; but the party convicted shall nevertheless be liable and subject to indictment, trial, judgment and punishment, according to law."—Section 9. of the same article, clause 2. "The privilege of the writ of *habeas corpus* shall not be suspended, unless when in cases of rebellion or invasion the public safety may require it."—Clause 3. "No bill of attainder or *ex post facto* law shall be passed."—Clause 7. "No title of nobility shall be granted by the United States: And no person holding any office of profit or trust under them, shall, without the consent of the congress, accept of any present, emolument, office or title, of any kind whatever, from any king, prince or foreign state."—Article III. section 2. clause 3. "The trial of all crimes, except in cases of impeachment, shall be by jury; and such trial shall be held in the state where the said crimes shall have been committed; but when not committed within any state, the trial shall be at such place or places as the congress may by law have directed."—Section 3, of the same article, "Treason against the United States shall consist only in levying war against them, or in adhering to their enemies, giving them aid and comfort. No person shall be convicted of treason unless on the testimony of two witnesses to the same overt act, or on confession in open court."—And clause 3, of the same section,

"The congress shall have power to declare the punishment of treason, but no attainder of treason shall work corruption of blood, or forfeiture, except during the life of the person attainted."

It may well be a question whether these are not upon the whole, of equal importance with any which are to be found in the constitution of this state. The establishment of the writ of *habeas corpus*, the prohibition of *ex post facto* laws, and of TITLES OF NOBILITY, *to which we have no corresponding provisions in our constitution*, are perhaps greater securities to liberty and republicanism than any it contains. The creation of crimes after the commission of the fact, or in other words, the subjecting of men to punishment for things which, when they were done, were breaches of no law, and the practice of arbitrary imprisonments have been in all ages the favourite and most formidable instruments of tyranny. The observations of the judicious Blackstone[a] in reference to the latter, are well worthy of recital. "To bereave a man of life (says he) or by violence to confiscate his estate, without accusation or trial, would be so gross and notorious an act of despotism, as must at once convey the alarm of tyranny throughout the whole nation; but confinement of the person by secretly hurrying him to goal, where his sufferings are unknown or forgotten, is a less public, a less striking, and therefore *a more dangerous engine* of arbitrary government." And as a remedy for this fatal evil, he is every where peculiarly emphatical in his encomiums on the *habeas corpus* act, which in one place he calls "the BULWARK of the British constitution."[b]

Nothing need be said to illustrate the importance of the prohibition of titles of nobility. This may truly be denominated the corner stone of republican government; for so long as they are excluded, there can never be serious danger that the government will be any other than that of the people.

To the second, that is, to the pretended establishment of the common and statute law by the constitution, I answer, that they are expressly made subject "to such alterations and provisions as the legislature shall from time to time make concerning the same." They are therefore at any moment liable to repeal by the ordinary legislative power, and of course have no constitutional sanction. The only use of the declaration was to recognize the ancient law, and to remove doubts which might have been occasioned by the revolution. This consequently can be considered as no part of a declaration of rights, which under our constitutions must be intended as limitations of the power of the government itself.

[a]Vide Blackstone's Commentaries, vol. 1, page 136.
[b]Idem, vol. 4, page 438.

It has been several times truly remarked, that bills of rights are in their origin, stipulations between kings and their subjects, abrigements of prerogative in favor of privilege, reservations of rights not surrendered to the prince. Such was MAGNA CHARTA [1215], obtained by the Barons, sword in hand, from king John. Such were the subsequent confirmations of that charter by subsequent princes. Such was the *petition of right* [1628] assented to by Charles the First, in the beginning of his reign. Such also was the declaration of right presented by the lords and commons to the prince of Orange in 1688, and afterwards thrown into the form of an act of parliament, called the bill of rights [1689]. It is evident, therefore, that according to their primitive signification, they have no application to constitutions professedly founded upon the power of the people, and executed by their immediate representatives and servants. Here, in strictness, the people surrender nothing, and as they retain every thing, they have no need of particular reservations. "WE THE PEOPLE of the United States, to secure the blessings of liberty to ourselves and our posterity, do *ordain* and *establish* this constitution for the United States of America." Here is a better recognition of popular rights than volumes of those aphorisms which make the principal figure in several of our state bills of rights, and which would sound much better in a treatise of ethics than in a constitution of government.

But a minute detail of particular rights is certainly far less applicable to a constitution like that under consideration, which is merely intended to regulate the general political interests of the nation, than to a constitution which has the regulation of every species of personal and private concerns. If therefore the loud clamours against the plan of the convention on this score, are well founded, no epithets of reprobation will be too strong for the constitution of this state. But the truth is, that both of them contain all, which in relation to their objects, is reasonably to be desired.

I go further, and affirm that bills of rights, in the sense and in the extent in which they are contended for, are not only unnecessary in the proposed constitution, but would even be dangerous. They would contain various exceptions to powers which are not granted; and on this very account, would afford a colourable pretext to claim more than were granted. For why declare that things shall not be done which there is no power to do? Why for instance, should it be said, that the liberty of the press shall not be restrained, when no power is given by which restrictions may be imposed? I will not contend that such a provision would confer a regulating power; but it is evident that it would furnish, to men disposed to usurp, a plausible pretence for claiming that power. They might urge with a semblance of reason, that the constitution ought not to be charged with the absurdity of providing against the abuse of an authority, which was not given, and that the provision against restraining the liberty of the press afforded a clear implication, that a power to prescribe proper regulations concerning it, was intended to be vested in the national government. This may serve as a specimen of the numerous handles which would be given to the doctrine of constructive powers, by the indulgence of an injudicious zeal for bills of rights.

On the subject of the liberty of the press, as much has been said, I cannot forbear adding a remark or two: In the first place, I observe that there is not a syllable concerning it in the constitution of this state, and in the next, I contend that whatever has been said about it in that of any other state, amounts to nothing. What signifies a declaration that "the liberty of the press shall be inviolably preserved?" What is the liberty of the press? Who can give it any definition which would not leave the utmost latitude for evasion? I hold it to be impracticable; and from this, I infer, that its security, whatever fine declarations may be inserted in any constitution respecting it, must altogether depend on public opinion, and on the general spirit of the people and of the government.[c] And here, after all, as intimated upon another occasion, must we seek for the only solid basis of all our rights.

There remains but one other view of this matter to conclude the point. The truth is, after all the declamation we have heard, that the constitution is itself in every rational sense, and to every useful purpose, A BILL OF RIGHTS. The several bills of rights, in Great-Britain, form its

---

[c]To show that there is a power in the constitution by which the liberty of the press may be affected, recourse has been had to the power of taxation. It is said that duties may be laid upon publications so high as to amount to a prohibition. I know not by what logic it could be maintained that the declarations in the state constitutions, in favour of the freedom of the press, would be a constitutional impediment to the imposition of duties upon publications by the state legislatures. It cannot certainly be pretended that any degree of duties, however low, would be an abrigement of the liberty of the press. We know that newspapers are taxed in Great-Britain, and yet it is notorious that the press no where enjoys greater liberty than in that country. And if duties of any kind may be laid without a violation of that liberty, it is evident that the extent must depend on legislative discretion, regulated by public opinion; so that after all, general declarations respecting the liberty of the press will give it no greater security than it will have without them. The same invasions of it may be effected under the state constitutions which contain those declarations through the means of taxation, as under the proposed constitution which has nothing of the kind. It would be quite as significant to declare that government ought to be free, that taxes ought not to be excessive, &c. as that the liberty of the press ought not to be restrained.

constitution, and conversely the constitution of each state is its bill of rights. And the proposed constitution, if adopted, will be the bill of rights of the union. Is it one object of a bill of rights to declare and specify the political privileges of the citizens in the structure and administration of the government? This is done in the most ample and precise manner in the plan of the convention, comprehending various precautions for the public security, which are not to be found in any of the state constitutions. Is another object of a bill of rights to define certain immunities and modes of proceeding, which are relative to personal and private concerns? This we have seen has also been attended to, in a variety of cases, in the same plan. Adverting therefore to the substantial meaning of a bill of rights, it is absurd to allege that it is not to be found in the work of the convention. It may be said that it does not go far enough, though it will not be easy to make this appear; but it can with no propriety be contended that there is no such thing. It certainly must be immaterial what mode is observed as to the order of declaring the rights of the citizens, if they are to be found in any part of the instrument which establishes the government. And hence it must be apparent that much of what has been said on this subject, rests merely on verbal and nominal distinctions, which are entirely foreign from the substance of the thing.

7

The Constitution: Debate Over Property, Class, and Government

THERE WERE SEVERAL MAJOR ECONOMIC
arguments made by the opposing parties in the debate over the Constitution. Federalists argued that the economy during the Confederation years was in disastrous condition and that the cause was the ineffective government under the Articles. The Confederation government was unable to coordinate a trade policy to respond to British restrictions on American commerce or to compel commercial treaties with other European powers. The Constitution, Federalists said, would permit a unified trade policy that would command respect from the world and permit retaliation against the British. This would benefit the merchant, the farmer, and the laborer. The state governments were engaged in economic policies—such as the emission of legal tender paper money and laws that prevented creditors from collecting debts owed to them—that protected dishonest debtors and violated the rights of property. These policies stifled economic incentives needed to restore prosperity. While the Confederation was powerless to stop these damaging policies, the Constitution by specific prohibitions on the states, would establish stable economic conditions that would protect and attract capital, thereby encouraging the growth of the American economy and restoring prosperity. The poor were the most hard hit by the policies of the states, and it was the poor who would benefit most from a rigorous government and the prosperity it would bring. Finally, Federalists argued that the new government, because of its complex structural checks and balances, would allow for the representation of all economic interests, but would allow none to dominate. Eco-

nomic factions, which had been ruinous to the political systems of other republics, would under the Constitution be controlled and constructive.

Antifederalists rejected these points of view. They denied that state economic policies were bad or that economic conditions were disastrous. They pointed out that the states were paying off state and national debts, that the prevalent condition of the country was widespread ownership of land, that property was secure, that the country was at peace, and that recovery from wartime destruction was steadily proceeding. The Confederation government was actually engaged in selling its huge national domain in the West and its credit was sufficiently sound to obtain a large loan from private Dutch bankers. Although Antifederalists favored retaliation against the British, they argued that the states were doing this on their own; to the extent that federal power had to be enhanced to allow coordinated trade policy, they favored a grant of specific power in the federal government to regulate trade and enact tariffs, but not the broad—they would argue unlimited—language of the Constitution to regulate commerce and impose taxes. Antifederalists were dubious that the myriad of economic interests in the country would be balanced and controlled by the government under the Constitution. They were persuaded that the new government would be dominated by a narrow aristocracy of the rich who would seek to control economic affairs so as to benefit themselves at everyone else's expense. A small House of Representatives of sixty-five members and a tiny Senate of twenty-six could never represent the many classes, occupations, and professions in America. Congress would be controlled by the wealthy and the lawyers to the exclusion of the broader population.

In short, Federalists and Antifederalists had different views of the state of the economy, of the appropriateness of state policies to deal with economic conditions, of the necessity for changing the Articles of Confederation to improve business and trade conditions, and of the ability of the Constitution to control economic factions or to allow the representation of the diverse economic interests of the people.

Outsiders View American Society

LOUIS GUILLAUME OTTO TO COMTE DE VERGENNES
New York, 10 October 1786*

My Lord. The Commissioners named by various States to propose a general plan of Commerce and to give to Congress the powers necessary to execute it were meeting in Annapolis over the last month. But, only five States being represented, they did not think they should broach the principal question, and they limited themselves to addressing to Congress and to the various Legislatures a report that characterizes the present spirit of this country's politics. In translating this report, I have taken care not only to put it into French but to render it intelligible. They endeavored to give the original an obscurity that the people will see through with difficulty, but which the powerful and enlightened Citizens will not fail to turn to account.

For a very long time, My Lord, they have felt the necessity of giving the federal Government more energy and vigor, but they have also felt that the excessive independence accorded to the Citizens with regard to the States, and to the States with regard to Congress, is too dear to individuals for them to be divested of it without great precautions. The people are not unaware that the natural consequences of a greater power accorded to the Government will be a regular collecting of taxes, a strict administration of justice, extraordinary duties on imports, strict actions against debtors, and lastly a marked preponderance of the rich men and the great proprietors. It is therefore in the interest of the people to preserve, as much as possible, the absolute liberty that was accorded to them at a time when they knew no other law than necessity, and when an English army laid, so to speak, the foundations of the political Constitution. It is in these tempestuous times that it was necessary to agree that all power should emanate only from the people, that everything be submitted to its supreme will, and that the Magistrates be only its servants.

Although there were no Patricians in America, there is a class of men known under the denomination of *Gentlemen*; who by their wealth, by their talents, by their education, by their families, or by the positions that they fill, aspire to a preeminence that the people refuse to accord them, and although several of these men have betrayed the interests of

---

*Correspondance Politique, États-Unis, Vol. 32, ff. 88–89, 94–95, Archives du Ministères des Affaires Étrangères, Paris, France. Otto had been France's chargé d'affaires since 1785 and continued to be its principal diplomat in America until the Comte de Moustier arrived as minister plenipotentiary in early 1788. Vergennes was France's Minister of Foreign Affairs.

their class in order to acquire popularity, there reigns among them a liaison all the more intimate, since they fear almost all the efforts of the people to despoil them of their possessions, and since they are in addition creditors, and consequently interested in strengthening the Government and attending to the execution of the laws. These men ordinarily pay the highest taxes, while the small proprietors escape the vigilance of the Collectors. Most of them being merchants, it is important to them to solidly establish the credit of the United States in Europe by the exact payment of debts and to have Congress given sufficiently extensive powers to make the people contribute thereto.

They have tried in vain, My Lord, by pamphlets and by other publications, to propagate notions of justice and of integrity, and to divest the people of a liberty of which they make such bad use. In proposing a new organization of the federal Government, they would have caused all minds to rebel. Ruinous circumstances for the Commerce of America have happily chanced to furnish the reformers a pretext to introduce some innovations. They represented to the people that the name American had become a disgrace among all the nations of Europe; that the flag of the United States was everywhere exposed to insults and vexations; that the farmer, no longer being able to freely export his produce, would soon be reduced to the last misery; that it was time to employ reprisals and to prove to foreign nations that the United States would not suffer this violation of the freedom of Commerce with impunity, but that vigorous measures could only be taken by unanimous Consent of the thirteen States and that, Congress not having the necessary powers, it was essential to form a general assembly charged to present it with the plan that it should adopt, and to indicate to it the means to execute it. The people, generally discontented with the difficulties of Commerce, and little suspecting the secret motives of their Antagonists, embraced this measure with ardor, and named Commissioners who were supposed to meet in Annapolis at the Commencement of September.

The authors of this proposition, My Lord, had no hope or even any desire to see this Assembly of Commissioners, which should only prepare a question much more important than that of Commerce, succeed. The measures were so well taken that at the end of September, there were no more than five States represented in Annapolis, and the Commissioners of the Northern States were held up for several days in New York in order to delay their arrival. The assembled States, after having waited almost three weeks, had broken up on the pretext that they were not numerous enough to enter into the matter, and to justify this dissolution, they sent the various Legislatures and Congress a report, of which I have the honor to send You the enclosed translation. In this document, the Commissioners make use of an infinity of circumlocutions and ambiguous phrases to explain to their constituents the impossibility of taking into consideration a general plan of Commerce and the powers relative thereto without touching at the same time on other objects intimately connected with the prosperity and the national importance of the United States. Without naming these objects, the Commissioners elaborate on the present crisis of public affairs, on the dangers to which the confederation is exposed, on the discredit of the United States in foreign countries, and on the necessity of reconciling under a single point of view the interests of all the States. They conclude by proposing for the month of May next a new Assembly of Commissioners charged not only with deliberating on a general plan of Commerce, but *on other matters that might interest the harmony and the well-being of the States and on the means of adapting the federal Government to the needs of the union.* In spite of the obscurity of this document, You will perceive, My Lord, that the Commissioners do not wish to take into consideration the grievances of Commerce, infinitely interesting to the people, without perfecting at the same time the fundamental constitution of Congress. It is hoped that new Commissioners will be named with powers sufficiently extensive to deliberate on these important subjects and to put Congress in a position not only to approve resolutions for the prosperity of the union, but to execute them.

COMTE DE MOUSTIER TO COMTE DE MONTMORIN
New York, 2 August 1788 (excerpt)*

The State of New York on the 25th of last month finally acceded to the new Constitution, which is now adopted by eleven States. The recommended amendments are so numerous and so important that if the new Congress takes them into account, this Constitution will barely resemble its first form. However, a great blow has been dealt to the individual Sovereignty of the States taken separately. The phantom of Democracy that has seduced the people is about to disappear. The credulous majority, intoxicated by the noblest hopes that it allowed itself to be fed, has itself forged the bonds by which sooner or later the Leaders of the people will be able to subjugate and control them after having appeared to want to obey them. The Constitution is taken on approval until a better one is found. This tendency always to perfect is infinitely favorable to the designs of the ambitious, who, by means of alterations, will manage to weary

*Correspondance Politique, États-Unis, Vol. 33, ff. 238–41, Archives du Ministères des Affaires Étrangères, Paris, France. Moustier arrived in New York City in January 1788 as France's minister to the United States. Montmorin had succeeded Vergennes as France's Minister of Foreign Affairs.

the American people and make them receive with indifference the yoke that is prepared for them and that they will probably endure much more patiently than expected. The proposed amendments offer a multitude of pretexts at the outset even for a reorganization of Government. This means is open to various parties. It is not doubted that each will profit from it according to its views.

Antifederalists

FEDERAL FARMER
c. 8 November 1787 (excerpts)*

The first principal question that occurs, is, Whether, considering our situation, we ought to precipitate the adoption of the proposed constitution? If we remain cool and temperate, we are in no immediate danger of any commotions; we are in a state of perfect peace, and in no danger of invasions; the state governments are in the full exercise of their powers; and our governments answer all present exigencies, except the regulation of trade, securing credit, in some cases, and providing for the interest, in some instances, of the public debts; and whether we adopt a change, three or nine months hence, can make but little odds with the private circumstances of individuals; their happiness and prosperity, after all, depend principally upon their own exertions. We are hardly recovered from a long and distressing war: The farmers, fishmen, &c. have not yet fully repaired the waste made by it. Industry and frugality are again assuming their proper station. Private debts are lessened, and public debts incurred by the war, have been, by various ways, diminished; and the public lands have now become a productive source for diminishing them much more. I know uneasy men, who wish very much to precipitate, do not admit all these facts; but they are facts well known to all men who are thoroughly informed in the affairs of this country. It must, however, be admitted, that our federal system is defective, and that some of the state governments are not well administered; but, then, we impute to the defects in our governments, many evils and embarrassments which are most clearly the result of the late war. We must allow men to conduct on the present occasion, as on all similar one's. They will urge a thousand pretences to answer their purposes on both sides. When we want a man to change his condition, we describe it as miserable, wretched, and despised; and draw a pleasing pic-

*The *Letters from the Federal Farmer* was a forty-eight-page pamphlet published in New York City around 8 November. It was one of the most significant Antifederalist publications, going through "four editions" with several thousand copies sold. The authorship is uncertain.

ture of that which we would have him assume. And when we wish the contrary, we reverse our descriptions. Whenever a clamor is raised, and idle men get to work, it is highly necessary to examine facts carefully, and without unreasonably suspecting men of falsehood, to examine, and enquire attentively, under what impressions they act. It is too often the case in political concerns, that men state facts not as they are, but as they wish them to be; and almost every man, by calling to mind past scenes, will find this to be true.

Nothing but the passions of ambitious, impatient, or disorderly men, I conceive, will plunge us into commotions, if time should be taken fully to examine and consider the system proposed. Men who feel easy in their circumstances, and such as are not sanguine in their expectations relative to the consequences of the proposed change, will remain quiet under the existing governments. Many commercial and monied men, who are uneasy, not without just cause, ought to be respected; and, by no means, unreasonably disappointed in their expectations and hopes; but as to those who expect employments under the new constitution; as to those weak and ardent men who always expect to be gainers by revolutions, and whose lot it generally is to get out of one difficulty into another, they are very little to be regarded: and as to those who designedly avail themselves of this weakness and ardor, they are to be despised. It is natural for men, who wish to hasten the adoption of a measure, to tell us, now is the crisis—now is the critical moment which must be seized, or all will be lost: and to shut the door against free enquiry, whenever conscious the thing presented has defects in it, which time and investigation will probably discover. This has been the custom of tyrants and their dependants in all ages. If it is true, what has been so often said, that the people of this country cannot change their condition for the worse, I presume it still behooves them to endeavour deliberately to change it for the better. The fickle and ardent, in any community, are the proper tools for establishing despotic government. But it is deliberate and thinking men, who must establish and secure governments on free principles. Before they decide on the plan proposed, they will enquire whether it will probably be a blessing or a curse to this people. . . .

The confederation was formed when great confidence was placed in the voluntary exertions of individuals, and of the respective states; and the framers of it, to guard against usurpation, so limited and checked the powers, that, in many respects, they are inadequate to the exigencies of the union. We find, therefore, members of congress urging alterations in the federal system almost as soon as it was adopted. It was early proposed to vest congress with powers to levy an impost, to regulate trade, &c. but such was known to be the caution of the states in parting with power, that the vestment, even of these, was proposed to be under several checks and limitations. During the war, the general confusion, and the introduction of paper money, infused in the minds of people vague ideas respecting government and credit. We expected too much from the return of peace, and of course we have been disappointed. Our governments have been new and unsettled; and several legislatures, by making tender, suspension, and paper money laws, have given just cause of uneasiness to creditors. By these and other causes, several orders of men in the community have been prepared, by degrees, for a change of government; and this very abuse of power in the legislatures, which, in some cases, has been charged upon the democratic part of the community, has furnished aristocratical men with those very weapons, and those very means, with which, in great measure, they are rapidly effecting their favourite object. And should an oppressive government be the consequence of the proposed change, posterity may reproach not only a few overbearing, unprincipled men, but those parties in the states which have misused their powers.

The conduct of several legislatures, touching paper money, and tender laws, has prepared many honest men for changes in government, which otherwise they would not have thought of—when by the evils, on the one hand, and by the secret instigations of artful men, on the other, the minds of men were become sufficiently uneasy, a bold step was taken, which is usually followed by a revolution, or a civil war. A general convention for mere commercial purposes was moved for—the authors of this measure saw that the people's attention was turned solely to the amendment of the federal system; and that, had the idea of a total change been started, probably no state would have appointed members to the convention. The idea of destroying, ultimately, the state government, and forming one consolidated system, could not have been admitted—a convention, therefore, merely for vesting in congress power to regulate trade, was proposed. This was pleasing to the commercial towns; and the landed people had little or no concern about it. September, 1786, a few men from the middle states met at Annapolis, and hastily proposed a convention to be held in May, 1787, for the purpose, generally, of amending the confederation—this was done before the delegates of Massachusetts, and of the other states arrived—still not a word was said about destroying the old constitution, and making a new one—The states still unsuspecting, and not aware that they were passing the Rubicon, appointed members to the new convention, for the sole and express purpose of revising and amending the confederation—and, probably, not one man in ten thousand in the United States, till within these ten or twelve days, had an idea that the old ship was to be destroyed, and he put to the alternative of embarking in the new ship presented, or of being left in danger of sinking—The States, I believe, universally supposed the convention would report alterations in the confederation, which would pass an examination in congress, and after being agreed to there, would be confirmed by all the legislatures, or be rejected. Virginia made a very respectable appointment, and placed at the head of it the first man in America:*—In this appointment there was a mixture of political characters; but Pennsylvania appointed principally those men who are esteemed aristocratical. Here the favourite moment for changing the government was evidently discerned by a few men, who seized it with address. Ten other states appointed, and tho' they chose men principally connected with commerce and the judicial department, yet they appointed many good republican characters—had they all attended we should now see, I am persuaded, a better system presented. The non-attendance of eight or nine men, who were appointed members of the convention, I shall ever consider as a very unfortunate event to the United States.—Had they attended, I am pretty clear that the result of the convention would not have had that strong tendency to aristocracy now discernible in every part of the plan. . . . We shall view the convention with proper respect— and, at the same time, that we reflect there were men of abilities and integrity in it, we must recollect how disproportionably the democratic and aristocratic parts of the community were represented. . . .

The essential parts of a free and good government are a full and equal representation of the people in the legislature, and the jury trial of the vicinage in the administration of justice—a full and equal representation, is that which possesses the same interests, feelings, opinions, and views the people themselves would were they all assembled—a fair representation, therefore, should be so regulated, that every order of men in the community, according to the common course of elections, can have a share in it—in order to allow professional men, merchants, traders, farmers, mechanics, &c. to bring a just proportion of their best informed men respectively into the legislature, the representation must be considerably numerous—We have about 200 state senators in the United States, and a less number than that of federal representatives cannot, clearly, be a full representation of this people, in the affairs of internal taxation and police, were there but one legislature for the whole union. The representation cannot be equal, or the situation of the people proper for one government only—if the extreme parts of the society cannot be represented as fully as the central—It is apparently impracticable that this should be the case in this extensive country—it would be impossible to collect a representation of the parts of the country five, six, and seven hundred miles from the seat of government. . . .

*George Washington.

The house of representatives, the democrative branch, as it is called, is to consist of 65 members; that is, about one representative for fifty thousand inhabitants, to be chosen biennially—the federal legislature may increase this number to one for every thirty thousand inhabitants, abating fractional numbers in each state.—Thirty-three representatives will make a quorum for doing business, and a majority of those present determine the sense of the house.—I have no idea that the interests, feelings, and opinions of three or four millions of people, especially touching internal taxation, can be collected in such a house.—In the nature of things, nine times in ten, men of elevated classes in the community only can be chosen—Connecticut, for instance, will have five representatives—not one man in a hundred of those who form the democrative branch in the state legislature, will on a fair computation, be one of the five—The people of this country, in one sense, may all be democratic; but if we make the proper distinction between the few men of wealth and abilities, and consider them, as we ought, as the natural aristocracy of the country, and the great body of the people, the middle and lower classes, as the democracy, this federal representative branch will have but very little democracy in it, even this small representation is not secured on proper principles. . . .

This subject of consolidating the states is new; and because forty or fifty men have agreed in a system, to suppose the good sense of this country, an enlightened nation, must adopt it without examination, and though in a state of profound peace, without endeavouring to amend those parts they perceive are defective, dangerous to freedom, and destructive of the valuable principles of republican government—is truly humiliating. It is true there may be danger in delay; but there is danger in adopting the system in its present form; and I see the danger in either case will arise principally from the conduct and views of two very unprincipled parties in the United States—two fires, between which the honest and substantial people have long found themselves situated. One party is composed of little insurgents, men in debt, who want no law, and who want a share of the property of others; these are called levellers, Shayites, &c. The other party is composed of a few, but more dangerous men, with their servile dependents; these avariciously grasp at power and property; you may discover in all the actions of these men, an evident dislike to free and equal governments, and they will go systematically to work to change, essentially, the forms of government in this country; these are called aristocrats, morrisites,* &c. &c. Between these two parties is the weight of the community; the men of middling property, men not in debt on the one hand, and men, on the other, content with republican governments, and not

*Supporters of former Confederation Superintendent of Finance Robert Morris.

188 FEDERALISTS AND ANTIFEDERALITS

aiming at immense fortunes, offices, and power. In 1786, the little insurgents, the levellers, came forth, invaded the rights of others, and attempted to establish governments according to their wills. Their movements evidently gave encouragement to the other party, which, in 1787, has taken the political field, and with its fashionable dependents, and the tongue and the pen, is endeavouring to establish in great haste, a politer kind of government. These two parties, which will probably be opposed or united as it may suit their interests and views, are really insignificant, compared with the solid, free, and independent part of the community. It is not my intention to suggest, that either of these parties, and the real friends of the proposed constitution, are the same men. The fact is, these aristocrats support and hasten the adoption of the proposed constitution, merely because they think it is a stepping stone to their favourite object. I think I am well founded in this idea; I think the general politics of these men support it, as well as the common observation among them, That the proffered plan is the best that can be got at present, it will do for a few years, and lead to something better.

CENTINEL III (SAMUEL BRYAN)
Philadelphia *Independent Gazetteer*, 8 November 1787 (excerpt)*

What then are we to think of the motives and designs of those men who are urging the implicit and immediate adoption of the proposed government; are they fearful, that if you exercise your good sense and discernment, you will discover the masked aristocracy, that they are attempting to smuggle upon you, under the suspicious garb of republicanism?—When we find that the principal agents in this business, are the very men who fabricated the form of government, it certainly ought to be conclusive evidence of their invidious design to deprive us of our liberties—The circumstances attending this matter, are such as should in a peculiar manner excite your suspicion; it might not be useless to take a review of some of them.

In many of the states, particularly in this and the northern states, there are aristocratic junto's of the *well-born few*, who had been zealously endeavouring since the establishment of their [state] constitutions, to humble that offensive *upstart, equal liberty*; but all their efforts were unavailing, the *ill-bred churl* obstinately kept his assumed station.

However, that which could not be accomplished in the several states, is now attempting through the medium of the future Congress.—Experi-

*Reprinted in the *Pennsylvania Herald*, 9 November; Philadelphia *Freeman's Journal*, 14 November; *New York Journal*, 20 November; Providence *United States Chronicle*, 3 January 1788; Boston *American Herald*, 7 January; and in a New York City pamphlet anthology printed in April 1788.

ence having shown great defects in the present confederation, particularly in the regulation of commerce and maritime affairs; it became the universal wish of America to grant further powers, so as to make the federal government adequate to the ends of its institution. The anxiety on this head was greatly increased, from the impoverishment and distress occasioned by the excessive importations of foreign merchandise and luxuries and consequent drain of specie, since the peace: thus the people were in the disposition of a drowning man, eager to catch at any thing that promised relief, however delusory. Such an opportunity for the acquisition of *undue* power, has never been viewed with indifference by the ambitious and designing in any age or nation, and it has accordingly been too successfully improved by such men among us. The deputies from this state (with the exception of two) and most of those from the other states in the union, were unfortunately of this complexion, and many of them of such superior endowments, that in an *exparte* discussion of the subject by specious glosses, they have gained the concurrence of some well-disposed men, in whom their country has great confidence, which has given a great sanction to their scheme of power.

A comparison of the authority under which the convention acted, and their form of government will show that they have despised their delegated power, and assumed sovereignty; that they have entirely annihilated the old confederation, and the particular governments of the several states, and instead thereof have established one general government that is to pervade the union; constituted on the most *unequal* principles, destitute of accountability to its constituents, and as despotic in its nature, as the Venetian aristocracy; a government that will give full scope to the magnificent designs of the *well-born*; a government where tyranny may glut its vengeance on the *low-born*, unchecked by *an odious bill of rights*: as has been fully illustrated in my two preceding numbers.

A PLEBEIAN
An Address to the People of the State of New York,
17 April 1788 (excerpt)*

It is insisted, that the present situation of our country is such, as not to admit of a delay in forming a new government, or of time sufficient to deliberate and agree upon the amendments which are proper, without involving ourselves in a state of anarchy and confusion.

*This twenty-six-page pamphlet was reprinted in four installments in the Philadelphia *Independent Gazetteer* on 23, 24, 27 and 28 May. About half of the pamphlet appeared in three installments in the Lansingburgh, N.Y. *Federal Herald* on 28 April and 5 and 12 May. Advertisements for the pamphlet appeared in the *New York Journal* and in newspapers in Wilmington, N.C. The authorship is uncertain.

On this head, all the powers of rhetoric, and arts of description, are employed to paint the condition of this country, in the most hideous and frightful colours. We are told, that agriculture is without encouragement; trade is languishing; private faith and credit are disregarded, and public credit is prostrate; that the laws and magistrates are contemned and set at naught; that a spirit of licentiousness is rampant, and ready to break over every bound set to it by the government; that private embarrassments and distresses invade the house of every man of middling property, and insecurity threatens every man in affluent circumstances; in short, that we are in a state of the most grievous calamity at home, and that we are contemptible abroad, the scorn of foreign nations, and the ridicule of the world. From this high-wrought picture, one would suppose, that we were in a condition the most deplorable of any people upon earth. But suffer me, my countrymen, to call your attention to a serious and sober estimate of the situation in which you are placed, while I trace the embarrassments under which you labour, to their true sources. What is your condition? Does not every man sit under his own vine and under his own fig-tree, having none to make him afraid? Does not every one follow his calling without impediments and receive the reward of his well-earned industry? The farmer cultivates his land, and reaps the fruit which the bounty of heaven bestows on his honest toil. The mechanic is exercised in his art, and receives the reward of his labour. The merchant drives his commerce, and none can deprive him of the gain he honestly acquires; all classes and callings of men amongst us are protected in their various pursuits, and secured by the laws in the possession and enjoyment of the property obtained in those pursuits. The laws are as well executed as they ever were, in this or any other country. Neither the hand of private violence, nor the more to be dreaded hand of legal oppression, are reached out to distress us.

It is true, many individuals labour under embarrassments, but these are to be imputed to the unavoidable circumstances of things, rather than to any defect in our governments. We have just emerged from a long and expensive war. During its existence few people were in a situation to increase their fortunes, but many to diminish them. Debts contracted before the war were left unpaid while it existed, and these were left a burden too heavy to be borne at the commencement of peace. Add to these, that when the war was over, too many of us, instead of reassuming our old habits of frugality and industry, by which alone every country must be placed in a prosperous condition, took up the profuse use of foreign commodities. The country was deluged with articles imported from abroad, and the cash of the country has been sent out to pay for them, and still left us labouring under the weight of a huge debt to persons abroad. These are the true sources to which we are to trace all the private difficulties of individuals: But will a new government relieve you from these? The advocates for it have not yet told you how it will do it—And I will venture to pronounce, that there is but one way in which it can be effected, and that is by industry and œconomy; limit your expences within your earnings; sell more than you buy, and every thing will be well on this score. Your present condition is such as is common to take place after the conclusion of a war. Those who can remember our situation after the termination of the war preceding the last, will recollect that our condition was similar to the present, but time and industry soon recovered us from it. Money was scarce, the produce of the country much lower than it has been since the peace, and many individuals were extremely embarrassed with debts; and this happened, although we did not experience the ravages, desolations, and loss of property, that were suffered during the late war.

With regard to our public and national concerns, what is there in our condition that threatens us with any immediate danger? We are at peace with all the world; no nation menaces us with war; nor are we called upon by any cause of sufficient importance to attack any nation. The state governments answer the purposes of preserving the peace, and providing for present exigencies. Our condition as a nation is in no respect worse than it has been for several years past. Our public debt has been lessened in various ways, and the western territory, which has always been relied upon as a productive fund to discharge the national debt, has at length been brought to market, and a considerable part actually applied to its reduction. I mention these things to show, that there is nothing special, in our present situation, as it respects our national affairs, that should induce us to accept the proffered system, without taking sufficient time to consider and amend it. I do not mean by this, to insinuate, that our government does not stand in need of a reform. It is admitted by all parties, that alterations are necessary in our federal constitution, but the circumstances of our case do by no means oblige us to precipitate this business, or require that we should adopt a system materially defective. We may safely take time to deliberate and amend, without in the mean time hazarding a condition, in any considerable degree, worse than the present. . . .

Before I close, I beg your indulgence, while I make some remarks on the splendid advantages, which the advocates for this system say are to be derived from it.—Hope and fear are two of the most active principles of our nature: We have considered how the latter is addressed on this occasion, and with how little reason: It will appear that the promises it makes, are as little to be relied upon, as its threatenings. We are amused with the fair prospects that are to open, when this government is put into operation—Agriculture is to flourish, and our fields to yield an hundred fold—Commerce is to expand her wings, and bear our productions to all the ports in the world—Money is to pour into our country through every channel—Arts and manufactures are to rear their heads, and every mechanic find full employ—Those who are in debt, are to find easy means to procure money to pay them—Public burdens and taxes are to be lightened, and yet all our public debts are soon to be discharged.—With such vain and delusive hopes are the minds of many honest and well meaning people fed, and by these means are they led inconsiderately to contend for a government, which is made to promise what it cannot perform; while their minds are diverted from contemplating its true nature, or considering whether it will not endanger their liberties, and work oppression.

Far be it from me to object to granting the general government the power of regulating trade, and of laying imposts and duties for that purpose, as well as for raising a revenue: But it is as far from me to flatter people with hopes of benefits to be derived from such a change in our government, which can never be realized. Some advantages may accrue from vesting in one general government, the right to regulate commerce, but it is a vain delusion to expect any thing like what is promised. The truth is, this country buys more than it sells: It imports more than it exports. There are too many merchants in proportion to the farmers and manufacturers. Until these defects are remedied, no government can relieve us. Common sense dictates, that if a man buys more than he sells, he will remain in debt; the same is true of a country.—And as long as this country imports more goods than she exports—the overplus must be paid for in money or not paid at all. These few remarks may convince us, that the radical remedy for the scarcity of cash is frugality and industry. Earn much and spend little, and you will be enabled to pay your debts, and have money in your pockets; and if you do not follow this advice, no government that can be framed, will relieve you.

As to the idea of being relieved from taxes by this government, it is an affront to common sense, to advance it. There is no complaint made against the present confederation more justly founded than this, that it is incompetent to provide the means to discharge our national debt, and to support the national government. Its inefficacy to these purposes, which was early seen and felt, was the first thing that suggested the necessity of changing the government; other things, it is true, were afterwards found to require alterations; but this was the most important, and accordingly we find, that while in some other things the powers of this government seem to be in some measure limited, on the subject of raising money, no bounds are set to it. It is authorized to raise money to any amount, and in any way it pleases. If then, the capital embarrassment in our present government arises from the want of money, and this constitution effectually authorizes the raising of it, how are the taxes to be lessened by it? Certainly money can only be raised by taxes of some kind or other; it must be got either by additional impositions on trade, by excise, or by direct taxes, or what is more probable, by all together. In either way, it amounts to the same thing, and the position is clear, that as the necessities of the nation require more money than is now raised, the taxes must be enhanced. This you ought to know, and prepare yourselves to submit to.—Besides, how is it possible that the taxes can be decreased when the expences of your government will be greatly advanced? It does not require any great skill in politics, or ability at calculation to show, that the new government will cost more money to administer it, than the present. I shall not descend to an estimate of the cost of a federal town, the salaries of the president, vice-president, judges, and other great officers of state, nor calculate the amount of the pay the legislature will vote themselves, or the salaries that will be paid the innumerable revenue and subordinate officers. The bare mention of these things is sufficient to convince you, that the new government will be vastly more expensive than the old: And how is the money to answer these purposes to be obtained? It is obvious, it must be taken out of the pockets of the people, by taxes, in some mode or other.

FEDERAL FARMER: AN ADDITIONAL NUMBER OF
Letters to the Republican, 2 May 1788 (excerpts)*

I shall proceed to consider further my principal position, viz. that there is no substantial representation of the people provided for in a government, in which the most essential powers, even as to the internal police of the country, are proposed to be lodged; and to propose certain amendments as to the representative branch: 1st, That there ought to be *an increase of the numbers of representatives:* And, 2dly, That the elections of them ought to be better secured.†

---

*This 136-page pamphlet is a continuation of the pamphlet published by "Federal Farmer" in early November 1787. Both pamphlets were widely distributed by the New York Federal Republican Committee. The authorship is uncertain.

†In commenting upon the discussion of representation and suffrage which follows, the reviewer of the *Additional Letters* in the May issue of the New York *American Magazine* (probably Noah Webster) states that "The author maintains that the federal representation will be too small, and that all orders of men, merchants, farmers, mechanics, &c. should be represented by some of their own professions. In these positions, especially in the latter, we do not agree with the Federal Farmer. The suffrages of the people must be left free. To restrict them to particular classes of men would be an abridgement of that liberty for which our author contends. But the principle that each order of men should be separately represented in the national Legislature, is not well founded. However it may be useful or necessary to represent each profession in the state assemblies, yet the principle will not apply to the federal legislature; for in the latter, *States* are represented, and not particular orders or districts. The people at large, it is true, choose the delegates of one branch; but the men chosen represent the *collective interest* of all orders—the State. Delegates, therefore, should understand, not merely the interest of *one order* of men, but the *combined interest* of the community. He should be a man of *general information.*"

1. The representation is unsubstantial and ought to be increased. In matters where there is much room for opinion, you will not expect me to establish my positions with mathematical certainty; you must only expect my observations to be candid, and such as are well founded in the mind of the writer. I am in a field where doctors disagree; and as to genuine representation, though no feature in government can be more important, perhaps, no one has been less understood, and no one that has received so imperfect a consideration by political writers. The ephori in Sparta, and the tribunes in Rome, were but the shadow; the representation in Great-Britain is unequal and insecure. In America we have done more in establishing this important branch on its true principles, than, perhaps, all the world besides: yet even here, I conceive, that very great improvements in representation may be made. In fixing this branch, the situation of the people must be surveyed, and the number of representatives and forms of election apportioned to that situation. When we find a numerous people settled in a fertile and extensive country, possessing equality, and few or none of them oppressed with riches or wants, it ought to be the anxious care of the constitution and laws, to arrest them from national depravity, and to preserve them in their happy condition. A virtuous people make just laws, and good laws tend to preserve unchanged a virtuous people. A virtuous and happy people by laws uncongenial to their characters, may easily be gradually changed into servile and depraved creatures. Where the people, or their representatives, make the laws, it is probable they will generally be fitted to the national character and circumstances, unless the representation be partial, and the imperfect substitute of the people. However, the people may be electors, if the representation be so formed as to give one or more of the natural classes of men in the society an undue ascendancy over the others, it is imperfect; the former will gradually become masters, and the latter slaves. It is the first of all among the political balances, to preserve in its proper station each of these classes. We talk of balances in the legislature, and among the departments of government; we ought to carry them to the body of the people. Since I advanced the idea of balancing the several orders of men in a community, in forming a genuine representation, and seen that idea considered as chimerical, I have been sensibly struck with a sentence in the marquis Beccaria's treatise: this sentence was quoted by congress in 1774, and is as follows:—"In every society there is an effort continually tending to confer on one part the height of power and happiness, and to reduce the others to the extreme of weakness and misery; the intent of good laws is to oppose this effort, and to diffuse their influence universally and equally."* Add to this Montesquieu's

*Cesare Bonesana, Marchese di Beccaria, *An Essay on Crimes and Punishments* (3rd ed., London, 1770), 1. This work was first published in Livorno (Leghorn) in 1764. The passage

opinion, that "in a free state every man, who is supposed to be a free agent, ought to be concerned in his own government: therefore, the legislative should reside in the whole body of the people, or their representatives."* It is extremely clear that these writers had in view the several orders of men in society, which we call aristocratical, democratical, merchantile, mechanic, &c. and perceived the efforts they are constantly, from interested and ambitious views, disposed to make to elevate themselves and oppress others. Each order must have a share in the business of legislation actually and efficiently. It is deceiving a people to tell them they are electors, and can choose their legislators, if they cannot, in the nature of things, choose men from among themselves, and genuinely like themselves. I wish you to take another idea along with you; we are not only to balance these natural efforts, but we are also to guard against accidental combinations; combinations founded in the connections of offices and private interests, both evils which are increased in proportion as the number of men, among which the elected must be, are decreased. To set this matter in a proper point of view, we must form some general ideas and descriptions of the different classes of men, as they may be divided by occupations and politically: the first class is the aristocratical. There are three kinds of aristocracy spoken of in this country—the first is a constitutional one, which does not exist in the United States in our common acceptation of the word. Montesquieu, it is true, observes, that where a part of the persons in a society, for want of property, age, or moral character, are excluded any share in the government, the others, who alone are the constitutional electors and elected, form this aristocracy;† this according to him, exists in each of the United States, where a considerable number of persons, as all convicted of crimes, under age, or not possessed of certain property, are excluded any share in the government; the second is an aristocratic faction, a junto of unprincipled men, often distinguished for their wealth or abilities, who combine together and make their object their private interests and aggrandizement; the existence of this description is merely accidental, but particularly to be guarded against. The third is the natural aristocracy; this term we use to designate a respectable order of men, the

---

quoted here represents the first two sentences of Beccaria's "Introduction." It was quoted in "An Address to the Inhabitants of the Province of Quebec," adopted by the First Continental Congress on 26 October 1774. Thomas Cushing, Richard Henry Lee, and John Dickinson composed the committee that drafted this address, which was printed in Philadelphia in both English and French by order of Congress. A German edition, for which Congress had made Pennsylvania's delegates responsible, was also printed in Philadelphia. The address was then reprinted in several other towns and cities.

Spirit of Laws, I, Book XI, chapter VI, 226.

†*Ibid.*, I, Book II, chapter II, 11–18. This chapter is entitled: "Of the Republican Government, and the Laws in relation to Democracy."

line between whom and the natural democracy is in some degree arbitrary; we may place men on one side of this line, which others may place on the other, and in all disputes between the few and the many, a considerable number are wavering and uncertain themselves on which side they are, or ought to be. In my idea of our natural aristocracy in the United States, I include about four or five thousand men; and among these I reckon those who have been placed in the offices of governors, of members of Congress, and state senators generally, in the principal officers of Congress, of the army and militia, the superior judges, the most eminent professional men, &c. and men of large property*—the other persons and orders in the community form the natural democracy; this includes in general the yeomanry, the subordinate officers, civil and military, the fishermen, mechanics and traders, many of the merchants and professional men. It is easy to perceive that men of these two classes, the aristocratical, and democratical, with views equally honest, have sentiments widely different, especially respecting public and private expences, salaries, taxes, &c. Men of the first class associate more extensively, have a high sense of honor, possess abilities, ambition, and general knowledge: men of the second class are not so much used to combining great objects; they possess less ambition, and a larger share of honesty: their dependence is principally on middling and small estates, industrious pursuits, and hard labour, while that of the former is principally on the emoluments of large estates, and of the chief offices of government. Not only the efforts of these two great parties are to be balanced, but other interests and parties also, which do not always oppress each other merely for want of power, and for fear of the consequences; though they, in fact, mutually depend on each other; yet such are their general views, that the merchants alone would never fail to make laws favourable to themselves and oppressive to the farmers, &c. the farmers alone would act on like principles; the former would tax the land, the latter the trade. The manufacturers are often disposed to contend for monopolies, buyers make every exertion to lower prices, and sellers to raise them; men who live by fees and salaries endeavour to raise them, and the part of the people who pay them, endeavour to lower them; the public creditors to augment the taxes, and the people at large to lessen them. Thus, in every period of society, and in all the transactions of men, we see parties verifying the observation made by the Marquis; and those classes which have not their centinels in the government, in proportion to what they have to gain or lose, must infallibly be ruined.

Efforts among parties are not merely confined to property; they contend for rank and distinctions; all their passions in turn are enlisted in

*See Alexander Hamilton's speech commenting on this passage in the New York Convention on 21 June 1788 (below).

political controversies—Men, elevated in society, are often disgusted with the changeableness of the democracy, and the latter are often agitated with the passions of jealousy and envy: the yeomanry possess a large share of property and strength, are nervous and firm in their opinions and habits—the mechanics of towns are ardent and changeable, honest and credulous, they are inconsiderable for numbers, weight and strength, not always sufficiently stable for the supporting free governments; the fishing interest partakes partly of the strength and stability of the landed, and partly of the changeableness of the mechanic interest. As to merchants and traders, they are our agents in almost all money transactions; give activity to government, and possess a considerable share of influence in it. It has been observed by an able writer, that frugal industrious merchants are generally advocates for liberty. It is an observation, I believe, well founded, that the schools produce but few advocates for republican forms of government; gentlemen of the law, divinity, physic, &c. probably form about a fourth part of the people; yet their political influence, perhaps, is equal to that of all the other descriptions of men; if we may judge from the appointments to Congress, the legal characters will often, in a small representation, be the majority; but the more the representatives are encreased, the more of the farmers, merchants, &c. will be found to be brought into the government.

These general observations will enable you to discern what I intend by different classes, and the general scope of my ideas, when I contend for uniting and balancing their interests, feelings, opinions, and views in the legislature; we may not only so unite and balance these as to prevent a change in the government by the gradual exaltation of one part to the depression of others, but we may derive many other advantages from the combination and full representation; a small representation can never be well informed as to the circumstances of the people, the members of it must be too far removed from the people, in general, to sympathize with them, and too few to communicate with them: a representation must be extremely imperfect where the representatives are not circumstanced to make the proper communications to their constituents, and where the constituents in turn cannot, with tolerable convenience, make known their wants, circumstances, and opinions, to their representatives; where there is but one representative to 30,000, or 40,000 inhabitants, it appears to me, he can only mix, and be acquainted with a few respectable characters among his constituents, even double the federal representation, and then there must be a very great distance between the representatives and the people in general represented. On the proposed plan, the state of Delaware, the city of Philadelphia, the state of Rhode Island, the province of Maine, the county of Suffolk in Massachusetts, will have one representative each; there can be but little personal knowledge, or but few communications, between him and the people at large of either of those districts. It has been observed, that mixing only with the respectable men, he will get the best information and ideas from them; he will also receive impressions favourable to their purposes particularly.

MELANCTON SMITH
Speech in New York Ratifying Convention, 21 June 1788 (excerpt)*

The number of representatives should be so large, as that while it embraces the men of the first class, it should admit those of the middling class of life. I am convinced that this government is so constituted, that the representatives will generally be composed of the first class in the community, which I shall distinguish by the name of the natural aristocracy of the country. I do not mean to give offence by using this term. I am sensible this idea is treated by many gentlemen as chimerical. I shall be asked what is meant by the natural aristocracy, and told that no such distinction of classes of men exists among us. It is true it is our singular felicity that we have no legal or hereditary distinctions of this kind; but still there are real differences: Every society naturally divides itself into classes. The author of nature has bestowed on some greater capacities than on others—birth, education, talents and wealth, create distinctions among men as visible and of as much influence as titles, stars and garters. In every society, men of this class will command a superior degree of respect—and if the government is so constituted as to admit but few to exercise the powers of it, it will, according to the natural course of things, be in their hands. Men in the middling class, who are qualified as representatives, will not be so anxious to be chosen as those of the first. When the number is so small the office will be highly elevated and distinguished—the style in which the members live will probably be high—circumstances of this kind, will render the place of a representative not a desirable one to sensible, substantial men, who have been used to walk in the plain and frugal paths of life.

Besides, the influence of the great will generally enable them to succeed in elections—it will be difficult to combine a district of country containing 30 or 40,000 inhabitants, frame your election laws as you please, in any one character; unless it be in one of conspicuous military, popular,

---

*The Debates and Proceedings of the Convention of the State of New-York . . . (New York, 1788), 32–33. Smith, who drew heavily from arguments in the "Federal Farmer," was answered immediately by Alexander Hamilton. (See below.)

civil, or legal talents. The great easily form associations; the poor and middling class form them with difficulty. If the elections be by plurality, as probably will be the case in this state, it is almost certain, none but the great will be chosen—for they easily unite their interests—The common people will divide, and their divisions will be promoted by the others. There will be scarcely a chance of their uniting, in any other but some great man, unless in some popular demagogue, who will probably be destitute of principle. A substantial yeoman of sense and discernment, will hardly ever be chosen. From these remarks it appears that the government will fall into the hands of the few and the great. This will be a government of oppression. I do not mean to declaim against the great, and charge them indiscriminately with want of principle and honesty.— The same passions and prejudices govern all men. The circumstances in which men are placed in a great measure give a cast to the human character. Those in middling circumstances, have less temptation—they are inclined by habit and the company with whom they associate, to set bounds to their passions and appetites—If this is not sufficient, the want of means to gratify them will be a restraint—they are obliged to employ their time in their respective callings—hence the substantial yeomanry of the country are more temperate, of better morals and less ambition than the great. The latter do not feel for the poor and middling class; the reasons are obvious—they are not obliged to use the pains and labour to procure property as the other.—They feel not the inconveniences arising from the payment of small sums. The great consider themselves above the common people—entitled to more respect—do not associate with them—they fancy themselves to have a right of preeminence in every thing. In short, they possess the same feelings, and are under the influence of the same motives, as an hereditary nobility. I know the idea that such a distinction exists in this country is ridiculed by some—But I am not the less apprehensive of danger from their influence on this account—Such distinctions exist all the world over—have been taken notice of by all writers on free government—and are founded in the nature of things. It has been the principal care of free governments to guard against the encroachments of the great. Common observation and experience prove the existence of such distinctions. Will any one say, that there does not exist in this country the pride of family, of wealth, of talents; and that they do not command influence and respect among the common people? Congress, in their address to the inhabitants of the province of Quebec, in 1775, state this distinction in the following forcible words quoted from the Marquis Beccaria. "In every human society, there is an essay continually tending to confer on one part the height of power and happiness, and to reduce the other to the extreme of weakness and misery. The intent of good laws is to

oppose this effort, and to diffuse their influence universally and equally."
We ought to guard against the government being placed in the hands of
this class—They cannot have that sympathy with their constituents which
is necessary to connect them closely to their interest: Being in the habit of
profuse living, they will be profuse in the public expenses. They find no
difficulty in paying their taxes, and therefore do not feel public burdens.
Besides if they govern, they will enjoy the emoluments of the government. The middling class, from their frugal habits, and feeling themselves
the public burdens, will be careful how they increase them.

But I may be asked, would you exclude the first class in the community, from any share in legislation? I answer by no means—they would be
more dangerous out of power than in it—they would be factious—discontented and constantly disturbing the government—it would also be
unjust—they have their liberties to protect as well as others—and the largest
share of property. But my idea is, that the Constitution should be so framed
as to admit this class, together with a sufficient number of the middling
class to controul them. You will then combine the abilities and honesty of
the community a proper degree of information, and a disposition to pursue
the public good. A representative body, composed principally of respectable
yeomanry is the best possible security to liberty—When the interest of this
part of the community is pursued, the public good is pursued; because the
body of every nation consists of this class. And because the interest of both
the rich and the poor are involved in that of the middling class. No burden
can be laid on the poor, but what will sensibly affect the middling class. Any
law rendering property insecure, would be injurious to them.—When therefore this class in society pursue their own interest, they promote that of the
public, for it is involved in it.

Federalists

JAMES MADISON TO THOMAS JEFFERSON
New York, 24 October 1787 (excerpt)*

A constitutional negative on the laws of the States seems equally
necessary to secure individuals against encroachments on their rights. The
mutability of the laws of the States is found to be a serious evil. The injustice of them has been so frequent and so flagrant as to alarm the most
stedfast friends of Republicanism. I am persuaded I do not err in saying

*Jefferson Papers, Library of Congress. For a similar argument by Madison, see *The Fed-
eralist* No. 10, pp. 26–32.

that the evils issuing from these sources contributed more to that uneasiness which produced the Convention, and prepared the public mind for a general reform, than those which accrued to our national character and interest from the inadequacy of the Confederation to its immediate objects. A reform therefore which does not make provision for private rights, must be materially defective. The restraints against paper emissions, and violations of contracts are not sufficient. Supposing them to be effectual as far as they go, they are short of the mark. Injustice may be effected by such an infinitude of legislative expedients, that where the disposition exists it can only be controuled by some provision which reaches all cases whatsoever. The partial provision made, supposes the disposition which will evade it. It may be asked how private rights will be more secure under the Guardianship of the General Government than under the State Governments, since they are both founded on the republican principle which refers the ultimate decision to the will of the majority, and are distinguished rather by the extent within which they will operate, than by any material difference in their structure. A full discussion of this question would, if I mistake not, unfold the true principles of Republican Government, and prove in contrediction to the concurrent opinions of theoretical writers, that this form of Government, in order to effect its purposes, must operate not within a small but an extensive sphere. I will state some of the ideas which have occurred to me on this subject. Those who contend for a simple Democracy, or a pure republic, actuated by the sense of the majority, and operating within narrow limits, assume or suppose a case which is altogether fictitious. They found their reasoning on the idea, that the people composing the Society, enjoy not only an equality of political rights; but that they have all precisely the same interests, and the same feelings in every respect. Were this in reality the case, their reasoning would be conclusive. The interest of the majority would be that of the minority also; the decisions could only turn on mere opinion concerning the good of the whole, of which the major voice would be the safest criterion; and within a small sphere, this voice could be most easily collected, and the public affairs most accurately managed. We know however that no Society ever did or can consist of so homogeneous a mass of Citizens. In the savage State indeed, an approach is made towards it; but in that State little or no Government is necessary. In all civilized Societies, distinctions are various and unavoidable. A distinction of property results from that very protection which a free Government gives to unequal faculties of acquiring it. There will be rich and poor; creditors and debtors; a landed interest, a monied interest, a mercantile interest, a manufacturing interest. These classes may again be subdivided according to the different productions of different situations & soils, & according to different branches of commerce, and of manufactures. In addition to these natural distinctions, artificial ones will be founded, on accidental differences in political, religious or other opinions, or an attachment to the persons of leading individuals. However erroneous or ridiculous these grounds of dissention and faction, may appear to the enlightened Statesman, or the benevolent philosopher, the bulk of mankind who are neither Statesmen nor Philosophers, will continue to view them in a different light. It remains then to be enquired whether a majority having any common interest, or feeling any common passion, will find sufficient motives to restrain them from oppressing the minority. An individual is never allowed to be a judge or even a witness in his own cause. If two individuals are under the biass of interest or enmity against a third, the rights of the latter could never be safely referred to the majority of the three. Will two thousand individuals be less apt to oppress one thousand, or two hundred thousand, one hundred thousand? Three motives only can restrain in such cases. 1. a prudent regard to private or partial good, as essentially involved in the general and permanent good of the whole. This ought no doubt to be sufficient of itself. Experience however shows that it has little effect on individuals, and perhaps still less on a collection of individuals; and least of all on a majority with the public authority in their hands. If the former are ready to forget that honesty is the best policy; the last do more. They often proceed on the converse of the maxim: that whatever is politic is honest. 2. respect for character. This motive is not found sufficient to restrain individuals from injustice, and loses its efficacy in proportion to the number which is to divide the praise or the blame. Besides as it has reference to public opinion, which is that of the majority, the Standard is fixed by those whose conduct is to be measured by it. 3. Religion. The inefficacy of this restraint on individuals is well known. The conduct of every popular Assembly, acting on oath, the strongest of religious ties, shows that individuals join without remorse in acts against which their consciences would revolt, if proposed to them separately in their closets. When Indeed Religion is kindled into enthusiasm, its force like that of other passions is increased by the sympathy of a multitude. But enthusiasm is only a temporary state of Religion, and whilst it lasts will hardly be seen with pleasure at the helm. Even in its coolest state, it has been much oftener a motive to oppression than a restraint from it. If then there must be different interests and parties in Society; and a majority when united by a common interest or passion can not be restrained from oppressing the minority, what remedy can be found in a republican Government, where the majority must ultimately decide, but that of giving such an extent of its sphere, that no common interest or passion will be likely to unite a majority of the whole number in an unjust pursuit. In a large Society, the people are broken into so many interests and parties, that a common sentiment is less likely to be felt, and the requisite concert less likely to be formed, by a majority of the whole. The same security seems requisite for the civil as for the religious rights of individuals. If the same sect form a majority and have the power, other sects will be sure to be depressed. Divide et impera, the reprobated axiom of tyranny, is under certain qualifications, the only policy, by which a republic can be administered on just principles. It must be observed however that this doctrine can only hold within a sphere of a mean extent. As in too small a sphere oppressive combinations may be too easily formed against the weaker party; so in too extensive a one, a defensive concert may be rendered too difficult against the oppression of those entrusted with the administration. The great desideratum in Government is, so to modify the sovereignty as that it may be sufficiently neutral between different parts of the Society to controul one part from invading the rights of another, and at the same time sufficiently controuled itself, from setting up an interest adverse to that of the entire Society. In absolute monarchies, the Prince may be tolerably neutral towards different classes of his subjects; but may sacrifice the happiness of all to his personal ambition or avarice. In small republics, the sovereign will is controuled from such a sacrifice of the entire Society, but is not sufficiently neutral towards the parts composing it. In the extended Republic of the United States, The General Government would hold a pretty even balance between the parties of particular States, and be at the same time sufficiently restrained by its dependence on the community, from betraying its general interests.

A Landholder I (Oliver Ellsworth)
Connecticut Courant, 5 November 1787*

To the Holders and Tillers of Land.

The writer of the following passed the first part of his life in mercantile employments, and by industry and œconomy acquired a sufficient sum on retiring from trade to purchase and stock a decent plantation, on which he now lives in the state of a farmer. By his present employment he is

---

*This was the first of thirteen essays written by "A Landholder" that appeared simultaneously in the Hartford *Connecticut Courant* and the Hartford *American Mercury* between 5 November 1787 and 24 March 1788. The author was Oliver Ellsworth, a lawyer, delegate to Congress (1778–83), judge of the Connecticut Superior Court (1785–88), delegate to the Constitutional Convention and to the state ratifying convention, U.S. Senator (1789–96), and Chief Justice of the United States (1796–1800). This essay was reprinted in the *Connecticut Gazette,* 16 November; the *Norwich Packet,* 22 November; the *Albany Gazette,* 22 November; and the Northampton, Mass., *Hampshire Gazette,* 28 November.

interested in the prosperity of Agriculture, and those who derive a support from cultivating the earth. An acquaintance with business has freed him from many prejudices and jealousies, which he sees in his neighbours, who have not intermingled with mankind, nor learned by experience the method of managing an extensive circulating property. Conscious of an honest intention he wishes to address his brethren on some political subjects which now engage the public attention, and will in the sequel greatly influence the value of landed property. The new constitution for the United States is now before the public, the people are to determine, and the people at large generally determine right, when they have had means of information.

It proves the honesty and patriotism of the gentlemen who composed the general Convention, that they chose to submit their system to the people rather than the legislatures, whose decisions are often influenced by men in the higher departments of government, who have provided well for themselves and dread any change least they should be injured by its operation. I would not wish to exclude from a State Convention those gentlemen who compose the higher branches of the assemblies in the several states, but choose to see them stand on an even floor with their brethren, where the artifice of a small number cannot negative a vast majority of the people.

This danger was foreseen by the Fœderal Convention, and they have wisely avoided it by appealing directly to the people. The landholders and farmers are more than any other men concerned in the present decision, whether the proposed alteration is best they are to determine; but that an alteration is necessary, an individual may assert. It may be assumed as a fixed truth that the prosperity and riches of the farmer must depend on the prosperity, and good national regulation of trade. Artful men may insinuate the contrary—tell you let trade take care of itself, and excite your jealousy against the merchant because his business leads him to wear a gayer coat, than your œconomy directs. But let your own experience refute such insinuations. Your property and riches depend on a ready demand and generous price for the produce you can annually spare. When and where do you find this? Is it not where trade flourishes, and when the merchant can freely export the produce of the country to such parts of the world as will bring the richest return? When the merchant doth not purchase, your produce is low, finds a dull market—in vexation you call the trader a jocky, and curse the men whom you ought to pity. A desire of gain is common to mankind, and the general motive to business and industry. You cannot expect many purchasers when trade is restricted, and your merchants are shut out from nine tenths of the ports in the world. While they depend on the mercy of foreign nations, you are the first persons who will be humbled. Confined to a few foreign ports they must sell low, or not at all; and can you expect they will greedily buy in at a high price, the very articles which they must sell under every restriction.

Every foreign prohibition on American trade is aimed in the most deadly manner against the holders and tillers of the land, and they are the men made poor. Your only remedy is such a national government as will make the country respectable; such a supreme government as can boldly meet the supremacy of proud and self-interested nations. The regulation of trade ever was and ever must be a national matter. A single state in the American union cannot direct, much less controul it. This must be a work of the whole, and requires all the wisdom and force of the continent; and until it is effected our commerce may be insulted by every overgrown merchant in Europe. Think not the evil will rest on your merchants alone; it may distress them, but it will destroy those who cultivate the earth. Their produce will bear a low price, and require bad pay; the labourer will not find employment; the value of lands will fall, and the landholder become poor.

While our shipping rots at home by being prohibited from ports abroad, foreigners will bring you such articles and at such price as they please. Even the necessary article of salt has the present year, been chiefly imported in foreign bottoms, and you already feel the consequence, your flax-seed in barter has not returned you more than two thirds of the usual quantity.—From this beginning learn what is to come.

Blame not our merchants, the fault is not in them but in the public. A fœderal government of energy is the only means which will deliver us, and now or never is your opportunity to establish it, on such a basis as will preserve your liberty and riches. Think not that time without your own exertions will remedy the disorder. Other nations will be pleased with your poverty; they know the advantage of commanding trade, and carrying in their own bottoms. By these means they can govern prices and breed up a hardy race of seamen, to man their ships of war when they wish again to conquer you by arms. It is strange the holders and tillers of the land have had patience so long. They are men of resolution as well as patience, and will I presume be no longer deluded by British emissaries, and those men who think their own offices will be hazarded by any change in the constitution. Having opportunity, they will coolly demand a government which can protect what they have bravely defended in war.

A LANDHOLDER II (OLIVER ELLSWORTH)
Connecticut Courant, 12 November 1787*

TO THE HOLDERS AND TILLERS OF LAND.

Gentlemen, You were told in the late war that peace and independence would reward your toil, and that riches would accompany the establishment of your liberties, by opening a wider market, and consequently raising the price of such commodities as America produces for exportation.

Such a conclusion appeared just and natural. We had been restrained by the British to trade only with themselves, who often re-exported to other nations at a high advance, the raw materials they had procured from us. This advance we designed to realize, but our expectation has been disappointed. The produce of the country is in general down to the old price, and bids fair to fall much lower. It is time for those who till the earth in the sweat of their brow to enquire the cause. And we shall find it neither in the merchant or farmer, but in a bad system of policy and government, or rather in having no system at all. When we call ourselves an independent nation it is false, we are neither a nation, nor are we independent. Like thirteen contentious neighbours we devour and take every advantage of each other, and are without that system of policy which gives safety and strength, and constitutes a national structure. Once we were dependent only on Great-Britain, now we are dependent on every petty state in the world and on every custom house officer of foreign ports. If the injured apply for redress to the assemblies of the several states, it is in vain, for they are not, and cannot be known abroad. If they apply to Congress, it is also vain, for however wise and good that body may be, they have not power to vindicate either themselves or their subjects.

Do not my countrymen fall into a passion on hearing these truths, nor think your treatment unexampled. From the beginning it hath been the case that people without policy will find enough to take advantage of their weakness, and you are not the first who have been devoured by their wiser neighbours, but perhaps it is not too late for a remedy, we ought at least to make a trial, and if we still die shall have this consolation in our last hours, that we tried to live.

I can foresee that several classes of men will try to alarm your fears, and however selfish their motives, we may expect that *liberty, the encroach-*

---

*This essay, with slight variations, was also printed on 12 November in the Hartford *American Mercury*. It was reprinted in the *Norwich Packet*, 22 November; the *Connecticut Gazette*, 23 November; and the Northampton, Mass., *Hampshire Gazette*, 5 December. The text at the end of the essay within angle brackets was printed in the *New Haven Gazette* on 22 November and reprinted in seven other newspapers by 2 February 1788: N.H. (2), Mass. (2), N.Y. (1), Md. (1), Va. (1).

ments of power, *and the inestimable privileges of dear posterity* will with them be fruitful topicks of argument. As holy scripture is used in the exorcisms of Romish priests to expel imaginary dæmons; so the most sacred words will be conjured together to oppose evils which have no existence in the new constitution, and which no man dare attempt to carry into execution, among a people of so free a spirit as the Americans. The first to oppose a federal government will be the old friends of Great Britain, who in their hearts cursed the prosperity of your arms, and have ever since delighted in the perplexity of your councils. Many of these men are still among us, and for several years their hopes of a re-union with Britain have been high. They rightly judge that nothing will so soon effect their wishes as the deranged state we are now in, if it should continue. They see that the merchant is weary of a government which cannot protect his property, and that the farmer finding no benefit from the revolution, begins to dread much evil; and they hope the people will soon supplicate the protection of their old masters. We may therefore expect that all the policy of these men will center in defeating those measures, which will protect the people, and give system and force to American Councils. I was lately in a circle where the new constitution was discussed. All but one man approved, he was full of trembling for the liberties of poor America. It was strange! It was wonderous strange to see his concern! After several of his arguments had been refuted by an ingenious farmer in the company, but says he, it is against the treaty of peace, we received independence from Great Britain on condition of our keeping the old constitution. Here the man came out! We had beat the British with a bad frame of government, and with a good one he feared we should eat them up.

Debtors in desperate circumstances, who have not resolution to be either honest or industrious, will be the next men to take the alarm. They have long been upheld by the property of their creditors and the mercy of the public, and daily destroy a thousand honest men who are unsuspicious. *Paper money* and *tender acts*, is the only atmosphere in which they can breathe and live. This is now so generally known that by being a friend to such measures a man effectually advertises himself a bankrupt. The opposition of these we expect, but for the sake of all honest and industrious debtors, we most earnestly wish the proposed constitution may pass, for whatever gives anew spring to business will extricate them from their difficulties.

There is another kind of people will be found in the opposition. Men of much self-importance and supposed skill in politics, who are not of sufficient consequence to obtain public employment, but can spread jealousies in the little districts of country where they are placed. These are always jealous of men in place and of public measures, and aim at making themselves consequential by distrusting every one in the higher offices of society.

It is a strange madness of some persons, immediately to distrust those who are raised by the free suffrages of the people, to sustain powers which are absolutely necessary for public safety. Why were they elevated but for a general reputation of wisdom and integrity; and why should they be distrusted, until by ignorance or some base action they have forfeited a right to our confidence.

To fear a general government on energetic principles least it should create tyrants, when without such a government all have an opportunity to become tyrants and avoid punishment; is fearing the possibility of one act of oppression, more than the real exercise of a thousand. But in the present case, men who have lucrative and influential state offices, if they act from principles of self-interest, will be tempted to oppose an alteration, which would doubtless be beneficial to the people. To sink from a controlment of finance, or any other great department of the state, thro' want of ability or opportunity to act a part in the federal system must be a terrifying consideration. <Believe not those who insinuate that this is a scheme of great men to grasp more power. The temptation is on the other side. Those in great offices never wish to hazard their places by such a change. This is the scheme of the people and those high and worthy characters who in obedience to the public voice offer the proposed amendment of our federal constitution thus esteemed it; or they would not have determined state Conventions as the tribunal of ultimate decision. This is the last opportunity you may have to adopt a government which gives all protection to personal liberty, and at the same time promises fair to afford you all the advantages of a sovereign empire. While you deliberate with coolness, be not duped by the artful surmises of such as from their own interest or prejudice are blind to the public good.>

RESOLUTIONS OF THE TRADESMEN OF BOSTON
7 January 1788

The tradesmen and mechanics were a significant force in Boston politics, and both Federalists and Antifederalists courted them during the debate over the ratification of the Constitution. In mid-November Antifederalists distributed a broadside signed "Truth" which speculated that Boston's tradesmen would be injured if the Constitution were ratified. Federalists countered by demonstrating how the tradesmen would benefit from ratification. As the election of Boston's delegates to the state Convention approached, both Antifederalists and Federalists filled the town's newspapers urging tradesmen to vote for their respective candidates. Both sides proposed slates of candidates, sometimes including a mechanic.

Some Federalists did not want Samuel Adams, the president of the state Senate, to be elected to the state Convention because they believed he opposed the Constitution, even though he had not declared himself publicly. Other Federalists wanted Adams elected despite his opposition to the Constitution. They felt that his opposition would intensify if he were not elected and would be tempered if he served in the Convention. Since Adams was still a significant political force and a "venerable" Revolutionary patriot, no organized opposition emerged to prevent his election, and on 7 December he was chosen one of Boston's twelve delegates. After Adams's election, his opposition became more widely known, and on 25 and 28 December the Massachusetts Gazette printed several items openly attacking him.

On 3 January 1788 ten of Boston's Convention delegates met at the home of former governor James Bowdoin to discuss the Constitution. At the meeting, Adams pointedly declared his opposition to the Constitution and vowed to oppose it in the Convention. Adams's views spread rapidly through Boston, and rumors circulated that Boston's tradesmen also opposed the Constitution. Alarmed leaders of the tradesmen caucused on the evening of 5 January "to consider what was to be done in consiquence of Mr Adams declaration" (Nathaniel Gorham to Henry Knox, 6 January). Two days later an announcement appeared in the Boston Gazette requesting the real tradesmen of Boston to meet at the Green Dragon Tavern that evening at six o'clock "on Business of the first importance." As requested, more than 380 tradesmen gathered, and they unanimously adopted five resolutions announcing their wholehearted support of the Constitution and warning that, if any delegate or delegates opposed ratification of the Constitution, such action would be considered "contrary to their best interest, the strongest feelings, and warmest wishes" of Boston's tradesmen. The warning seemed to be directed primarily at Samuel Adams.

Three slightly different versions of the tradesmen's resolutions were printed in the Massachusetts Gazette, 8 January; Massachusetts Centinel, 9 January; and Boston Gazette, 14 January. The Massachusetts Gazette's version of the resolutions and its concluding paragraph were not reprinted. The Boston Gazette's version of the resolutions appeared in the Newport Herald on 17 January. The Massachusetts Centinel's version of the resolutions was reprinted in thirteen newspapers by 13 February: Mass. (3), R.I. (1), N.Y. (2), N.J. (1), Pa. (5), Md. (1). Excerpts from the Centinel's version were also reprinted in the January issue of the nationally circulated Philadelphia American Museum and in two New York newspapers. The Centinel prefaced the resolutions with two original paragraphs and followed them with a third. Eight newspapers reprinted the first paragraph; thirteen the second; and twelve the third.

MASSACHUSETTS GAZETTE, 8 JANUARY
Resolutions of the TRADESMEN of the Town of BOSTON.

Boston, January 7, 1787 [1788].

AGREEABLE to an advertisement inserted in the papers of this day, the TRADESMEN of this town convened at Mason's-hall, Green Dragon, when John Lucas, Esquire, Paul Revere, Esquire, and Mr. Benjamin Russell,* were chosen to draft certain resolutions, expressive of the sense of this body. The committee, after having retired for that purpose, returned, and reported the following—which, being read, was UNANIMOUSLY accepted, and ordered to be printed in the several publick papers—viz.

WHEREAS some persons, intending to injure the reputation of the tradesmen of this town, have asserted, that they were unfriendly and adverse to the adoption of the constitution of the United States of America, as proposed on the 17th September last, by the Convention of the United States assembled in Philadelphia: Therefore, to manifest the falsehood of such assertions, and to discover to the world our sentiments of the proposed frame of government,

Be it RESOLVED,

1. THAT such assertions are false and groundless; and it is the sense of this body, that all those, who propagate such reports, have no other view than the injury of our reputation, in the attainment of their own wicked purposes, on base and false grounds.

2. THAT, in the judgment of this body, the proposed frame of government, is well calculated to secure the liberties, protect the property, and guard the rights of the citizens of America; and it is our warmest wish and prayer that the same should be adopted by this commonwealth.

3. THAT, it is our opinion, if said constitution should be adopted by the United States of America, trade and navigation will revive and increase, employ and subsistence will be afforded to many of our townsmen, who are now suffering from want of the necessaries of life; that it will promote industry and morality; render us respectable as a nation; and procure us all the blessings to which we are entitled from the natural wealth of our country; our capacity for improvement, from our industry, our freedom and independence.

4. THAT it is the sense of this body, that if the proposed frame of government should be rejected, the small remains of commerce yet left us, will be annihilated, the various trades and handicrafts dependent thereon, must decay; our poor will be increased, and many of our worthy

---

*John Lucas was commissary of pensioners for Massachusetts, Paul Revere, a silver-smith, and Benjamin Russell, the printer of the *Massachusetts Centinel.*

and skillful mechanicks compelled to seek employ and subsistence in strange lands.

5. THAT, in the late election of delegates to represent this town in Convention, it was our design, and the opinion of this body, the design of every good man in town, to elect such men, and such only, as would exert their utmost ability to promote the adoption of the proposed frame of government in all its parts, without any conditions, pretended amendments, or alterations whatever: and that such, and such only, will truly represent the feelings, wishes, and desires of their constituents: and if any of the delegates of this town should oppose the adoption of said frame of government in gross, or under pretence of making amendments, or alterations of any kind, or of annexing conditions to their acceptance, such delegate or delegates will act contrary to their best interest,* the strongest feelings, and warmest wishes of the Tradesmen of the town of Boston.

JOHN LUCAS.

After the above resolutions were passed, John Lucas, Esq. Mr. Joseph Clark, Paul Revere, Esq. Mr. Rhodes, Mr. William Boardman, Joshua Witherlee, Esq. and Captain David Spear,† were appointed a standing-committee, to notify a meeting of the Tradesmen of this town in future. After which the meeting was dissolved.

It was with pleasure, says a correspondent, he observed the perfect order, unanimity, and intelligence, that pervaded the body of respectable Tradesmen which met last evening at the Green-Dragon. Notwithstanding the number exceeded three hundred and eighty, as appeared by an enumeration made at the time of their retiring from the Hall, as much regularity and propriety were discovered throughout all their proceedings, and deliberations, as ever were observed in any legislative body.

Massachusetts Centinel, 9 January

The TRADESMEN and MECHANICKS of the town of Boston, have always manifested their attachment to the principles of the Revolution—with steadiness and perseverance they pursued the prize of Independence—that object obtained, they have patiently, though anxiously, waited for the blessings of good government; that those happy scenes which they were led to anticipate from the success which crowned the arms of

---

*In the *Massachusetts Centinel* and *Boston Gazette* versions of the resolutions, "their best interest" reads "the best interests."

†William Boardman was a hatter, Joshua Witherle was a coppersmith, and David Spear was a cooper.

America, might be realized:—From the first appointment of the late Continental Convention, they looked up to that honourable Body, as to the *enlightened* and *distinguished patriots* of their country, from whose deliberations and decisions they had EVERY THING to hope—nor have they been disappointed.—The CONSTITUTION which they have proposed to the UNITED STATES, they consider as the result of much wisdom, candour, and those mutual concessions, without which America cannot expect ever to harmonize in any system of COMMERCE or GOVERNMENT.*

Proceedings of the TRADESMEN of the town of BOSTON.

The enemies to good government, finding that their flimsy arguments against the new constitution would avail nothing, when opposed by the fair arguments of reason and common sense, adopted a new fallacy to injure the system proposed, by asserting that the democratick part of the community, viz. the Tradesmen of the seaports, and OUR BRETHREN the Yeomen of the country were opposed to its adoption—Certain of the falsity of such reports as far as they respected the Tradesmen of this town, and feeling their reputations hurt thereby, a number of Tradesmen met, and agreed to request a general meeting of their brethren on Monday evening, at the Green-Dragon, in order that their opinions might be had on the subject.—Accordingly advertisements for that purpose were inserted in the papers of Monday last.—At about six o'clock, near four hundred of the most respectable *real* Tradesmen of this town—men who obtain their support from the sweat of their brow, and the labour of their hands—men who are constantly employed in the hive of the Commonwealth for their own subsistence and the dignity of the state, met at the Green-Dragon—when the subsequent spirited and patriotick proceedings took place. Although convened together at a short notice, and forming a large body when met, the whole business was conducted with as much propriety and regularity, we venture to say, as ever marked the proceedings of the best organized and well regulated assembly whatever.† The proceedings follow. [The tradesmen's resolution appear at this point.]

---

*This paragraph was reprinted eight times by 5 February: R.I. (1), N.J. (1), Pa. (4), Md. (2).
†This paragraph was reprinted thirteen times by 13 February: Mass. (3), R.I. (1), N.Y. (2), N.J. (1), Pa. (5), Md. (1).

BENJAMIN RUSH TO JEREMY BELKNAP
Philadelphia, 28 February 1788 (excerpt)*

Some of the same reasons have operated upon me, that have influenced you to admire & prefer the new government. If it held forth no other advantages that a future exemption from paper money & tender laws, it would be eno' to recommend it to honest men. To look up to a government that encourages Virtue—-establishes justice ensures order, secures property—and protects from every Species of Violence, affords a pleasure that can only be exceeded by looking up in all circumstances to a *general providence*. Such a pleasure I hope is before us & our posterity under the influence of the new Government.

FRANCIS HOPKINSON TO THOMAS JEFFERSON
Philadelphia, 6 April 1788 (excerpt)†

We are in a high political Fermentation about our new proposed federal Constitution. There are in every State People who have Debts to pay, Interests to support, or Fortunes to make—these wish for scrambling Times, paper Money Speculations, or partial Commercial advantages—An effective general Government will not suit their Views, & of Course there are great oppositions made to the new Constitution—but this opposition chiefly arises from a few leading Party Men in the Towns & Cities, who have been very industrious in holding it up as a political Monster to the Multitude who know nothing of Government, & have gained many Proselytes in the back Counties.—The Lees†† & Mr. Mason have so exerted themselves in Virginia as to make the Determination of that State doubtful—-Maryland is infected with a Mr Martin—but I am told the Constitution will be adopted there. We shall know in a few Weeks—The Convention met in New Hampshire & adjourn'd to sometime in June—The City of New York is federal, but the Country much opposed, under the Influence of Govr. Clinton.—Altho' Pennsylvania has long since adopted the proposed System, yet in no State have the People behaved so scandalously as here—George Bryan & his Party (formerly called the Constitutional Party) have been moving Heaven & Earth against the Establishment of a federal Government—Our Papers teem with the most opprobrious Revilings against the System & against all who befriend it—These Scribblers began with Arguments against the proposed Plan, such

*Belknap Papers, Massachusetts Historical Society.
†Jefferson Papers, Library of Congress.
††Arthur and Richard Henry Lee.

Arguments as would stand with equal Force against every or any Government that can be devised—they were Arguments against Government in
general, as an Infringement upon natural Liberty—they then poured forth
a torrent of abuse against the Members of the late general Convention
personally & individually—You will be surprized when I tell you that our
public news Papers have announced General Washington to be a Fool
influenced & led by that Knave Dr. Franklin, who is a public Defaulter for
Millions of Dollars, that Mr. Morris has defrauded the Public out of as
many Millions as you please & that they are to cover their frauds by this
new Government*—What think you of this.—Some of the Authors of
these inflammatory Publications have been traced, & found to be Men of
desperate Circumstances.

DAVID RAMSAY ORATION
Charleston *Columbian Herald,* 5 June 1788 (excerpt)†

While legislative assemblies interfered between debtors and creditors, what security could there be for property? He that sold, did not know
that he should ever get the stipulated price. he that parted with his money
could not tell when it would be replaced.—hence a total want of confidence
and of credit. From this day forward, these evils will be done away; creditors knowing that they can recover payment, will be less disposed to distress
their debtors than when under a fluctuating system which might induce
them to make the most of present opportunities, lest future laws should
create new impediments to the course of justice. Debtors, despairing of

---

*"Centinel" I had charged that Washington had been duped into signing the Constitution.
"Centinel" XVI accused Benjamin Franklin and Robert Morris of being public defaulters.

†The South Carolina Convention, meeting in Charleston, ratified the Constitution on 23
May. The next day a "Federal Committee" planned a celebration for Charleston on 27 May,
"weather permitting," and the chairman of the "Federal Committee" asked David Ramsay to
prepare an oration. Ramsay, who had voted to ratify the Constitution in the state Convention,
composed his oration in six hours, but he said that he was unable to deliver it because "the
crowd was so great that it could not be spoken with convenience." More than 2,800 people took
part in the procession alone.
   The oration first appeared in print, without any indication that Ramsay was the author, in
the Charleston *Columbian Herald,* 5 June, and as a twelve-page pamphlet struck by Bowen &
Co., the printers of the *Herald.* The pamphlet was entitled *An Oration, Prepared for Delivery
before the Inhabitants of Charleston, Assembled on the 27th May, 1788, to Celebrate the Adoption of the
New Constitution by South-Carolina.* Ramsay identified himself as the author of the oration when
he sent a copy to Benjamin Lincoln of Hingham, Mass., on 20 June.
   The oration was reprinted in whole or in part in the New York *Daily Advertiser,* 17 July;
Pennsylvania Mercury, 17 July; *New Haven Gazette,* 24 July; Baltimore *Maryland Gazette,* 29 July;
Charleston *City Gazette,* 29 July; and *Virginia Centinel,* 13, 20 August, all of which noted that
Ramsay was the author and that the oration had been prepared for the celebration of South
Carolina ratification. Surprisingly, the Charleston *City Gazette* reprinted the oration from the
New York *Daily Advertiser,* almost two months after it had first been published in Charleston.

farther legislative indulgences, and knowing that they can be compelled to pay, will be stimulated to double exertions for acquiring the means of discharging their debts. The gold and silver which have long rusted in the desks of the cautious, will once more see the light and add to the circulating medium of our country. That useful order of men, formerly called money lenders will be revived, and the distresses of the unfortunate relieved without sacrificing their property, or administering to the rapacity of usurers. Time would fail me in dilating at full length on that section of the constitution which declares, that "no state shall emit bills of credit, make any thing but gold and silver a tender in payment of debts, pass any bill of attainder or ex post facto law, impairing the obligation of contracts." This will restore credit; and credit is a mine of real wealth, far surpassing those of Mexico and Peru. It will soon bring back the good old times under which we formerly flourished and were happy.

EDMUND PENDLETON
Speech in Virginia Ratifying Convention, 12 June 1788 (excerpt)*

On the subject of Government the worthy member (*Patrick Henry*) and I differ at the threshold. I think Government necessary to protect liberty. He supposes the American spirit all-sufficient for the purpose. What say the most respectable writers—Montesquieu, Locke, Sidney, Harrington, &c.? They have presented us with no such idea. They properly discard from their system, all the severity of cruel punishments, such as tortures, inquisitions, and the like—-shocking to human nature, and only calculated to coerce the dominion of tyrants over slaves. But they recommend making the ligaments of Government firm, and a rigid execution of the laws as more necessary than in a Monarchy—to preserve that virtue, which they all declare to be the pillar on which the Government, and liberty its object, must stand. They are not so visionary, as to suppose, there ever did or ever will exist a society, however large their aggregate fund of virtue may be, but hath among them persons of a turbulent nature, restless in themselves, and disturbing the peace of others—Sons of rapine and violence, who unwilling to labour themselves, are watching every opportunity to snatch from the industrious peasant the fruits of his honest labour. Was I not then correct in my inference, that such a Government and liberty were friends and allies, and that their common enemy was turbulence, faction, and violence? 'Tis those therefore that will be offended by good Government, and for those I suppose no Gentleman

*Debates and Other Proceedings of the Convention of Virginia . . . (3 vols., Petersburg, Va., 1788–89), II, 92–94.

will profess himself an advocate. The writers just mentioned, point out licentiousness as the natural offspring of liberty, and that therefore all free Governments should endeavor to suppress it, or else it will ultimately overthrow that liberty of which it is the result. Is this speculation only? Alas! reason and experience too fatally prove its truth in all instances. A Republican Government is the nursery of science. It turns the bent of it to eloquence, as a qualification for the representative character, which is, as it ought to be, the road to our public offices. I have pleasure in beholding these characters already produced in our councils—and a rising fund equal to a constant supply—May heaven prosper their endeavors, and direct their eloquence to the real good of their country. I am unfortunate enough to differ from the worthy member in another circumstance. He professes himself an advocate for the *middling* and *lower* classes of *men*. I profess to be a friend to the *equal* liberty of *all men*, from the palace to the cottage, without any other distinction than between *good* and *bad* men. I appeal to my public life and private behaviour, to decide whether I have departed from this rule. Since distinctions have been brought forth and communicated to the audience; and will be therefore disseminated, I beg Gentlemen to take with them this observation, that distinctions have been produced by the opposition. From the friends of the new Government, they have heard none.—None such are to be found in the organization of the paper before you.

Why bring into debate the whims of writers—introducing the distinction of *well born* from others?*—I consider every man *well born* who comes into the world with an intelligent mind, and with all his parts perfect. I am an advocate for fixing our Government on true republican principles, giving to the poor man free liberty in his person and property. Whether a man be great or small he is equally dear to me. I wish, Sir, for a regular Government, in order to secure and protect those honest citizens who have been distinguished—I mean the industrious farmer and planter. I wish them to be protected in the enjoyment of their honestly and industriously acquired property. I wish commerce to be fully protected and encouraged, that the people may have an opportunity of disposing of their crops at market, and of procuring such supplies as they may be in want of. I presume that there can be no political happiness,

---

*On 11 June George Mason criticized the small number of representatives that Virginia would have in the U.S. House of Representatives. Although Virginia had 160 members in its House of Delegates, it would only have ten U.S. Representatives "chosen, if not wholly, yet mostly from the higher order of the people—from the great—the wealthy—the *well-born*. The *well-born*—that Aristocratic idol—that flattering idea—that *exotic* plant which has been lately imported from the ports of Great-Britain, and planted in the luxuriant soil of this country." Mason refers to John Adams's *Defence of the Constitutions*, which was criticized by some because it praised the British Constitution, supported a powerful executive, diminished the role of the people, and attached too great a prominence to the rich and well born.

unless industry be cherished and protected, and property secured.—Suppose a poor man becomes rich by honest labour, and increases the public stock of wealth, shall his reward be the loss of that liberty he set out with? Will you take away every stimulus to industry, by declaring that he shall not retain the fruits of it? The idea of the poor becoming rich by assiduity is not mere fancy. I am old enough, and have had sufficient experience to know the effects of it. I have often known persons commencing in life without any other stock but industry and economy; by the mere efforts of these, rise to opulence and wealth. This could not have been the case without a Government to protect their industry.—In my mind the true principles of republicanism, and the greatest security of liberty, is regular Government. Perhaps I may not be a republican, but this is my idea. In reviewing the history of the world, shall we find an instance where any society retained its liberty without Government? As I before hinted, the smallest society in extent, to the greatest empire, can only be preserved by a regular Government, to suppress that faction and turbulence so natural to many of our species. What do men do with those passions when they come into society? Do they leave them? No—they bring them with them.— These passions which they thus bring into society will produce disturbances which without any check will overturn it.

ALEXANDER HAMILTON
Speech in New York Ratifying Convention, 21 June 1788 (excerpt)*

Sir, we hear constantly a great deal, which is rather calculated to awake our passions, and create prejudices, than to conduct us to truth, and teach us our real interests.—I do not suppose this to be the design of the gentlemen [opposing the Constitution].—Why then are we told so often of an aristocracy? For my part, I hardly know the meaning of this word as it is applied. If all we hear be true, this government is really a very bad one. But who are the aristocracy among us? Where do we find men elevated to a perpetual rank above their fellow citizens; and possessing powers entirely independent of them? The arguments of the gentlemen only go to prove that there are men who are rich, men who are poor, some who are wise, and others who are not—That indeed every distinguished man is an aristocrat.—This reminds me of a description of the aristocrats, I have seen in a late publication, styled the Federal Farmer.—The author reckons in the aristocracy, all governors of states, members of Congress, chief

*The Debates and Proceedings of the Convention of the State of New-York . . . (New York, 1788), 39–40. Hamilton was responding to remarks made by Melancton Smith. (See above.)

magistrates, and all officers of the militia.—This description, I presume to say, is ridiculous.—The image is a phantom. Does the new government render a rich man more eligible than a poor one? No. It requires no such qualification. It is bottomed on the broad and equal principle of your state constitution.

Sir, if the people have it in their option to elect their most meritorious men; is this to be considered as an objection? Shall the constitution oppose their wishes, and abridge their most invaluable privilege? While property continues to be pretty equally divided, and a considerable share of information pervades the community; the tendency of the people's suffrages, will be to elevate merit even from obscurity—As riches increase and accumulate in few hands;—as luxury prevails in society; virtue will be in a greater degree considered as only a graceful appendage of wealth, and the tendency of things will be to depart from the republican standard. This is the real disposition of human nature: It is what, neither the honorable member nor myself can correct—It is a common misfortune, that awaits our state constitution, as well as all others.

There is an advantage incident to large districts of election, which perhaps the gentlemen, amidst all their apprehensions of influence and bribery, have not adverted to. In large districts, the corruption of the electors is much more difficult:—Combinations for the purposes of intrigue are less easily formed: Factions and cabals are little known. In a small district, wealth will have a more complete influence; because the people in the vicinity of a great man, are more immediately his dependents, and because this influence has fewer objects to act upon. It has been remarked, that it would be disagreeable to the middle class of men to go to the seat of the new government. If this be so, the difficulty will be enhanced by the gentleman's proposal. If his argument be true, it proves, that the larger the representation is, the less will be your choice of having it filled. But, it appears to me frivolous to bring forward such arguments as these. It has answered no other purpose, than to induce me, by way of reply, to enter into discussions, which I consider as useless, and not applicable to our subject.

It is a harsh doctrine, that men grow wicked in proportion as they improve and enlighten their minds. Experience has by no means justified us in the supposition, that there is more virtue in one class of men than in another. Look through the rich and the poor of the community; the learned and the ignorant.—Where does virtue predominate? The difference indeed consists, not in the quantity but kind of vices, which are incident to the various classes; and here the advantage of character belongs to the wealthy. Their vices are probably more favorable to the prosperity of the state, than those of the indigent; and partake less of moral depravity.

After all, Sir, we must submit to this idea, that the true principle of a republic is, that the people should choose whom they please to govern them. Representation is imperfect, in proportion as the current of popular favour is checked.—This great source of free government, popular election, should be perfectly pure, and the most unbounded liberty allowed. Where this principle is adhered to; where, in the organization of the government, the legislative, executive, and judicial branches are rendered distinct; where again the legislative is divided into separate houses, and the operations of each are controuled by various checks and balances, and above all, by the vigilance and weight of the state governments; to talk of tyranny, and the subversion of our liberties, is to speak the language of [religious] enthusiasm.

Index